John Houghton is the pseudonym of a distinguished writer. He lives in Britain.

Praise for *A Forever Family*

'This is a brave account, with all the untidiness of real life. Some images are very real indeed. Imagine one small boy collapsing in hysteria at the sight of a delivery van; another boy standing out in the cold, obsessively washing coal; and the isolation, desperation and rage of an adoptive father who realises that "there are all sorts of hells hidden behind suburban doors, and we were living in one of them." '
Judith Palmer, *Independent*

'Houghton's thoughtfulness, humanity and obvious love for his very challenging children make this a powerful book.'
Rebecca Loncraine, *Times Literary Supplement*

'It is an invaluable glimpse into a side of adoption rarely exposed; what happens when adopted children are so damaged that normal family life is impossible.'
Irish Times

'A frank and touching account which reveals the complexities of adoption and fragility of the human spirit . . . There is no happy ending, just survival and that, in itself, is the strange optimism with which you are left.'
Maria Garner, *Tribune*

'It is no exaggeration to say that [the Houghtons] entered an emotional war zone . . . This book offers a heartrending, no-holds-barred account of adoption that is remarkable for its searing honesty and immediately engaging in that it offers a rare insight into the perspective of the adoptive parents of older children . . . A compelling and controversial read.'
Evening Herald

A Forever Family

A TRUE STORY OF ADOPTION

John Houghton

faber and faber

First published in 2006
by Faber and Faber Limited
3 Queen Square London WC1N 3AU
This paperback edition first published in 2007

Typeset by Faber and Faber Limited
Printed in England by Mackays of Chatham plc,
Chatham, Kent

A CIP record for this book
is available from the British Library

ISBN 978-0-571-22779-2

4 6 8 10 9 7 5 3

For the five of us

All the names have been changed.
The dates are deliberately vague.
It could have happened anywhere in the country.

This is only one version of the story, or perhaps only one of many different stories about the same thing. Marina would tell it differently, as our memories of certain events are surprisingly divergent. One day, our three children – Kieran, Paul and Cate – will tell their own stories to their friends, lovers and partners. They will tell them to their own children. All those stories will be slightly different too. Other versions already exist in various places, but they are unlikely to be complete. There are files held by the Social Services Departments of the city where we now live and the town where we used to live, one set dealing with an adoption that took place fourteen years ago, the other with the aftermath that came ten years later. Our experience of Social Services Departments strongly suggests that these files will provide the least complete version of the story. Details will be missing because they were never recorded in the first place, because they were recorded wrongly, because files are missing or because files have been lost. Two primary schools and one high school hold records of our children's time with them. There are medical files on all of us, telling of minor illnesses and major problems. Mine also contain references to overuse of alcohol and tobacco, to prescriptions for antidepressants, to a referral to hospital for the removal of cataracts, and a lot else besides. There are court records and police files. The after-adoption unit of the local Department of Social Services will have records of our attempts to find help and support, and of their attempts to provide it. They tell of a family, and a couple, on the edge of complete dysfunctionality and even collapse. The psychotherapist I saw on a weekly basis for nineteenth months no doubt has her case notes, but they will remain confidential. Our friends will have their own tales to tell about us, and they must include some strange (and often ill-informed) speculation. A very few close friends know most of the story; our relatives do not. We have not told them it because we do not know how they might react, how it might shift their perception of our children or how they might treat them as a result.

No one is in a position to bring all these stories together or to tell the whole story, and no one knows how it will end. My version of our story is not a complete or photographic record of fourteen years of our lives. I did not keep a diary and I do not have total recall. My memories are sometimes blurred and confused. I cannot always recall the precise sequence in which events occurred.

I

Two or three years ago, I came across a display in the local shopping mall. It was in a space that is usually occupied by displays of garden furniture or motorised scooters for the disabled, and had been put up by one of the national adoption agencies. I stopped to look, to read the appeal asking people to adopt or at least foster children, and to glance at some of the photographs of the children who were looking for a 'forever family'. Few other passers-by were taking much interest and I was quickly approached by a smart young woman holding a clipboard and some leaflets. She smiled: 'Have you ever thought about adopting, sir?' I don't normally speak to anyone like this, but I couldn't resist it: 'Done it, love. Three times.'

We were approaching our late thirties when we finally learned that we could not have children. The reasons why we could not do not really matter much now, and they are as banal as they are painful. We did not want a lot – just a baby. Most couples can manage it without too much difficulty. It is still hard to come to terms with the paradox of having used contraception for so long, only to learn that we didn't need to after all, but I'm used to living with paradoxes and ironies now, some of them cruel, some of them bordering on the comical. Not the least of them is that we have three children in their teens without ever having had a baby. Other ironies are a source of amusement. When Cate whines and whines that she wants a sister, we can, in all seriousness, ask her,

'Do you want an older one or a younger one?' That usually shuts her up.

Never having had a baby still hurts. The beginnings of our family are so different from those of other families. There are a lot of absences, and there are things that were never there and that are still not there. There are no baby clothes carefully folded away in a cupboard and no tiny shoes kept in a box. I have no photographs of a sweaty Marina with our newborn child in a delivery suite. Our baby was fifteen months old, and she was brought to us by car. In the case of our two elder children, there are no memories of a baby's first words or of a baby's first attempts to walk, as they were, respectively, aged five and three when they came to live with us. Marina and I have never been on excited shopping trips to buy all the things a new baby needs. We have never spent dreamy hours choosing names. We've never been able to discuss whether our children look like their father or their mother because there cannot be any family likeness. There are things that can never happen. I will never have made love with my pregnant wife and I will probably never be present at the birth of a baby. I will never have held our baby minutes after he or she was born. I will never have watched Marina breast-feeding our baby. She has never been able to stand at the school gates and join in with the other mothers as they exchanged horror stories about how long they had been in labour. She still finds it awkward when she is teased about the bad timing that led to all three children being born in the same month of the year. After all, it wasn't her bad timing.

Of course we rejoiced when friends had their babies, but there was always a stab of jealousy. There still is. Going into town on the bus one morning, I sat opposite a young woman with her baby in a buggy. They were lovely to watch. They were completely in love with each other and they smiled, laughed and cooed at each other. For the twenty minutes it took to get into town, that mother never lost eye contact with her baby. I've never seen that look on Marina's face and our children never had that kind of contact with their birth mother. Neither I nor Marina can ever provide that experience for them because it has always been too late. Cate went into foster care when she was five days old, and remained with the same family until she was placed with us. At about sixteen months, she sat on Marina's lap, looking up at her. The expression on her face said that she knew: wrong eyes, wrong colour hair, wrong smell, wrong woman. Not mum.

There are so many little reminders that we are not a family like any other. We can never forget. More than once, I have had to admit that I have no idea why Cate's name is written as it is. If pushed, I suppose that I'd have to say that, given that she was born before Cate Blanchett came on the scene, I can only assume that her birth mother could not spell. 'Does your daughter have the same colour hair as you?' asks my hairdresser in an attempt to make conversation. Do I explain that Cate is adopted and does not have my colouring, or do I just laugh and say no? I never know what to do. I take two of the children for an eye test; the optician asks if there are any conditions, such as glaucoma or cataracts, that run in the family, and I have to explain that we are not genetically related. We don't really know if the children suffered any diseases in early childhood, and have to explain to doctors why we don't know. Their early medical records are as fragmentary as the rest of their early history. We certainly do not know anything about their birth mother's state of health while she was pregnant, though it could well be relevant to their health. There are a great many things we will probably never know.

Facing up to the impossibility of having a baby in the 'normal' manner, we decided that nature was not going to stand in our way and that we would adopt. And we would adopt children, and not just one child. We quickly learned that we would probably not be allowed to adopt a young baby. Quite apart from the fact that so few babies are available for adoption, we were too old. This is pragmatism rather than ageism: adoptive parents are expected to live long enough to see their children into young adulthood, and whilst no legislation or policy can guarantee that they will do so, the odds can be improved. We had already learned that we were too old for some things when we began to look for a medical explanation for our inability to conceive. For many young doctors in a hurry to climb the ladder, a couple approaching their late thirties are so old as to be almost geriatric, and far too old to be of much medical interest.

Once we had accepted that we were too old to adopt a baby, we began to investigate the possibility of adopting older children and contacted the city's Social Services Department. We were invited to attend a meeting for prospective adopters and fosterers in the Town Hall. All I remember is that it was scary as well as sad. Couples willing to adopt or foster are like gold dust, and all the agencies are desperate to find new recruits. They advertise for them on the sides of buses and on billboards. I say 'couples', but there has never been anything to prevent single people from adopting or fostering. And I seem to recall that a man at that meeting did express an interest in becoming a foster-carer. He was unmarried and had a lot of experience of working with boys in the voluntary sector. I have no idea as to whether or not he was gay. It wouldn't have mattered anyway. One issue that did concern those running the meeting was that so few non-white people had turned up. That all the social workers present were white can't have helped.

That most agencies now discourage inter-ethnic adoption, or at least do not actively encourage it, makes things more difficult for ethnic-minority children. So far as I recall, this was not an issue that came up when we began to explore adoption, but had we been asked if were willing to consider a non-white child, we would no doubt have said yes. In retrospect, I think we might have been wrong to do so. Whatever else we may have to put up with, we will never be called 'black bastard' or 'black bitch' as we walk down the street. How easy would it be for us to empathise with a boy or girl who has been called just that in the playground? At some point, all adoptive fathers are confronted by an angry, frightened child who spits at them: 'You can't tell me to do anything – you're not even my real dad.' It is meant to hurt, and it does hurt. We learn to live with it and eventually we learn not to react by saying, 'Tough, but I'm the only dad you've got.' It must be much harder not to react to 'You're not my real mum. You're not even black.' It is very easy for a teacher to put an adopted child in an embarrassing situation. Even basic lessons on family history can be difficult. How are our children supposed to react when they are asked to talk about their grandparents given that, to all intents and purposes, they have none and have never had any? An inter-ethnic adoption could make such lessons even more difficult. A girl could be asked in front of a whole class: 'If both your parents are white, how come you're black?' She may never have told any of her thirty classmates that she was adopted as a baby and she may not want to do so now.

Because so few babies are available for adoption in this country, some couples do look elsewhere, though inter-country adoption is much less common than some media reports might suggest. In any given year, there are no more than two or three hundred cases in Britain. Whilst we were as moved as anyone else by the television footage from the Romanian orphanages, we never wanted to adopt those children. We never even considered the inter-country option and we never became fixated on the idea of adopting a baby. In subjective terms, this presumably means that our desire to become parents had become greater than our desire for a baby, and that must mean that, almost without realising it, we had come to terms with our infertility. There are still brief moments when I wonder what it would have been like to have children of our own and times when I ask myself if that wouldn't have been easier. These are, however, no more than fleeting moments. We have three children of our own, and they became our children very quickly. At some early stage, one of the social workers involved asked if we felt we were dealing with a problem on someone else's behalf. We could quite honestly say, after only a matter of weeks of living with our children, that we were not. If there was a problem, it was our problem and no one else's.

Emma is almost five. She is a pretty girl with long dark hair, big eyes and a ready smile. She likes cats and dogs and would love to have a pony of her own. Emma happily goes to nursery but is a little nervous about starting school proper in the autumn. She sometimes finds it difficult to get on with other children but does try to make an effort. At times, she finds it hard to concentrate on her work. Emma is looking for a forever family but wants to stay in touch with her older brother and younger sister. Emma must be the only or youngest child in her new family and needs clear, firm boundaries.

Emma's picture smiles from a website, from newspaper adverts, and from the newsletters put out by the various adoption agencies. Sometimes, her face smiles from a display like the one I saw in the shopping mall. She can be seen in the adverts on the buses that say 'The city's children need adopters and foster-carers.' 'Emma' may well be her real name but the website makes it clear that the picture is of a model. Not yet five, Emma is already an 'older child' and it will therefore be difficult to place her with the forever family she needs so badly. At the moment, she is living with foster-parents and has also spent periods in institutional care. A ward of court, she has no contact with either of her birth parents, and her birth mother has said that she will not contest any application for adoption. No one knows where Emma's father is. She no longer has regular contact with either her brother or her sister, who are also in the care of a local authority. Little is known about her early life.

Adoptions have always taken place, but the present system came into being thanks to the Adoption Act of 1926, which established a legal framework for the adoption of children. There is a spontaneous association between 'baby' and 'adoption' and many prospective adopters do initially hope to become the new parents of a baby. Their hopes will probably be dashed by reality. The peak year for the adoption of babies was 1968 (a vintage year with a record total of almost 25,000 adoptions), and the numbers have been falling ever since. The vast majority of the babies adopted in 1968 were under one year old, and many were the children of girls and very young women who were coerced by a very cruel system into giving them up for adoption. In extreme cases, their mothers were not even allowed to hold or feed their children before they were taken away. Many women lost their children to 'third-party' adoptions, which were facilitated by sympathetic doctors or priests who privately arranged for a child to be handed over to a childless couple of their acquaintance. There was no paperwork, and many of the children grew up not knowing they had been adopted. Many of the mothers were assured that no one would ever know that they had had an illegitimate child. Such private arrangements are now illegal, but informal adoptions still take place on a scale that no one can even estimate.

The average age of a child at the point when it is decided that adoption is in his or her best interest is now two years and six months, and it is only in exceptional circumstances that a newborn baby will, like Cate, be taken from its mother. The availability of contraception and abortion, together with the fact that there is now relatively little stigma attached to being a single mother, means that girls no longer give birth in mother-and-baby units and then 'give up' their babies for adoption. Most mothers whose children are removed from their care are not teenagers. They were aged between twenty-five and thirty-four when they gave birth and, on average, they are aged twenty-four years and eleven months when their children are taken into care.

In a city of this size, roughly 1,300 children are being cared for, or 'looked after' to use the current jargon, by the Department of

Social Services, and a further 400 are living with approved foster-carers. Nationally, about 40,000 children are living in foster-homes on any given day. In 2002, 3,600 children were placed for adoption in England as a whole, and roughly half of them were categorised as difficult to place. The figures are slowly rising, and in the year ending 31 March 2003, 3,700 looked-after children were adopted. Their average age was four years and five months. It is to be hoped that the resources devoted to supporting adoptive families increase proportionately. If they do not, there will be a high casualty rate.

Emma's chances are not good, even though she does have things going for her. She is a pretty girl. That should not matter, but it does. The agency trying to place her for adoption is not looking for a forever family for both her and her siblings. That makes her easier to place, but it suggests that there are problems elsewhere as a lot of effort goes into trying to keep sibling groups together. That her adoption will not be contested means that there will be no ugly courtroom battles. Emma is not physically disabled, has no medical problems and does not appear to have any special educational needs. She is white and, tragically, that too is to her advantage. What hope is there for a child who is described as being 'of Irish-Nigerian parentage' and who needs to be placed with a family 'from the same background'?

The website's description of Emma hints at other reasons why she is hard to place, but prospective adopters are unlikely to be able to crack the code. The caveat that she must be the only or youngest child in her new family strongly suggests that she is likely to harm a younger child – either physically or sexually. She needs 'clear, firm boundaries', sometimes finds it difficult to get on with other children and is nervous about starting school. Non-adoptive parents of children of Emma's age will object that most, if not all, children are nervous about starting school. That is no doubt true, but they are not nervous for the same reasons as Emma. Emma suffers from acute separation anxiety and knows, just knows, that, if she leaves the house and goes to school, something dreadful will happen to either her or her carers. Emma's inability to concentrate may mean that she is easily distracted because she is always watching out for danger; she has already been hurt in some way and fears that she will be hurt again. This, together with her need for clear, firm boundaries could mean many things. They suggest that she will probably be on methylphenidate by the time she is seven. Methylphenidate hydrochloride, better known as Ritalin, is widely used to control Attention Deficit Hyperactivity Disorder. In the five years up to 2003, the number of prescriptions for the drug rose by 102 per cent. One of those prescriptions was written for our son Paul, who is now seventeen. He does not actually have ADHD, but the drug does help to control his mood swings and does something to calm his outbursts of violence. It does appear to improve his concentration at school, but it is the mood-changing effect that is really important. Without the Ritalin, he quickly becomes our very own Mr Hyde. I have always found the idea of giving mood-altering drugs to children quite abhorrent, but we've learned to be much less high-principled than we used to be, and the Ritalin works.

The original prescription was written by a clinical psychiatrist but we now get the Ritalin through our GP. This is always slightly tricky as methylphenidate is a controlled substance – a Class II amphetamine – and therefore cannot be put on a standard repeat prescription. Every prescription has to be written by hand and when I go to order a new supply, I have to remind the receptionist about this. She almost always forgets and I have to wait until a doctor is free to write the prescription. Collecting the prescription is not straightforward either. A controlled substance has to be locked away in the chemist's safe and only a qualified pharmacist can give it to me and, if he or she has gone to lunch, I either have to wait or come back later. Walking home with a three months' supply of this stuff in my pocket always feels slightly uncomfortable because it is addictive and has a street-value; girls who are worried about their weight use it as an appetite-suppressant, and there are reports of black markets operating in school playgrounds.

At first, Paul was taking three 10mg pills a day, which meant that one had to be taken during the school day. He would go to school after taking his first dose and leave a second with the receptionist-secretary, without whom the school would rapidly collapse into chaos. At lunchtime, Paul would go to her desk and ask for his second pill. He was always on time and faultlessly polite, but it could be a struggle to get him to take it at home. The dose has now been changed, and Paul takes the drug in a form that allows the 36mg dose to be released into his system over a twelve-hour period, and that makes everyone's life a lot easier. We have not observed any side-effects. Paul has regular check-ups and no problems with the drug have even been identified. We still do not like giving it to him and we do not know how long he will have to go on taking it.

That so little is known about Emma's early life is disturbing. If a human life is to a large extent a story, understanding how it began is of crucial importance. A lot will be known about Emma's life, but the fragments will be scattered throughout social service records and reports, medical records, perhaps even psychiatric reports. The problem is that no one has put the fragments together, that no one has tried to tell the whole story. It is no one person's job to do that. Everyone who deals with Emma – her social workers, her nursery teacher and whoever else is involved – is working with flawed and fragmentary information and there is no one to collate it all. Emma has lived with foster-carers and in institutions and there has therefore been little continuity in her life, and there will be gaps in her story. Her adoptive parents may eventually be able to help her tell her story, but before they can do that they will have to learn a lot of things they do not want to know. They will have to visit some very dark places and they will not emerge unscathed.

Emma does know her story but she cannot tell it yet. Perhaps she will never be able to do so, or at least not without a lot of help. The help may have to be professional and she may have to work with a psychotherapist. Fragments will emerge unexpectedly (and always at the most inconvenient moment). She will have confused memories of why she first came into care, of why her birth parents are not there, and of why she has had so little contact with her siblings. But she will have to be helped to sort out the confusion and to remember properly. Her adoptive parents will have to help by making a 'life story' book. This is an important aspect of working with adopted children, as words, pictures and any other fragments of the past can be combined to produce at least a tentative account of their histories, though there will almost inevitably be gaps and inconsistencies. Without that account, it will be hard for Emma to understand just who she is, or how she became who she is.

Children are taken into care for many different reasons, and their removal from their birth parents is by no means always permanent. Most will return to their families within a matter of weeks. A single parent (almost inevitably a mother) without a support network of friends and relatives may fall ill and be hospitalised. She may go into hospital to have another baby. A parent (usually a father) may be in jail ('working abroad' or 'on the oil rigs'), leaving his partner unable to cope. A parent may have been injured or disabled in an accident, or may be suffering from incapacitating mental illness. A family may be experiencing great stress or breakdown. A child's behaviour may have become so uncontrollable that he or she is a danger to others. A parent or family may not be able to cope with a child suffering from ADHD. Such children cannot settle and cannot concentrate on anything, and living with them is like being trapped inside a jam jar with a wasp that buzzes and buzzes with malevolent energy. There is no escape from them and their demands, and there may come a point where it is no longer humanly possible to live with them despite the Ritalin.

In the vast majority of cases, there has been some form of neglect or abuse, either physical or sexual. Cruelty to children is horrifically common: every week, a child dies at the hands of its parents or carers, just as two women are killed by their partners each week. The sexual abuse of children is horrifyingly common, as we have known since the Cleveland Inquiry of 1987. Sensational tales of ritual and even satanic abuse do not help because they detract attention from a reality that is as drab as it is horrific. Precisely because they are sensational, such tales can desensitise us to the realities. The hysterical witch hunts do not help anyone. In the vast majority of cases, the abuser is not someone in the robes of a devil-worshipper or the man in the dirty raincoat who hangs around the school gates. He is almost always someone who is close to the child and in a position of trust. He might be the child's father or uncle, or her mother's new boyfriend. He could be a priest, a teacher or the baby-sitter's boyfriend, and he could be either gay or straight. As it is with violence against women, so it is with the abuse of children. It occurs on sink estates and in expensive houses in desirable suburbs.

A lot is said about sexual abuse, but it is easy to forget just what the words mean. 'Daddy used to come into my room . . . He hurt me in my bottom . . . There was a nasty taste in my mouth . . .' A child who begins such sentences, and who may not be able to complete them, has almost certainly been raped or forced to perform some form of oral sex. When a young child, even a baby, is raped, an erect adult penis is forced into its rectum. With a very young girl, anal penetration is, I am told, 'easier' than vaginal penetration, which will begin when she is older. The physical effects of sexual abuse often lead to hospitalisation and the internal injuries caused can be long-lasting, but they can be treated. The psychological effects cannot be treated so easily and there may be no way to compensate for the damage that has been done. The scars may never heal. Victims of torture say that anyone who has been tortured remains tortured; children who have been sexually abused remain sexually abused. There are no magic spells to un-abuse them and yet, as a psychiatric social worker with a lot of experience in this most difficult of fields convinced me, there is a very real sense in which there is no such animal as a Sexually-Abused Child. The girl who was sexually abused at a very early age is also the girl who likes dancing and who, without meaning to, often neglects to feed and water her guinea pig. The boy who was abused is also the boy who is mad about the local football team and who wants to be a fire-fighter when he grows up. The abuse is part of their history, but there are other parts to it. Abuse often takes the form of a cycle that is difficult to break. The men (and the mercifully few women) who abuse have often been abused themselves, and they are often victims as well as perpetrators. That does not justify their behaviour and whilst they do need help, it does not mean that they should not also be punished and removed from circulation. Children who have been abused can grow up to be abusers. Some do not even grow up before they become abusers, and that, perhaps, is why Emma must be the only or youngest child in her new family.

Pictures like that of Emma and the thumbnail sketches that accompany them are designed to be heartbreaking because they represent a shameless attempt to recruit adopters. For a long time, we subscribed to the monthly newsletter published by one of the national adoption agencies, and we went on receiving it once our children had been placed with us. It was a very helpful source of information and advice and we learned a great deal from it, but we were always drawn to the 'be my parent section', with its pathetic little pictures. The worst were of a boy; call him George. One issue published his photograph with a caption saying that the last time George was featured, there were no responses to his appeal for a forever family. Not one. George did appear to have his fair share of problems but the real difficulty was that he was ten years old. In adoption terms, he was, in other words, a very old child indeed. Some pictures of these 'older' children appear month after month. We eventually cancelled our subscription to the newsletter because we were finding it too painful to go on looking at the photos. We were also worried that, if our children saw them, they might conclude that we were thinking of adopting another child, or even other children. And we certainly did not want them to think that we were going to advertise them for adoption. That is one of the fears an adopted child lives with: she has already been given away once, so why shouldn't it happen again?

A child of ten is unlikely to find adoptive parents and will therefore remain in the care of a local authority or go on being looked after by foster-carers. Looked-after children tend to perform badly at school and are not high-achievers. Truancy is often a major problem. They will leave school with few, if any, qualifications and will be ill-prepared for work, adult life and lasting relationships. All children in care are officially deemed to be at risk and all the indicators are poor: rates of literacy and numeracy, social skills, and employment prospects. For looked-after children, all the dangers that lie in wait for young people in general are magnified: drugs, alcohol, petty criminality, inappropriate sexual behaviour and relationships, homelessness, unemployment . . . and the list goes on.

Girls face particular risks. They are likely to become sexually active at an early age, and risk early pregnancy or sexually transmitted diseases. Some will put themselves in danger again and again. Some will be very promiscuous because their self-esteem is so poor and their sense that there is no future for them so great that everything about them says, 'I'm not worth shit, anyone can fuck me.' A lot of older boys, and a lot of men, can read the signs and they respond to the message accordingly, whilst the girls mistake sexual predation for a demonstration of affection. It is not a long way from this to an apprenticeship in prostitution. Girls in this position are very vulnerable and very self-destructive. It is a dangerous combination. Many a foster-carer and many an adoptive parent has answered the doorbell to find that the girl they are trying to care for has been brought home (again) by the police, very drunk, clothing disturbed and vomit all over her. In some cases, the girl is pregnant. If that is the case, the cycle may well begin again. Some rent-boys got where they are today by following the equivalent route: one day, the friendly man offered to buy the lost and lonely boy in the bar a drink, and then another.

The statistics are appalling. Of the 28,000 children looked after in the period ending March 1999, almost 12,000 had been looked after for at least five years. If a child has been looked after for eighteen months, he or she has an 80 per cent chance of remaining in care for at least another four years, and it is probable that he or she will remain in care until he or she leaves the care-system aged between sixteen and eighteen. Seventy per cent of young people leave the care-system without any educational qualifications. They are ten times more likely than other children to be excluded from school. Seventeen per cent of the girls leaving care are pregnant or are already mothers; only three per cent of twenty-year-old women in the population at large have children. The children of these girls are sixty-six times more likely to need local authority care than the children of those who have not been in care. Thirty-nine per cent of all male prisoners under the age of twenty-one have come out of the care system. Some 80 per cent of them have mental health problems such as depression, anxiety, psychosis or personality disorders. When they are released, they will probably face homelessness and long-term unemployment. At best they will become part of the transient population that drifts from hostel to hostel. They will sleep on the floors of friends. Sometimes they will live in squats, and they will spend some nights on the streets. The transients are always going to get it sorted. The flat or bedsit is always going to be sorted next week, 'by Monday'. And another Monday comes and goes. A few of the transients were adopted as children. The adoptions ended in disaster, the children went back into care and it all started again.

We were visited at home by a warm, friendly woman who was very enthusiastic about her job as a fostering and adoption officer. There will be a lot of women in this story, and relatively few men. Whether this is simply a reflection of our experience or of the way roles are distributed in social services and related professions is not entirely clear to me, but I strongly suspect it is the latter.

Maggie was a fostering and adoption officer and she began to explain what was involved in adopting children. She was glad to learn that we were married because that would make things easier. She confirmed that we probably could not adopt a baby but told us that we should certainly look into adopting an older child or children, that sibling groups were particularly difficult to place and that, if we thought we were prepared to take one on, we might improve our chances. We would, in any case, have to have medicals and police checks would have to be run on us. A parking fine is not an obstacle to adopting, and nor are most minor convictions, but any convictions for scheduled sexual offences or offences against children mean that no approval to adopt or foster can ever be granted. We were told that how much we earned was irrelevant. Living on state benefits should be no obstacle to adoption, and the days when working-class girls gave up babies for adoption to childless middle-class couples are long gone. Adoption no longer satisfies the desires of the childless; it attempts to meet the needs of children. In theory, it is true that the socio-economic status of the prospective adopters is irrelevant but most cases of adoption known to me have involved social promotion for the children concerned. The majority of adopters are either in professional, managerial or technical occupations, and most of the rest have skilled or partly skilled jobs. Only 2 per cent are unemployed.

Maggie went on to explain that we would have to have a series of 'home study' visits from a social worker to assess our suitability. If our initial application was approved, we would be placed on the appropriate register and attempts would be made to match us with children in search of a family. If all went well, children would be placed with us for fostering with a view to adoption. We would then have to work closely with a social worker for a period of up to three or four years. There would be a lot of paperwork to deal with and there were no guarantees of success. She strongly recommended that we attend some day schools about fostering that were to be held in a few weeks' time. They would be very informative and helpful. She was very sorry but there was nothing specifically designed for prospective adopters. It was an exhausting but exciting evening. We were enthusiastic, and very, very frightened, and we decided to go ahead. We signed up for the day schools. We began to read relevant publications and we began to speculate, or rather fantasise, about a future that was going to change everything. We were going to find our forever family. It was a hot summer and I remember the sweaty night when neither of us could sleep. We had just made love (without any more cruel illusions about making babies) and were talking softly as we finally drifted off. 'Do you think it will ever happen? Do you think we can do it?' 'We can do anything.'

We attended the day schools on two consecutive weekends. They took place in a Children's Centre on the edge of the city. The grounds were extensive but the buildings themselves had a truly institutional sadness about them. About thirty or forty people had turned up and were standing around, looking very nervous. We were taken into a large hall. When we were all seated, we were asked to turn to the person sitting next to us ('No, not your partner, please!'), introduce ourselves and then explain why we were interested in fostering. There were bursts of laughter, gasps of fear and mumbled expressions of shyness, but somehow we all managed to do it. The ice had been broken and we could relax. We had ceased to be individuals and couples, and had become a group with a purpose and an agenda.

We began to listen very attentively. The meeting was chaired by social workers, but they left most of the talking to two experienced foster-carers who had seen a lot of children in their time. They told us horror stories about how and why children come into the care system. They told us of the children in their care who had never seen an apple, and of those who had never been given enough to eat. They talked about the five-year-old boy who walked up their garden path with his bloated belly sloshing from side to side, almost as though it were an autonomous thing rather than part of his body. He'd been living mainly on fizzy soft drinks containing vast amounts of sugar, and had turned into a walking bottle of pop that was pretending to be a boy. We were told about the difficulty of living with children with severe behavioural problems, with children who could simply not control their tempers and who would lash out at anyone who came near them and who had no idea of what made them angry. We were asked to imagine life with children who had never attended school on a regular basis, with children who would steal anything in sight or with children who would deliberately soil their bedclothes and the walls and curtains in their bedrooms. They told us about children who could not sleep because something terrible once happened in the darkness of what should be the safest place in the world: a child's bedroom. Perhaps worse still, we were told of children who had forgotten how to laugh or even smile, and of children who had never learned to laugh or smile in the first place. Two foster-carers with years of experience explained why they could no longer keep a pet: one of the children placed in their care had tortured their old cat to death.

We moved on to a new exercise. We were asked to remember important or significant things – good or bad – from our own childhood. The memories came fast: the first car we ever bought . . . a baby's christening . . . the day dad inadvertently got drunk at a wedding . . . the industrial accident that almost killed my father . . . the first foreign holiday we had . . . deaths, births, marriages. Our memories were written down in felt tip on a flip chart. When the big sheet of paper was full, the facilitator ripped it down, tore it, scrunched it into a ball and kicked it into a corner of the room: 'Those are the memories of a child in foster-care. Torn in pieces and thrown away. That's her past.' We had trusted someone with important, even precious memories, and he had betrayed our trust by trashing them. We could begin – but only begin – to imagine how children who have made the same mistake must feel, and to understand why they cannot trust any adult.

We watched a film about fostering in which a teenaged girl turned on the foster-mother she had been living with for two or three years: 'Don't fucking expect me to love you.' We were then asked to imagine that we were fostering a thirteen-year-old girl with a reputation for promiscuity. She has become involved with a thirty-year-old man who is very well known to the local police. Late one evening, he turns up on the doorstep asking to see our foster-child. What do we do? Invite him in? Call her to the door to speak to him? Shut the door in the face of a man with a reputation for violence? Argue with him? Call the police, knowing full well that no offence has been committed? The answer was that there was no right answer but that there were some wrong ones. Most of the group concluded that the 'least wrong' answer was 'Call the social workers.' That sounds sensible but the reality is that the only worker available late in the evening is a duty officer who is covering for a large area. He or she will be quite unable to leave the office and will have no knowledge of this particular girl. The cavalry will not come. The reality is that adoptive parents or foster-carers who find themselves in this position are on their own, but we were not told that. We were not told that there is no one out there.

We were on the point of formally applying to be approved when we suddenly had to take a difficult decision. There was a job opportunity in another town that would mean a big promotion for Marina: should she go for it, and what would happen to the adoption plans if she did get the job? We talked and talked, decided 'yes', decided 'no', and then changed our minds. Finally, we talked to Maggie, who saw no reason why anyone should object if we began the formal application process here and then transferred the application to the other town. We were, after all, a rare commodity. We wanted to adopt, were willing to consider older children, and even a sibling group. There were not many of us.

Marina applied for the job and got it. We went for a last walk on the hills we loved so much and prepared to move. I am a self-employed freelance and can work virtually anywhere and was looking forward to moving back to the region where I grew up. Then we discovered that we could not find a buyer for our house, and all our plans fell through. Marina rented a flat in the town where she was going to work, and I stayed where I was. We had become part of the curious category of the single married. Marina came back almost every weekend – the house was a good deal more comfortable than her rented accommodation, though I did spend some weekends there with her – but it always felt as though we were adjusting to being together, and then adjusting to being apart. Weekday evenings were long for both of us, and the nights were lonely. It was at this point that we started a ritual that we still observe. This was the only good thing about being 'single-married'. I began to prepare special and increasingly elaborate meals (with lots of wine) for Marina on Friday evenings to celebrate her homecoming. I still make special meals for her every week, but we have now moved them to Saturday. During the week, we all eat together in the evening. Saturday evening is for the two of us. Well, that's the theory. The reality is that small vultures scent something, gather, circle and descend.

Weeks and months went by and we still had no buyer. We eventually found the solution after months of this semi-detached existence: we bought a cheap flat and waited for the house market to pick up. For six months, we had two mortgages and lived in a flat while our house stood empty. It was an expensive arrangement, but it did allow us to go ahead with our adoption plans. We phoned another Social Services Department and explained our situation. We said that we were looking to adopt children, realised that there was almost no possibility of a baby, and would be willing to consider a sibling group. We had no real gender preferences, but thought that it would be nice for there to be a daughter in our family. The friendly social worker we were put in touch with was called Sarah, and she at once made it clear that she was very interested in us.

The home-study visits began in the early summer and lasted for six weeks. Regular visits from a social worker who is evaluating your suitability to become prospective adopters are nerve-racking. We were not on probation – that would come later. For the moment, we were on trial. The two-hour sessions once a week were not unpleasant, but nor were they easy. We got to like Sarah and soon became very fond of her. We almost began to think of her as a friend but she never became one, regardless of the real affection we had for her. Sarah would become one of our most important supports, but for the moment she was our assessor. She provided information about a system we did not yet understand, encouraged us, and quietly went on with her assessment of us. How would we cope? We both intended to go on working and had time-consuming jobs, so what arrangements would we make for daytime child-care? What would we do if a child was caught stealing from the local corner shop? How would we cope with illness? Did we approve of the smacking of children? How much television should they watch? Would I give up smoking? What about a child who had been sub-jected to sexual abuse? What if it was discovered that the child was HIV-positive? The questions went on. There was a point to even the most trivial of them: could we meet the needs of a child or children? Would placing a child or children with us be in their best interest? None of this was about our needs. We described ourselves. We talked about our own childhood. How did we meet, and where? What were we like? As individuals? As a couple? What were our strengths? What were our weaknesses? We answered as best we could. We were forced to think about ourselves in a way that we had rarely had call to do before. We had to know who we were, and we were learning a lot about ourselves. It was one thing to know that I loved Marina very deeply and had absolute trust in her, but it was quite another thing to have to put it into words and say it to a third party, and in Marina's presence. Hearing her say the same thing about me was almost as overwhelming as hearing her say she would marry me.

The end of the home-study phase ends, like every other phase in the adoption process, with the filling-in of forms. There are two and both are long and complicated. Form E is about the child or children, and includes a short history and a psychological profile. Form F deals with the prospective adopters. It contained factual information about us, as well as our profiles and of Sarah's assess-ment of our suitability, but it also demanded a statement of our basic beliefs. We were stumped. An Anglican could, I suppose, state in all honesty: 'I believe in the Thirty-Nine Articles (with all the usual mental reservations).' We could not say any such thing. Just what did we believe in? We believed in each other, and not a lot else, really. We talked, racked our brains and talked some more. We both have decades of school and university behind us. And so, eventually and with much heart-searching, we at last agreed on a statement of belief. We believed that we were free, within the obvious limits, and that we were therefore responsible for our own actions. That was about it and it could have come from a first-year student essay on philosophy. Form F was completed and sent off, together with the results of our medicals and those of the criminal records search, to a panel consisting of social workers from the local authority, a councillor, a doctor and up to three independent panel members. We waited. We waited very anxiously. In retrospect, I don't think we needed to be as anxious as we were. In terms of our class and social backgrounds, we were very typical would-be adopters. The mean age of a couple at approval is thirty-seven years and eight months. The age gap between adopters and adopted children averages thirty-five years and seven months. Give or take a few months, we were, without knowing it, identikit adopters.

We are from very different backgrounds. Marina was born in the suburbs, though her father was originally from much the same background as mine. I am from the industrial working class, or what used to be the industrial working class. I am a stereotype: grammar-school boy, first in the family to go to university and all the rest of it. I have a professional job, but I am very proud of where I come from. Most of my personal values must come from my family and class. I have always believed that I am no better than anyone else, and that no one is better than me. I will call no man 'sir', but I try to despise no one and will not knowingly humiliate anyone. Work matters to me and, whilst I don't care what anyone actually does for a living, I do care that they do it well and I believe that there probably is a perfect way to empty dustbins. I do not believe that wealth and influence make those who possess them any better than anyone else. At university, we were taught by an academic with a brilliant international reputation who, in terms of the way he lived his life, was a perfect shit who treated other people abominably. I still respect his academic work, but I've known unemployed labourers who were better men. I do mourn the passing of the industrial working class. I am horrified by what has been done to the world I came from, and still find it hard to believe that the old industrial areas are now blighted by heroin and cocaine. But I do not want the past back. Precisely what my dad did for a living does not matter. The steel, the coal, the iron and the shipbuilding . . . it was all much the same: long hours worked in dirty, dangerous jobs that killed and maimed husbands, fathers and sons. As a boy, I saw and learned to love the harsh beauty of heavy industry. I saw the metal skeletons on the river being fleshed out to become great ships. I saw the molten steel glowing red. I saw the gleaming black diamonds in the coal wagons. And I grew up knowing what happens when the high staging inside the hull gives way, when the molten metal spills and slops from the ladle, when the methane explodes hundreds of feet below ground.

Everyone knew of someone who had been killed or injured, and my father almost died in an industrial accident that left him with a fractured skull and spine. I was five and a half when I nearly lost my father. When he had his accident, he was reading *Alice in Wonderland* with me and it was six months before he could come home to finish it. For the first of the many weeks he spent in hospital, I was not even allowed to see him: a ward like that was, we were told, no place for a child. Part of me has never really recovered from that. It never will. I have no memory of actually being told that my dad had been hurt, probably because some things are too hard to remember. I do remember the visits. My mother, my sister and I travelled by bus – one and a half hours each way – to an isolated hospital on top of a hill. We travelled in the snow and in the rain. The hospital had until recently been a military establishment, and most of the nursing staff were male. It was a grim destination, but once I had got over the initial fear I quite enjoyed going to that surreal place where bed-ridden men used chest expanders to catapult bars of chocolate from one end of the ward to the other. If I caught a bar, I could keep it.

Astonishingly, my dad survived and lived for another thirty-five years. He was a strong man, and we were a lucky family. But he could never go back to his old job, which was both highly skilled and well paid. He was found various jobs in his old workplace: switchboard operator, assistant medical orderly, stores porter. He did them all well and never lost the respect of his workmates or bosses. This must have been how I learned that we should never knowingly humiliate anyone. As a student in London, I once queued at the fishmonger's behind an old lady. It was a cold day and a long queue. When the old lady reached the front of the queue, she saw the price of the eels she wanted, knew that she could not afford them and silently turned away with the hurt and the humiliation etched on her face. If my father had been there, he would have bought her the eels. I could not afford to do so.

After the accident, we had much less money than we had before. There was financial compensation, but not a lot. I could not have the shiny new bikes my friends had and I suspect that my mother and sister could not have many of the things they would have liked either. Yet I have never thought of myself as coming from a poor family and I am convinced that there is more (or perhaps less) to poverty than having little money. We had each other. The house was warm and there were always books. Somehow, my parents paid off a mortgage and modernised the house. We had holidays. When my father died, he left my mother comfortably off. We always lived in the same small terraced house. I always thought it was a good house; it was warm and safe, and I always liked going back there. When my mother could no longer cope and moved into sheltered housing, I sat alone in the house for the last time. All the furniture had been moved out, and I suddenly saw that it was not a good house after all. It was smaller than I had ever realised and it had not been well maintained; in the bedrooms, there were patches of damp that I had never seen. This was a poor house, and it always had been. We had turned it into the warm, safe house I grew up in. And now it was just the empty, tatty little house where I was sitting in tears because our warm, safe house had gone.

Marina lives with her own experience of loss. She wasn't even in her teens when her mother died of a thyroid condition that would not kill anyone these days. She was sent to a convent boarding school, and thought she had been banished into exile. She says that she never had an adolescence. Her years at boarding school have, on the other hand, left her with the ability to eat and digest almost anything, and she laughs as she recalls being one of the very few girls to have been unaffected by an outbreak of food poisoning that laid most of the school low ('I think it was the corned-beef hash'). It was a simple choice: she either ate what was on her plate, or she did not eat. Marina and I now enjoy a prosperous life on good incomes and, whilst we are by no means wealthy, we live comfortably. I don't want more than that. In material terms, we can give our children a good life and that is important, but it does not matter that we cannot give them a life of luxury. We have all the things we need and most of the things we want, and having more would not change our situation.

Just what Marina and I do is irrelevant. It is not social class that creates the problems experienced by so many adoptive families and being rich or poor makes no difference. The way in which we live our life is, on the other hand, very relevant. Marina works outside the home in a demanding profession and a harsh commercial environment; I am freelance and work mainly from home. My work can be very demanding too. I often have to do things at very short notice and that puts me under a lot of pressure but I can usually organise my work as I see fit, and no one cares which hours of the day or night I work. This must have some impact on how the children see us and on how they see themselves: Mum goes out to work, and Dad stays in his work room. This is not the pattern they observe in their friends' families but they rarely make anything of it. This may be because they regularly mix with children living in non-standard families. They have friends who are being raised by grandparents, by single parents, by foster-carers, by mums with boyfriends and by dads with girlfriends, and the list goes on. Paul announced one day that 'two lesbians' were moving into the street. Whilst he obviously thought that the arrival of 'two lesbians' was cause for comment, the fact that they were bringing up two girls together was not. It was simply not worth mentioning. I'm not sure that our children have much idea of what a 'normal' nuclear family is. And they are remarkably tolerant and accepting of all the different families they encounter; so far as they are concerned, that's just the way things are.

As I am at home, I do most, if not all, of the cooking, especially during the week. As Marina is off to work by eight most days, and often does not get home until six or seven, she can scarcely be expected to start cooking then. In any case, I like cooking and I'm good at it. The children very quickly got used to the idea of 'Dad in the kitchen' and do seem to have learned that gender roles have to be flexible. A very angry young Cate once screamed at me: 'You get back in the kitchen, Dad!' We eat well, and that is important to us. We eat freshly cooked food. Very little of it comes out of tins. Take-aways are a treat, and so are ready-prepared meals from supermarkets. We do not buy food from burger joints on the way home. The children have had their share of visits to McDonald's and Burger King, and they enjoyed them. So did I, but I am glad they can go by themselves now. But such visits have never been a substitute for good fresh food made at home. We have tried to bring up our children to eat well and to enjoy doing so, and I think we have succeeded. Kieran used to come home from school saying, with some pride, that we ate things his friends had never heard of. Paul and Cate can come to blows over who stole the last of the green salad. On what must have been one of our first holidays in France, Cate watched me eating mussels and chips, cautiously tried a mussel and was immediately hooked. Watching our little girl work her way through a bowl of mussels and a mound of freshly cooked chips was pure delight. Seeing the three of them devour huge helpings of couscous for the first time was an enormous pleasure. By the time they'd finished, there was not a grain left.

The psychotherapist I saw for so long sometimes asked me what I saw as my role in the family. I never really knew how to answer that question, except by saying 'being a parent'. I've been so many things over the years: keeper of small mammals, applier (and remover) of sticking plasters, changer of nappies, the sea monster in the swimming pool and a thousand other things too. Marina has been all those things too. I genuinely don't think that we have ever thought in terms of strongly defined roles for 'Mum' and 'Dad'. There is only one area in which this is not true: I do not drive. I accept that this is grossly unfair and that it places a burden upon

Marina, but I am far too frightened of today's traffic to do anything about it. Other than that it's always been a matter of loosely defined 'parent' roles, though in some confused way I think that I probably do want to be the children's mother. Whatever bizarre fantasy lies behind that, I do play an important nurturing role, even though 'Dad in the kitchen' is as much a result of the way we organise our lives as of any decision on my part. On the whole, our arrangements work, but it has to be said that we are not good at housework and live in a terrible mess. There are the days when I stomp around complaining that 'If I don't do it all, nothing ever gets done!' There are the days when Marina stomps around saying precisely the same thing.

There are also problems with the way we have cast me in the role of cook. Food does not just have a nutritional value. It also has a symbolic value: it means being together and looking after each other, and this puts any cook in a vulnerable position. The children very quickly learned that one way to upset me and hurt me is to reject the food I put in front of them; as they well know, a lot of effort goes into it. I can make a joke of being told to get back in the kitchen, but not of being told 'I'm not eating that crap.' That hurts, and they know it. It is a trap of my own making, and I fall into it quite regularly. I should have learned the lesson by now but I haven't.

We have made many mistakes in bringing up our children, but we have done some things right. Feeding them properly is one of them. Unlike many of the children I see on the street and at school, they are not overweight. They are roughly the size and shape that children of their age should be. They will not be obese children and they will not grow up to be obese adults. They do not expect or demand to be given industrial quantities of sweets. They sail through dental checks-ups and medicals.

We made an offer for a house and it was accepted. We started packing. Predictably, we could not sell the flat and for several months we still had two mortgages, as the ability to read and exploit the property market has never been one of our strengths.

We moved on 5 November. As we sat amongst a chaos of packing cases, the phone rang. When we finally found where the phone was in all the mess, we heard Sarah's voice. We had been approved to foster up to three children with a view to their adoption. She might, she said, have something in mind for us. We scarcely knew what to say, but we immediately found someone to say it to. The man who knocked at the door was our new neighbour, come to introduce himself as the local vicar. After the introductions had been made, Malcolm asked if we had children. Stumbling over our words, we explained that we hadn't, but had just been approved as prospective adopters. 'Oh, congratulations! Our two are adopted as well.'

We began to wait again. This time, it was a very different kind of waiting. We were waiting to become a family. We were waiting for the process of matching us to potential adoptees to begin. It was a delicious agony. We talked constantly about what the future might be. We made plans, changed them and then made new plans. We began to think about schools and about childcare. Mothercare and the Early Learning Centre suddenly became very interesting places. Toy shops took on a new meaning and soft toys became almost impossible to resist. But resist we did: we had to wait, and be patient. We were patient, but our level of anxiety was rising precipitously.

The last Christmas we spent without children was unforgettable. We were in a new house and we felt very cosy together. Just before Christmas, our car was stolen. We'd gone into the town centre by train, and when we got back to the car park where we had left the Fiesta, it was gone and it was never recovered. Either it was torched somewhere, or it is still rotting at the bottom of the river and providing a home for whatever aquatic monsters can survive that degree of pollution. Having no car for a couple of weeks proved to be a wonderful blessing. I had family in the region – my mother and sister – but they had no car at the time. Public transport was not operating over the holiday, so we couldn't go anywhere, and no one could come to us. We were cut off and it was wonderful. I don't recall much sex that Christmas, or at least not much 'complete' sex. I do remember lots of hugs, cuddles and love.

Sarah contacted us after the holidays. There were two possible matches. Two brothers aged three and five were looking for a new family. So were a boy aged five, his half-brother aged three and his half-sister aged fifteenth months. From time to time, I still wonder what happened to those two little boys.

II

According to the government's National Adoption Standards, 'adopters will be given full written information about the child before matching or an opportunity to consider it'. For some time now, Marina and I have been part of a support group for the adoptive parents of teenagers. How the group would laugh if someone read that out to us! We would laugh until we cried. To save time, some of us would just cry without bothering to laugh first. In this context, 'full written information' is a very relative concept and in extreme cases, all the information could be given on two scraps of paper. It is also quite conceivable that there is no 'full information' about a child in search of a family. What full information can there be about a baby who was found abandoned in a public toilet?

We certainly did not have anything like full information about our children before we were matched with them or even when we first met them, but the little information that we did have was grim enough. We knew that Kieran was the first child of Viv and her husband Kevin, and that Viv was in her early twenties when she had Kieran. We knew that the relationship with Kevin turned violent and that both Viv and Kieran suffered as a result. We knew about the many accidents that occurred during Kieran's first years, about the cups of coffee that were spilled on him and the cupboard that fell on him, and about how he was found playing on the pavement only inches away from heavy lorry traffic. We knew that there had been several changes of address, that Viv and Kevin split up and that, after a number of affairs with abusive partners, Viv embarked on a relationship with Andy, though we are not sure whether or not they actually lived together. We knew that this relationship turned violent too. We knew that Andy was the father of Paul and Cate, and also the man who sexually abused Kieran. How often the abuse occurred is not on record, but it was known that the physical injuries Kieran suffered required medical attention. When we first met him, one of the boy's most prized possessions was the little teddy bear he had been given by the nurse who had looked after him in hospital.

We were told the basic story. Immediately after the discovery of the abuse, Kieran, who was three, and Paul, who was just over a year old, were taken into the care of the local authority. Cate, who was conceived after the boys had been removed from Viv's care, was automatically deemed to be 'at risk' and was placed with foster-parents within days of being born. All three children were made wards of court, and Viv lost her parental rights. When we first met the children, no one knew where Kevin was. Andy, on the other hand, was still around, and a lot of social workers and police officers would have been only too happy to find grounds for arresting him. The children were all being looked after by different foster-parents and had never lived together as a family, but they knew of each other's existence and there was regular but limited contact between Paul and Kieran. All three were the youngest in their respective foster families. Viv remained in contact with her children and visited them fairly regularly, usually accompanied by a social worker, but, according to the foster-carers, who were not necessarily the best or most reliable of informants, she took little interest in her children, rarely played with them and spent most of the time talking about her own problems.

The story got worse as we learned more. Viv had been taken into care at the age of five months. She was a slow learner and appears to have had special educational needs as a child. Her carer died when she was a young woman, and her life immediately became chaotic; there were a number of different men, most of them violent, and a lot of alcohol. Her marriage to Kevin should have been the starting point for a more stable kind of existence, but the break-up destroyed all hope of that. Andy was a shadowy figure, but he was rumoured to have had an incestuous relationship with his sisters who had, he claimed, tried to 'force themselves on him'. One of the very few people to believe that story was Viv, who refused to accept that Andy had abused Kieran, and went on having a sexual relationship with him while her son was hospitalised for fifteen days before being taken into care. All this was hard to assimilate and harder still to come to terms with. Marina and I began to realise that we had led very sheltered lives and felt that we were looking into darkness, and we were.

We were looking into the darkness that the poster-child Emma came from. It is always there in the places where the stolen cars are found torched, where strangers are not welcome in the pubs where 'Who are you looking at?' can be the prelude to a glassing. Out here, violence is almost the norm, and much of it is directed against women and children. Sexuality is governed by different codes, and sometimes appears to be governed by no code at all. There are families here with a tradition of incest that goes back generations. There are men here who have had children by a score of women, and men who have had children by three different generations of women in a single family.

If the little information we had was difficult to take in, it was almost impossible to relate it to the children we actually met. Sarah introduced us to three perfectly ordinary children. They did not have tails and there were no visible stigmata; they were simply gorgeous. They all looked different, as Kieran was dark-haired whilst Cate was a sort of mousy blonde. Paul had bright red hair, though it has lost its flame-like quality over the years. Although they did look physically different, there was and is a likeness too: they all have the same beautiful blue-grey eyes and the same long lashes that give the two boys a delicious hint of femininity. At times, Kieran looks like Cate, and then he looks like Paul. It's almost as though they could pass the likeness to each other, or as though the likeness changed as the light changed. The same thing happens with mannerisms and facial expressions: they share a common repertoire.

Kieran was living with a couple who both had good jobs in the public sector. When we first saw him, he was playing on the carpet with his toy cars but looked up and gave us a big smile when we entered the room. He was very happy with his foster-carers and adored their daughter, who was four years older than him, even though (or because) she bossed him about. He told us that he liked going to help his grandfather on his allotment and that the beetroot was what he liked best. Kieran was, we were told by his foster-parents, well-behaved, and always tidied his bedroom and made his own bed. He was settling in well to his first year at school and enjoyed going to church on Sundays. Kieran was well-spoken, very articulate and seemed to be very self-possessed. He was five.

Paul was living with Joan, recently widowed and now a full-time foster-carer who had looked after many children over the years. One of them had simply refused to leave her when he reached eighteen, and he was still there. Danny looked just the kind of lad you do not want to meet coming out of the pub late on a Friday night, and may well have been, but he adored both Joan and the three-year old Paul, and spoiled him rotten. Paul himself was a red-headed squiggle of a boy who said little to us – 'Me a good boy' was about it – as he scrambled over the furniture, half-wearing a pair of pyjamas. There was a foster-daughter in the room too. She must have been about eight and she had the wary look of some wild animal. Her eyes were sad and she always seemed to make sure that there was a piece of furniture between her and everyone else. Sarah later told us that Keelie had been sexually abused, as had her brother, who was also in the care system. Her face is one I cannot forget.

When we first saw Cate, she was crawling over the carpet in pursuit of a white cat that had no intention of being caught. She was chubby, overdressed for that warm room, and very eager to be cuddled by anyone who picked her up. The room was crowded, and I can't remember her foster-family as well as the others. There were two older girls, one walking with a stick, but I can't see their faces now.

These first meetings were joyous – to put it simply, we fell in love three times over – but also incredibly fraught. We all knew what was going on, but it was different for all of us. Marina and I were meeting children who might become ours; their carers were meeting the people who were almost certainly going to take their foster-children away from them. Kieran's carers had in fact thought of adopting him, but had always put off the decision. And now it was too late, and he was going to be adopted by someone else. The children, with the possible exception of Kieran, obviously had no idea of what was happening. What does a three-year-old actually hear when he is told by the foster-mother he has been living with for the last eighteen months: 'Marina and John are going to be your new mum and dad'? What can the words mean?

We began to visit regularly, at first with Sarah and then on our own. On the whole, all the foster-carers were, given the circumstances, remarkably friendly and hospitable. We were all very polite to one another and tried to pretend to ourselves, and to each other, that we could cope with all these conflicting emotions. We took the boys on outings and we went to a fairground. We went to the beach and came back with wet feet, and they came to tea at our house, where they were horrified to find that we had not got around to buying any toys, and met our ginger cat, who did not know what was going to hit him. Both Kieran and Paul were easy to like, chatty and friendly. The four of us were getting on well together, but we were seeing much less of Cate, whose foster-mother was making it very obvious that she did not want to let her go.

As it began to look more likely that the children would be placed with us – and sooner rather than later – I realised that I had to go away for a while to complete the project I was working on because it would be almost impossible to find the time once they were with us. I went, and felt terrible about doing so as it meant leaving Marina in such a difficult position. After a full day in a very demanding job – to which she was still adjusting – she went out to visit the children, and then back to an empty house, late, tired and hungry. She described the evening on which she was left to give Paul his bath, and of the reaction she got; Joan told her with some amusement that she had done it 'just like us'. She had, in other words, got down on her knees by the side of the bath. Now, there are only so many positions in which one can bathe a small child, and standing up is not one of them. The source of the amusement, which presumably masked some very mixed emotions, was the sight of Marina on her knees. It was a funny sight simply because Marina was 'posh'. Although it was never said in so many words, I am convinced that the children's foster-carers perceived us as 'rich' and possibly even 'upper-class'. They probably did think that this would be to the children's advantage, but it almost certainly also fuelled their resentment. Not only were their children being taken away from them, they were being taken away by a rich couple.

I sensed something strangely familiar about all three houses – and especially Joan's – but couldn't pin it down at first. And then I realised what it was: the heat. The rooms in which we met the children were all overheated, but other rooms were cold. That was what I remembered: one hot room in a cold house. I grew up in a house like that. That was how skilled industrial workers used to live. The background of all the foster-carers was very similar to my own. There was something familiar about Danny too or, more accurately, about the pairing of young man and small boy. It took me a while to work it out. When my father was hospitalised for all those months after his accident, I was regularly taken out by one of his young workmates. He would turn up on the doorstep in the full teddy-boy regalia of drape-jacket, drainpipe trousers and brothel-creepers. To a lot of people, he must have looked menacing, but he cared enough to look after a little boy. So that was it: there had been a Danny in my life too.

We went on visiting as the winter became a cold spring and in the course of one visit, Kieran picked up a photograph and said: 'That's Cate. She's coming too.' It was now obvious that the children were going to be placed with us. There was more paperwork, and more forms to be filled in. We began to make preparations and to get both very excited and very anxious. Social Services provided a cot and a buggy for Cate, and Sarah, a woman with no children of her own, told us that she had great fun looking for them. We bought two beds for the boys, who would be sharing the large front bedroom, and we bought a wardrobe, which proved to be a disaster. It would have been fine in an adults' room; we just failed to anticipate how much wear and tear two small boys can inflict on anything that is not made of reinforced concrete.

We visited two local primary schools, with very little idea of what to look for, and tried to ask meaningful questions about the teaching of phonics. One school was at the top of a hill and the fence around the playground succeeded in attracting every piece of waste paper for miles around. I found it all too reminiscent of the playing fields where I had almost frozen to death as a boy. The alternative was slightly closer to home, much easier to get to and rather less exposed. It was an old building but it had a good feel to it; the classrooms were bright with posters and pictures, and the headteacher and her staff were welcoming. We also had to think of the needs of two pre-school children, and it was probably the nursery – purpose-built and at a slight distance from the main school – that swayed our decision. We'd already met the nursery teacher when she came to the door on Easter Sunday to give us a little chocolate egg at the suggestion of Malcolm the vicar. Before long, she would become the young woman Paul knew as 'My Miss Vaughan'. A year later, she became Cate's Miss Vaughan.

Everything was moving terrifyingly fast now. Most parents have an indeterminate period of 'trying' and then the nine months of a pregnancy to prepare for the arrival of a baby, but we had only a few weeks to prepare for the arrival of three children who were certainly not babies. And then everything accelerated again. We had been told that the boys would be placed with us during the third week of March, whilst Cate would be placed with us a week later. That was not quite how it worked out. The boys were placed with us on schedule but Cate came to us only two days later. Twelve hours before she arrived, we were still trying to assemble her cot. Both days were fraught; for us they were joyous events, but the children's foster-carers experienced them as calamitous events. We were establishing a family, but they were losing children they had lived with and loved for a long time. On those two days, the house was full of powerful and confused emotions as joyous events and calamitous events took place simultaneously. The house was full of frightened children, foster-carers on the point of letting their children go, social workers trying to ensure that everything went smoothly and two people on the point of becoming parents for the first time, and three times over. Our joy was blunted by the sight of foster-carers in tears; their anguish was made worse by our happiness. Those are days I would not care to live through again.

We were given a fostering allowance and allocated a social worker. It was agreed that Sarah would go on working with the children, but Marina and I would also have a worker of our own. He was a perfectly nice man in most respects and would, I am sure, have been good company in the pub, but was not a great deal of help to us in professional terms. He did, however, give us one valuable piece of advice. We should not, he told us, try to keep in touch with the children's foster families. At first I was surprised by this, but he was right; a lot of the past had to go, even though it was hard for the children. In moments of fear or anxiety, Kieran and Paul would cry and ask for their foster-carers because that is who they wanted, not us. Still unable to say who or what she wanted, Cate just cried and cried because of her feeling of the bitter loss. They went on crying for almost a year.

For several weeks, the children's foster-carers regularly rang to see how they were getting on, to say hello to them and, no doubt, to check up on us. Marina and I soon began to resent the calls and to see them as an unwanted intrusion; this was our family and we wanted to get on with learning how to live together as a family. Eventually, the calls became less regular and then ceased. The only contact we have now is through the Christmas cards we exchange with the couple who fostered Kieran, and we have had no contact at all with the other carers. We have never had any direct contact with our children's birth mother, and have never wanted to have any. We are, on the other hand, quite happy to have 'letter-box' contact, which is facilitated by social workers and works on a strictly confidential basis. Every year, we send off a brief letter describing the children's progress and a few photographs, but neither I nor Marina appear in the photos and we cannot be identified or traced. In exchange, we receive photographs and a short letter from Viv, though we usually have to ask for them. Viv now has four more children, each by a different father. Our children are intrigued to know that they have four half-sisters somewhere out there, but the photos can also upset them and they always ask why Viv could not keep them too. Kieran will glance at the photos we receive but he always refuses to read the accompanying letter: 'She never asks about me.' He is quite right: the letter, which is written on the semi-literate Viv's behalf by a social worker, is always about her. Although the photos are helpful to the children, they can also feed some uneasy fantasies. When she was just fourteen, Cate told us that the social workers had a vast collection of letters written to her by Viv and that they would give them all to her 'when I'm eighteen'. We did not have the heart to disillusion her and left that job to the professionals.

We have never avoided the issue of the past and the children have always known that they are adopted. We could, I suppose, have avoided telling Cate, but we could scarcely conceal anything from a five-year-old and a three-year-old, and we did not want to. We have always tried to explain to them that Viv did love them and wanted to keep them with her, but just could not do so. We do not blame her, though I do think she allowed a lot of harm to be done to Kieran in particular (or perhaps she just could not prevent it from being done). Even so, there is no question of malice on our part. From the little we know about Viv's own life, it is quite obvious that she never really stood a chance. It is also quite obvious that she and her daughters are receiving a high level of support from Social Services; if they were not, four more little girls would be looking for forever families. The children do ask about their birth mother and we answer their questions as best we can. The questions usually come at holiday times. The children perceive holidays as an upheaval and, at the level of fantasy, as a prelude to being 'moved on' yet again, and they inevitably dredge up submerged memories of real upheavals and of the times when they really were moved on. From time to time, they have talked of trying to contact their birth mother, though I suspect that it is, especially for Cate, the four half-sisters who are the real attraction. Cate once said that she wanted to see Viv: 'So I can tell her how mad I am at her for sending me away.' When Paul and Cate reach eighteen, they will have a legal right to have access to all the adoption papers, and to look for Viv. If they do decide to try to trace her, we will do our best to support them though I'm not sure that we will encourage them in their efforts. It would not be hard to trace Viv, as some social worker must know where she is and would be able to act as an intermediary. Whether or not she wants to be traced is a different matter altogether. Neither Paul nor Cate has ever said much about trying to find their father Andy, which is probably just as well, given that finding their father would mean finding Kieran's abuser. Kieran is now old enough to ask to see all the files but has shown no interest whatsoever in tracing Viv. He went through a phase of talking about trying to find his father but it never went further than that.

Until at least the mid-1970s, the theory was that adoption marked a 'clean break' with the past and the start of a new life. The past was gone, and that was that. The theory now looks terrifyingly naive: the past exists and will not just go away, and even babies store up memories. Any move away from that naivety is to be welcomed, but I fear that it may be a move towards a new naivety. Birth mothers and fathers now have the right to trace their adopted children, and the new emphasis on more open forms of adoption in which at least some contact with the past is maintained sometimes seems to suggest that the three parties most closely involved in an adoption – birth mother, child, adoptive parents – can coexist. This seems naive to me, as their interests are not necessarily the same, and as the emotions involved are hard to reconcile. Viv, Marina and I, and our three children, can never be some sort of extended family, and I sincerely hope that no one encourages Viv to take advantage of the new legislation and to try to trace Kieran, Paul and Cate.

A past had to go, and a future had to be organised, or at least improvised. We had to make childcare arrangements. Marina was granted three months of 'adoption leave' by her employers. I am still not entirely sure whether that was a statutory right or a discretionary privilege but we could not have coped without it. In the longer term, the best arrangement would, we decided, be to employ a nanny. We did not have room for a live-in nanny or au pair, and in any case we did not want to have a stranger living in our house as adapting to life with three children was going to be difficult enough. We began the search in time-honoured manner and bought a copy of *The Lady*, which we found to be a very odd publication. No one suitable was looking for a nanny's job in our area. And then, Sarah had the brilliant idea of contacting a local Further Education College that ran a National Nursery Examining Board course to see if it could find us someone.

We were lucky enough to find an eighteen-year-old who had just completed her two-year diploma course and was looking for a first job. She was lucky too, as she turned out to be the only 'applicant' for the post. We decided terms: for five days a week,

Angie would arrive at eight-thirty, or in time to get Kieran to school, look after the other two for the morning and afternoon, bring Kieran back from school and look after all three children until about five. Then, I would take over until Marina got back from work. Angie would do the children's washing and keep their rooms tidy. Angie agreed to feed Cate and Paul at lunch time, and even offered to make a meal for me too. I turned down the offer, mainly because I felt embarrassed at the idea of an eighteen-year-old cooking for me in my own home. In the end, I was glad I turned her down because, whilst Angie proved to have many talents, none of them were culinary. She established a strong relationship with the children and they grew very fond of her indeed. Life without Angie would have been very difficult to cope with, but her main role was not one covered by any job description: she absorbed a lot of the day-to-day turbulence of our family life, mopped up a lot of the tempestuous emotions and allowed us to save some of the strength we needed to have.

Marina woke me at two or two-thirty in the morning. There was a dragon in Kieran's room and he had woken her to ask her to get a knife from the kitchen to kill it. She asked me what I thought we should do. I really did not know, but even to someone who had just woken up, knives did not sound like a good idea. Kieran was sitting bolt upright on his bed, staring at something with fierce attention. He was sweating and his heart was racing, and he could certainly see something that was not there for us to see. It was a dragon and he had to kill it before it killed us. Kieran's speech was rapid but clear. We pretended that we could at least hear the dragon breathing, but Kieran told us not to be stupid: 'That's just Paul snoring.' Yes, we could see the dragon now and it was a big one. What could we do? I suddenly thought of something. If we knew its name, we could talk to it and tell it to go away and leave us alone. But I somehow knew that no dragon will tell a stranger its name, or at least not its real name. We had to trick it. We began to ask it questions and riddles. Eventually, we realised that the dragon had made the mistake of letting slip its real name. Solemnly but politely – offending a dragon can be a risky business – I addressed it by name and told it to go, and it obediently left the room. As an afterthought, I warned it never to come back: 'Remember, I know your name. Your real name.' We have never seen that dragon again. Next morning, Kieran could remember absolutely nothing about the incident.

We had just witnessed an attack of 'pavor noctis' or night terrors, which occur during the later phases of sleep. I don't really know why I reacted as I did that night, but everything suggests that I acted correctly. Pavor noctis is not in itself dangerous, though it is certainly alarming to see. Nor is sleepwalking dangerous in itself, but a sleepwalking child is in danger of falling downstairs or out of a window that has been left open. Getting a knife could have been disastrous as Kieran might well have used it in some imaginary battle and hurt himself or one of us. Shouting at a child in this condition is futile: she won't hear, but may well retain some unconscious memory of having been shouted at in the middle of the night. The idea of asking the dragon riddles in order to trick it into telling us its name came to me, I thought, unbidden but I gradually worked out that it came from a vague memory of the dangerous game Bilbo plays with Gollum in the 'Riddles in the Dark' chapter of *The Hobbit*, whilst the notion that knowing the real name of a creature gives one power over it was a very confused memory of Ursula Leguin's *Earthsea* books. I hadn't read either Tolkein or Leguin for at least fifteen years.

Days later, we took delivery of a pine table for the kitchen. Paul was looking out of the window when he saw the van pull up. Two men got out. Arms locked at the elbows and fists clenched tight, Paul began to scream and he went on screaming in total panic. When we finally calmed him down, he was quite unable to explain what had happened. No one has ever been able to do so. All we know is that an everyday occurrence had caused Paul to panic, and we can only speculate as to why this happened. Did Paul once see someone being taken away by two men in a van? Was it a police van? Did he see Andy being arrested and taken away? Did he see Kieran being taken away? Was he freaked by a memory of something that had happened to him? There is no way of knowing, and we will never find this missing piece of the jigsaw. This, we had been told by a social worker who had known Paul since birth, was a calm little boy who could take anything in his stride, and who could easily adapt to changing circumstances. But one day when we went to the beach with friends and, at the end of a happy day, Kieran asked them if he could get into their car, Paul could not take it in his stride. Our friends said that they would take Kieran home and he grinned all over but Paul, who was sitting in the back of our car, suddenly began to scream in fear. He had overheard the exchange and had jumped to the conclusion that our friends were taking Kieran to their home. He knew what was going on: someone was taking his brother away from him, and not for the first time. Nothing we had been told had allowed us to anticipate this pattern of behaviour.

I am not suggesting that information was deliberately withheld from us. But more of it could certainly have been provided, and it would have helped. When Kieran told us that he had moved many more times than Paul, and that he had therefore had the harder life, we more or less told him that he was talking nonsense. When we mentioned this in the course of a review meeting, the senior social worker present fumbled through his briefcase and finally produced a sheet of paper. After consulting it, he told us that Kieran was quite right: he had moved fifteen times in the three years he was with Viv. Casual conversations with Kieran himself gradually taught us more about the nature of these moves. There had been a big house with lots of women with children, but he could not remember any men being present. It was very crowded, and he remembered having to share a room. Kieran was describing a women's refuge.

When we did finally see the document describing Kieran's fifteen moves, we learned other things we had not been told about. When Viv went into hospital to have Paul, Kieran was taken into care for a few days. Presumably he then went home to find that all at once he had a little brother and concluded that he was being replaced. We later learned that Kieran's visits to see Paul at Joan's were always followed by long and violent tantrums. With a little more knowledge about this, we might have understood more about the boys' often tempestuous relationship. We would also have been able to believe what Kieran told us, and he would have been more prepared to talk to us as a result. The withholding of knowledge, or simply the failure to share it, is a way of exercising power and it is a way of ensuring that adoptive parents remain dependent upon their social workers. The withholding of information may not be deliberate, but it does reflect the inequality of the adoptive parents' relationship with social workers. It is, for instance, quite possible to imagine a worker saying to a case conference, 'Oh, they don't need to know that. It's not important,' or even 'Better not tell them that.' We have not found it easy to find information about our children's past, and at times we have had to fight hard for the little we have. To her immense credit, Sarah always did her best to ensure that we were kept as fully informed as possible and to avoid 'magic circles' of 'experts in the know', but there were things that she did not know either. We began to piece some things together from what Kieran told us himself. Each of his moves had meant a new separation from an environment – and presumably people – with which he had just become familiar. It meant a new experience of loss. At the age of only five, he had already experienced the trauma of loss on at least fifteen different occasions.

We did know in advance about the abuse Kieran had experienced and we were therefore quite ready for his 'disclosure'. It came one teatime and was perfectly matter of fact: 'Andy put a stick up my bottom. He squirted lemon juice in my face and mouth.' There was no need to ask Sigmund Freud for an interpretation. On other occasions, Freud might have been helpful. What did the fear of masks, and especially clown masks, mean? Did Andy wear a mask when he abused Kieran? Did someone come into Kieran's room wearing a clown mask? If so, what happened next? Were there other abusers too? I don't know, but Kieran went on being afraid of masks and clowns for a surprisingly long time. Watching *ET* for the first time terrified him. There is a scene in which scientists wearing protective clothing and helmets come to collect the alien, who has fallen ill, and Kieran screamed and burst into tears when he saw it. Had it triggered a memory? Was he seeing something that had happened to him? Was he seeing the van that may, we think, have terrified Paul? We have no answers to these questions.

Other bits and pieces emerged from the games he played. The way Kieran liked to play tying-up games with Paul strongly suggested that he had witnessed both oral sex acts and scenes of bondage involving his birth mother. There was also a much more complicated game involving a bed sheet that clearly represented a river. Someone had to lie in the river, and then die there; they then had to come back to life, sing and suck Kieran's penis. The only 'someone' available to play the game was Paul. We discussed all this with Sarah and she agreed that he was acting out and repeating the abuse and other traumatic experiences in an attempt to control and then exorcise memories that frightened him. But who else was involved in the scenes he had witnessed? Kevin? Andy? Other men? What did the singing mean? Could it possibly be a distorted memory of a woman coming to orgasm? There had been hints of sexualised behaviour during his foster-care placement, when Kieran had had to be very firmly told that it was not acceptable for him to lie on top of his foster-sister and ask her to open her legs. Marina, Sarah and I now began to explain to him that he should not be playing these games with Paul. We did not want him to be asexual, and we were not worried about sex play as such; what worried us was the way Kieran was acting out and reproducing the past. Between ourselves, we liked to joke that he could have all the oral sex he wanted when he was sixteen, but preferably not with his half-brother.

As a result of incidents like this, we became very watchful. Anything might tell us something about the past history of our children, and of Kieran in particular. And so we began to interpret everything they did or said, as though every gesture and every word had a hidden meaning. We also began to watch our children like hawks. We were acquiring one of the characteristic traits of adoptive parents: hyper-vigilance. All adoptive parents watch constantly. We all watch present behaviour because it might tell us something about the past, and because watching what the children are doing now might tell us what they are going to do next. When adoptive families meet or gather together, all the parents watch their own children, the other parents and all their children too. Our hyper-awareness means that we rarely relax and that we can rarely allow ourselves to be spontaneous because we are constantly reading the signs and waiting for the next explosion. We make store detectives look unobservant. Hyper-vigilance is also a characteristic feature of children who have been traumatised by abuse, loss or violence. They are always watching for signs of the danger that once threatened them and that will, at some point, threaten them once more. When the threat materialises, it will trigger the very primitive response of 'fight or flight'. That was Paul's response when he saw two men delivering our table and when he thought Kieran was being taken away from him. That was Kieran's response when he asked for a knife to kill the dragon.

According to the folklore of adoption, placement is followed by a honeymoon period in which everyone purrs in the bosom of their new and perfect family. In the case of Kieran, we learned almost at once that the period of bliss was already over, and that the few meetings at the home of his foster-carers and our days out together had been the honeymoon. Within days of his placement with us, it was well and truly over. Violent tantrums were not just a daily occurrence: they occurred at least three – sometimes four – times a day, and they were never over quickly. Toys would regularly fly through the air, and they were thrown with considerable violence. Kieran was frequently rude, offensive even, to both of us. We could not understand why, but the well-spoken and polite boy we had met was turning into someone very different, and we could not tell who or what he was becoming. In retrospect, it was obvious that he had been traumatised by yet another separation and yet another move; he did not want to be where he was. There were other signs that not all was well. There was the phone call from school asking if Kieran really should have ten pounds in his pocket. A few pieces of Marina's jewellery disappeared, and we think they were given to a little girl at school. Kieran was trying to buy himself friends.

We gradually began to observe a pattern in Kieran's behaviour. Many of his actions seemed calculated to annoy and irritate us and other people. They invited an angry response, and they certainly got it. Again and again, Kieran would behave in such a way that we felt we had no option but to punish him. We would confiscate toys, put him in the sin bin or on the 'naughty stair'. We threatened worse punishments: we would take his bike away, or whatever else we could think of. Nothing worked. We just could not understand why a boy of his age seemed to want to be punished and to make us so angry with him that we could spit verbal abuse at him. Kieran tapped into internal reserves of rage and anger whose existence we had never suspected. What we did not realise until a very long time later was that we were allowing him to write the rules of the game. If we were angry with him, he was the centre of our attention and could control the situation. Our anger, which was a natural reaction, just made everything worse. That is what he wanted. We had allowed ourselves to be drawn into his game, and he was much better at it than we were. We would eventually learn that adoptive parents cannot afford to have natural reactions.

Although Kieran settled into school to some extent, it was obvious that he was having problems. He was finding it difficult to make friends and the playground was not a comfortable place for him to be. There was not much we could do about that, as no adult can teach a child the code of the playground. At home, Kieran had his siblings. The longer they were with us, the closer the children became and Kieran did emerge as a charismatic older brother for Paul and Cate, but relations between the three of them could also be very strained. Paul in particular was on the receiving end of a lot of aggression which could turn into violence. One evening, we heard screams and found Paul on the floor of the boys' bedroom, bleeding from a cut to his head. It looked as though he had fallen out of bed and banged his head on the skirting board, but Kieran could easily have pushed him out of bed. This was not the only incident of the kind. It isn't easy to know what goes on in a bedroom but it was perfectly clear that Paul had not climbed into the toy box and closed the lid all by himself. We reworked the sleeping arrangements and moved Paul into a room with Cate. Kieran played with his siblings but he also spent time alone. The previous owners of our house had left behind a supply of coal and washing it became one of Kieran's favourite games.

Sometimes that was all he wanted to do. On cold days, a little boy would spend hours outside washing coal in cold water. It was a bleak sight.

Kieran had been accustomed to going to church with his foster-carers and made it clear that he would like to go on doing so. He said he liked the singing. We were perfectly happy to let him go but neither I nor Marina was willing to go with him, as we are both born-again atheists who cannot bring ourselves to sit through a church service without feeling we are complete hypocrites. We explained the problem to Malcolm the vicar, who said that he quite respected our views, and assured us that there was no problem; Kieran could go to Junior Church, which was integrated into the main morning service, and one of the helpers or teachers could take care of him. The arrangement worked and we had a short but very welcome break from the tantrums on Sundays, until the morning when a ruffled-looking Malcolm brought Kieran home. Kieran had objected to being asked to do something (or being told not to do something, which sounded more likely), lost his temper and head-butted his Sunday school-teacher. She was not hurt, but she was deeply shocked. We apologised to Malcolm and helped Kieran to write a letter of apology to the woman he had hurt. We remained on friendly terms with both her and Malcolm, but that was the end of Kieran's church-going.

That we were dealing with a seriously damaged little boy was becoming more and more obvious. The early weeks and months of the placement were horrifically stormy, and only bath times and story times provided welcome interludes of something approaching 'normality'. A warm steamy bathroom with three soapy wet children in it smells and feels like heaven. And then one evening, it became somewhere hellish. Still wet from the bath, Kieran was lying on his back on a towel on the floor. He arched his legs back over his shoulders until his feet touched the floor; his anus was exposed and dilated. His smile had turned into a nasty leer, and his body and his facial expression said only one thing: 'Fuck me.' This is how children who have been sexually abused try to please adults, because this is how they have been taught to please adults. We had always known that Kieran had been sexually abused. He had disclosed to us and we had taken it in our stride. We thought we had successfully resolved the issue of the sex games he'd been playing with Paul, but what we saw that evening left us feeling physically sick and shaken to the core. We were not disgusted with Kieran himself because we knew that his behaviour was beyond any conscious control. What was so shocking was that we were being confronted with the abuse itself: this was the reality of what had happened to Kieran and of what we were living with. It had not gone away, and Marina, Paul, Cate and I were all being dragged back into the original trauma of the sexual abuse of a young boy who was reliving it as we watched.

We began to look for help. My memories are none too clear here. That is not really surprising, as we were living in a blur of upsetting events and had few signposts. I do, however, remember that it was on the advice of Sarah that we contacted the Community Mental Health service at a local hospital. We were visited at home by a psychiatric nurse and a male sister who listened quietly as we described our situation, rarely intervening to interrupt what must have been a confused jumble of words and emotions. When we had finished, there was a deep silence for a few minutes, and then the sister simply said: 'You need help.' We sighed in relief. Our case was referred to the relevant consultant, but it took him a while to reply. He eventually told us that, because we were fostering the children and had yet to adopt them formally, any report written or any recommendation made would have to be seen by a court of law, but he did not explain why he refused to have dealings with a court. He simply said that the legal position made it impossible for him to do anything for us. That was that. A lifeboat had come, circled us and sailed away. We would have to swim.

Sarah finally came up with an informal arrangement that at least appeared to offer a solution. She arranged for us to see a junior doctor who was working for a postdoctoral qualification under the supervision of a psychiatrist she had known for a long time. After an initial interview with the three of us, the junior psychiatrist agreed to see Kieran on a regular basis. We explained to Kieran that seeing a specialist doctor was going to help to take away the anger that was inside him; Kieran asked if the doctor could take away the sadness too. Every week, I took a bewildered boy to his office and waited for an hour while Dr Morley worked with him. Kieran was cooperative enough but had little idea of what was going on. According to his version of events, he was left to play in a corner while the doctor watched and said almost nothing, and I suppose that is one way of describing play therapy. The informal arrangement proved not to be satisfactory because sessions were sometimes cancelled at very short notice. On one occasion, Kieran and I actually arrived to find that the session had been cancelled without anyone even bothering to let us know. We had the impression that we were being shoe-horned into the schedule of a young man in a hurry who really could not be bothered. There was never any real conclusion to any of this, but a final meeting left us with some disturbing impressions. Dr Morley appeared to us to think that the real problem lay with Marina; she was, he hinted, the classic hysterical professional woman who wanted it all, and who was finding out the hard way that she could not cope with it. He acknowledged that Kieran did have problems but thought that there was little that could be done about them now; for the moment, it was probably best to let sleeping dogs lie. As we now know, the only trouble with sleeping dogs is that they do wake up eventually. They have sharp teeth and they can bite.

The pattern has often been repeated over the years. We have been told again and again that we needed help, and been told then that it would not or could not be provided. Again and again, we have been made to feel that we were not coping simply because we were inadequate and incompetent. Sometimes this was the result of what I now know to be poor judgement on the part of those we approached for help. More generally, it was a side-effect of the prevailing view of adoption. Although perceptions are now changing, it was for a long time assumed that all that was required was tender loving care from reasonably competent adults who were willing to devote themselves to the admittedly difficult children they were fostering or adopting. Any further problems that did arise probably resulted from the failings, incompetence or inadequacy of the parents. That is not the case: adoptive parents have difficulties because they are trying to deal with the impossible.

Marina and I were also living with a fear we could hardly bring ourselves to put into words. There were moments when it looked as though Kieran would have to go back into care. The official figures report that about one in ten of all placements breaks down before an adoption order is granted, whilst other reports and anecdotal evidence suggest that the rate of disruption is considerably higher. Marina and I were not familiar with the statistics but we did sense that placements could go wrong and end badly. As bravely as we could, we sat there discussing whether or not this was 'the right placement' for Kieran, trying desperately to go on believing that we were strong enough to cope, and never daring to voice the fear that, if we lost Kieran, we would lose Paul and Cate too.

Within a very short space of time, we experienced a whole range of childhood mishaps, accidents and emergencies. Cate rocked so hard in her high chair that she sent it – and herself – flying and landed head first on the floor. In our panic, we got her to a doctor, though there was probably no real need to do so. Paul came in screaming and bleeding profusely from a cut to the head. Being naive, inexperienced and scared, we rushed him to the nearest Accident & Emergency department, not realising that the amount of blood that flows from a head wound is no indication of how serious it is. Next day, I asked Paul how he did it. I was teasing him, but Paul lowered his head and began to run towards the stone wall around the garden: 'Me show you, Dad.' Luckily, I was able to grab him before any more damage was done. 'Me show you, Dad' quickly became something of a family joke, and we still laugh at it. Paul finds it very funny indeed.

It is a funny story, but it might be more than that. Paul's psychology remains something of a mystery to this day. He has been subjected to all sorts of tests and examinations over the years, but no coherent psychological pattern has ever emerged. We do know that he has special educational needs and it has often been suggested that he might suffer from some form of autism. Autism is probably not a single condition but a spectrum ranging from extreme isolation and total indifference to others to a compulsion to repeat stereotypical gestures or phrases. The minor forms are not uncommon. Trainspotters, with their endless lists of engine numbers, can reasonably be described as suffering from a very mild form of autism. Paul's habit of reeling off football statistics probably comes into the same category. People with autism often display a tendency to take things absolutely literally and fail to understand figurative language. The autistic boy who is told by his teacher to 'pull his socks up' will do precisely that. A character in something we were watching on TV said she was 'snowed under'. A genuinely puzzled Paul turned to Marina and said that he could not see any snow.

The third member of our childless family was Jolly, our much-loved and pampered ginger tom, who never really recovered from Paul's bellowed YOUOFFMYBEDCATYOUOFFMYBED. This was Jolly's introduction to his new status at the bottom of the domestic food chain and he did not like it one little bit. Kieran had lived in a household with a dog, and Cate in one with cats, but Paul's acquaintance with the animal kingdom was restricted to a goldfish and a tankful of nasty-looking terrapins. I'm not even sure that he had seen a cat at close quarters and he was probably as surprised to find Jolly on his bed as Jolly was surprised to be ordered off it so roughly; being a cat, he had just assumed that all these nice new beds had been bought to give him a choice of comfortable places to sleep. Jolly and the children did, somewhat grudgingly, learn to live together but Jolly was never again the cat he used to be. Jolly is long gone and we currently live with a new generation of cats: Pussa and her three kittens, all middle-aged by now. The children have always adored them. Paul and Cate can still fight bitterly over who has Pussa to sleep on their bed and, given that she is the mother cat, it's not hard to see what those squabbles are really about.

All our three children are very fond of animals and none of them has ever hurt one. I don't think I could live with a child, or anyone else for that matter, who deliberately hurt an animal, and I am convinced that living with pets is good for children. Even at his most turbulent, Kieran would sit for long quiet periods with a cat purring on his lap and the animal seemed to communicate a sense of calm to him. Over the years, we've had other animals. We've had fish, mice, gerbils, and hamsters and we still have two guinea-pigs – often neglected, to be sure, but never hurt in any way. The trouble with mice and other small creatures is that they are so short-lived. There are all sorts of creatures buried in the back garden. They were given decent burials and had flowers placed on their graves. I never had mice or guinea-pigs as a boy but there has almost always been a cat in my life, and I find a home without one almost as forlorn as a home without books. I think the children would find a catless home strange too. They also like dogs, even though they sometimes find them a little frightening. Cate in particular would love to have a dog but we've always said no to that. I know who would have to take it for walks on wet nights in February. We'll stick with cats.

Of the three of them, it has always been Cate who has had most feeling for animals. For a long time, she went to a Farm Club at a rare-breeds centre just outside the city where we now live. She collected eggs, watched chicks hatching and mucked out horses and pigs. One Sunday morning, she came home almost hysterical with laughter. She had been sneezed upon by a Gloucester Old Spot pig that was at least three or four times her size and had been soaked. She thought this was very funny at the time, but the memory has since become a source of disgust. She has learned to be fastidious, and the girl who used to take the fresh fish I brought home from the market, prise open their mouths and ask for all the parts to be named is now a teenager who cannot bring herself to touch a fish. But animals remain a great source of pleasure. Paul's concentration is not always good, but he will sit by the pond in our present garden for ages, watching for the fish, the frogs and, best of all, the newts. A little pond measuring one metre by little more than half a metre has given us all more pleasure than many an expensive toy. I sometimes took a jar of frog spawn to their nursery class at school. One day, a group of kids from school came up to us and asked what was in the jar. They did not know what spawn was, and yet they lived five minutes' walk away from ponds that are alive with frogs and newts in springtime. No one had ever taken them to see them.

Paul and Marina were discussing what he could buy me for my birthday: 'Dad likes playing with my pet mouse. Perhaps we should get him a mouse of his own.'

Inevitably, our memories of this phase in our lives are dominated by images of turmoil, anger and fear. We were living through very difficult times and we tend to forget that there were other things too. Kieran was never an easy child to live with, but he was a bright lad who was always good company and who was interested in the world around him. The boy who threw things and swore at us was also the boy who performed in a school play at Christmas, and who would have been a much better cat if someone had not stood on his tail so heavily that it fell off. Most of the time Paul and Cate were not a lot of trouble. They could certainly be hard work, but they could also be the delightful children Marina called 'honeybuns'. All three children were very affectionate and enjoyed their hugs and cuddles. We had bad times and hard times, but we were a happy family too.

Cate must have been at most eighteen months when I first took her into town by myself. Getting there was something of a struggle involving some difficult negotiations between the buggy and the bus, and I don't think I'd ever realised how small a child is, or how big adults are in comparison. It was a perfectly banal morning out, and its high point was having a pee in the alley behind the central Methodist Church (her, not me). And then we came to the windows of a big department store, and saw the display of wedding dresses. Cate was transfixed, stared with huge eyes and flatly refused to move. If I hadn't picked her up and carried her away, we'd have been there yet. Wedding dresses are of course spectacular creations, but that in itself does not explain her reaction. It was almost as though she could see herself wearing one, as though she knew she could look like a princess too. By this time, the boys were certainly very keen on having new clothes but they would never have stared in this way at a window display of suits. Not yet two, Cate knew far more than they did about the attraction of beautiful clothes. Many things – and not least Cinderella – teach little girls about looking beautiful and about the importance of being a princess, and Cate had learned the lesson well.

We have very fond memories of the house we lived in then, but it was not really ideal for three young children. We soon found that we were quite lonely. None of the few friends we had in the area had young children. Malcolm and his wife Jen had children, and so did our other next-door neighbours, but they were just too old to be really interested in our three. A couple living over the road had children of the right age and they all got on well together. It was the road that posed the problem; relatively little traffic came through the village, but what traffic there was came far too fast for young children to be left to cross the road unsupervised. The children could not be allowed to get on with it by themselves, and arranging for them to play with friends who lived almost opposite us required planning and organisation. Our front garden was the size of a handkerchief, and certainly not big enough for proper games. To the rear of the house, there was what an estate agent would call a patio garden and what most people would call a yard with a raised flower bed. Half-way up the yard there was a step that cannot have been more than few inches high. For Cate, it was an obstacle as insurmountable as the Pyrenees. To cross it, she would sit down, raise her legs and swivel round on her bottom, swing her legs until they were over the obstacle, and then gradually struggle into a standing position on the far side of it. Just watching her was exhausting.

Most of the children's social life was engineered by our nanny Angie. The couple over the road employed a nanny called Debby and the two young women became good friends. Somehow, the two of them became the nucleus of a whole network of nannies and young children. I would come down from my study to find the kitchen or lounge full of young women and children I'd never seen before. At the end of the afternoon, an armada of buggies would come up the street with a mob of kids trailing behind and looking like remnants of a strange tribe that had somehow lost or mislaid its elders.

Like so many parents with young children, we were becoming cut off. The children absorbed all our energy and there was none left for socialising. We worked and we tried to look after our children, and that was all we did. The house had suddenly been taken over by our new and noisy family, and the neighbours must have been grateful for its thick stone walls. The nature of time changed and the days that started so early were long and tiring. We began to learn to live as parents and learned to change nappies. We learned to change wet beds in our sleep. We learned which types of ground would take Cate's pushchair, and which would not. That was an important lesson, as the pushchair was as heavy as a battle tank and almost as difficult to manoeuvre. Get bogged down in sand with that thing, and we really were in trouble, but it was handy for bringing home the shopping. We learned to eat, and almost to enjoy eating, fish fingers and oven chips. I realised just how much our lives had changed when I noticed at nine o'clock one Sunday morning that I was about to put on the second load of washing.

It is not just that we have three children without ever having had a baby. We have never had just one child. For a couple of days, we had two children. Ever since then, we have had three. We never had the time to learn from the mistakes we made with our first child because we've never had one. We made a lot of mistakes, and Kieran was probably the worst affected by them. With two younger and demanding children on our hands, we sometimes forgot that he was only five and saw him just as 'the eldest', and it did not help that he was apparently so mature and self-sufficient. Paul and Cate's needs were greater, and they were much more immediate and physical. Someone once told us that no one should have more children than they have hands. Between us, Marina and I have four hands but we have only two each. If one

64

of us took our children anywhere by ourselves, there was always one child who did not have a hand to hold, and it was inevitably Kieran. Some of his aggression towards the others, and especially Paul, must have stemmed from that.

It is likely that Kieran, Paul and Cate have all suffered from never having been the focus of individual attention and care. So far as we can tell, they never had that attention and care from their birth mother. And now, there was always another child in the way. No adoptive parent – mother or father – can ever give what was never given to a child in the first place. As adopters, we try but we cannot do it. All adoptive parents feel guilty about this; we all feel that we are failing, and that we can never be good enough. Most of the time, we forget this and just get on with things as best we can, but there are the grim moments when we feel it strongly. At a garden party given by a neighbour we met a baby who gurgled and laughed as she was passed from mother to father, from grandfather to grandmother and back again. She crawled across the lawn but always looked back at her mother, already sensing that she had a safe base to go back to: mum was there and would not go away. This was a very happy baby. Our children never had that safe base when they were a few months old. And we could not recreate it for them when they were fifteen months, three and five. What we were watching in our neighbour's garden was a child building the safe and secure attachment or bond with her mother that is the basis for a healthy childhood and, eventually, a healthy adulthood. No adopted child starts out with secure attachments. There is always something missing because it was never there in the beginning.

I know that the decision to remove our children from the care of their mother was not taken lightly, that it was taken in all good faith and that it was in their best interest. But I also know that something terrible was done to them, and that we cannot undo it. I know that our children have had incomparably better lives than they would otherwise have had. I don't think that anyone could deny that. But I also know that there will always be something that will never be there because it was never there in the first place. Kieran, for instance, went through a phase in which there was never enough to eat. We fed him well, but there was never enough. There were never enough biscuits in the cupboard, never enough sweets in the jar, never enough pop in the bottle, never enough food in the fridge. There was just never enough. Later, he began to steal compulsively. He usually stole from me and there was an element of aggression in his behaviour. There was also more to it than that. He did not need the money, and he was not hungry. He was stealing and eating in order to fill a gap that should never have been there. He just wanted, endlessly, painfully and hopelessly.

We bought an Andy Pandy *video for Cate. She loved it. She would jump and dance along with Andy and Teddy, and did so with a solemn grace. But not if anyone was watching. To see her, we had to keep very quiet and peek round the door.*

A much older Cate did something very similar. As she moved into adolescence, she began to lose interest in her collection of Barbies and soft toys and put most of them away in a cupboard. One day, I heard her singing and peaked around the door of her room. She was playing with her Barbies, but blushed scarlet when she saw me. But if I peered through the crack in the door, I would still see her playing with them.

The playing fields over the road were a godsend. Amateur sides played football there on Sunday mornings, but we had the area to ourselves for the rest of the time. Football is one of the many games I am not good at and my skills had not improved since I was a boy, but I could hold my own against Kieran and Paul. To a distant observer, it must have been an almost eerie sight: a man and two small boys on a big football field under a wide sky as the afternoon light faded. This is where we built snowmen and threw snowballs at each other. This is where, in the space of an afternoon and with almost no assistance, Kieran learned to ride his first bike. This is where I found the hedgehog I took home for the children to see. We often see them where we live now, but this was the first hedgehog. It was the spikiest hedgehog there has ever been, and no other hedgehog has ever curled up into such a tight ball. No other hedgehog has ever had such a pointed nose or such bright eyes. The children have seen a lot of hedgehogs since then but I've not forgotten the look on their faces as they tentatively touched the spikes of our first one.

There were other big spaces under wide skies. We spent most of our Sunday afternoons on the nearby beaches. Even when it was cold, the children loved going there. They had the freedom to run, and they ran. They dug holes in the sand and Kieran built elaborate castles. They all liked the water, even though it was rarely warm enough to do more than paddle in apprehensively. Cate, on the other hand, was convinced that she could reach the other side of the sea on foot, and regularly set off into the waves in her red

Postman Pat wellies. She discovered that the dead crabs she found on the tide line were not good to eat, though it took more than one experiment to convince her. There was a December day when we suddenly realised that we really did have to go home because Cate's lips were turning blue in the cold. The boys, meanwhile, were hunting for hermit crabs in a rock pool, quite oblivious to the temperature. One of the beauties of a big empty beach is that there is little or nothing for a child to want. Kieran, Paul and Cate are all very good at wanting things, and at demanding them. Here, there was almost nothing to want, so they didn't want anything. At most, there was an ice-cream van on summer days. I tried to tell them that all the five pound notes in my wallet had been overprinted with the message: 'These notes cannot be used to purchase ice cream.' They never believed me.

Beyond the playing fields, there was a large area of overgrown semi-wilderness. According to local legend, no one had ever succeeded in tracing the owners and it was therefore impossible for it to be either sold or bought, much less built over. If that tale is true, this must have been one of the very few 'un-owned' places in the entire country. What is definitely true is that the land had once been a market garden. There were cultivated plants that had gone wild. There were extensive patches of raspberry canes. Gathering fruit is something I have always enjoyed, and the children began to enjoy it too. On fine days, we gathered raspberries and, later in the year, huge blackberries. Predictably, we always ate more berries than we took home but we usually had enough to make a pie. One of my fondest memories of this time is the day we were caught in a heavy shower. We sheltered beneath the canes and bushes, ate fresh raspberries until the rain stopped and then went home wet, mouths and fingers stained bright red, hair full of bits of vegetation, tired and happy.

Those early days were crowded but very happy as well as turbulent. I remember Cate's 'oooh' of delight when I popped her first grape into her mouth. We remember how she almost jumped vertically out of her high chair the first time we used the coffee grinder. After that, we were always careful to warn her: 'Big noise coming now, Cate.' We remember Paul's grumblings about the pair of collared doves that used to sit on the window sill outside the bedroom: 'Damned cuckoo clock waked me again.' We remember his struggles with the English language. 'No, Paul, not "Her put hers hat on." You mean "she".' 'Right, her put she's hat on.'

In terms of the adoption process, we were still on probation and had to live by the rules. Sarah visited regularly and one of her duties was to check the state of the children's bedrooms. We all liked Sarah and looked forward to seeing her, but the visits did sometimes feel like interrogations. Every three months, we had an official review, which was attended by both social workers, their line manager, and a minute-taker. These were serious occasions and they were not always pleasant, especially when things were rough. For some reason or other, we were looking at photographs together and Sarah's line manager suddenly asked if he could take one to give to Viv. Marina was very fond of that photo; we had only one copy and she did not want to lose it. 'Why not? After all, Viv has given you an important gift.' That was not quite how we regarded the fostering of three very difficult children we were hoping to adopt, and they were certainly not Viv's gift to us: we'd never even met her. Later in the meeting, Marina admitted to having smacked Kieran, and was formally warned that she was putting everything at risk: foster-parents are not allowed to smack (but they do). Sarah's line manager quite rightly went on to argue that smacking does nothing to change a child's behaviour, but he had missed the point. Kieran had not been smacked as a punishment; the smack had been an expression of anger and frustration. At one point or another, we have struck all our children in anger and frustration, and we have always felt sick afterwards. Never again will I look askance at the woman who slaps her toddler's leg in the check-out queue at the supermarket. For all I know she has been living for hours and hours in that bubble of anger in which the only things that exist are an angry, frightened parent and an angry, frightened child. There is nothing outside it.

All our children had a talent for driving people to despair. Paul and Cate still have it, but Kieran had it in spades. Even Angie, who was normally so even-tempered that I began to wonder what she was on, swore that she would kill him after one particularly disastrous trip into town; Kieran had provoked a nasty scene in the middle of a big department store and then thrown a spectacular tantrum. Angie was a very good nanny, but she was eighteen and she reacted to public embarrassment in the same way as any eighteen-year-old.

Sarah did her best and, although it was probably not in her job description, began to try to do some individual therapeutic work with Kieran. This involved filling buckets at the outside tap, pouring the water from one bucket to another and measuring its volume. The water represented Tender Loving Care, and Sarah was trying to find out how Kieran wanted it to be distributed. I seem to recall that Kieran incorporated some coal-washing into the game. I'm not sure about the long-term therapeutic effects, but the immediate physical effects were comically visible: one damp Fostering and Adoption Officer and one very wet boy. Sadly, Sarah was not with us long enough to go on with this work. Her own life was hit by tragic events and she left the area. We lost a very skilled and experienced specialist and gained a social worker who was almost as out of her depth as we were. This is not unusual; Juliet was well meaning but, like most social workers, she knew surprisingly little about adoptive families and their problems. By the time they have learned something about them, they have either been promoted out of the front line or have fallen prey to professional burn-out.

We realised that we would have to move sooner rather than later, as Cate could not go on sharing a room for ever and would eventually need a space of her own. Building an extension was one obvious solution, but adding a brick extension to an old stone house would have bordered on the criminal and building in stone was far beyond our means. As it happens, it never came to a choice between building and moving. There was a very senior position vacant at Marina's old place of work in the city. Getting it would not make her God, but it would give her a seat at his right hand. She got it. We now faced the problem of finding a house and then moving into it with three small children on our hands. It proved to be surprisingly painless. We could easily drive down to the city and back in a day, and Angie would baby-sit if we were late. If we went down at the weekend, we took the children with us. Most prospective vendors were surprisingly accommodating, letting them play in the garden and even digging out videos to keep them occupied. After looking at various properties, we decided to go for the house we still live in. We held a last party for the few children we knew well and said goodbye. We said a tearful farewell to Angie, who had already found a new job to go to. We gave her good references and she deserved them. For a first job, it had certainly been a demanding one.

III

We have been living here for ten years now and it has been a good place to bring up the children. We live in a street of large semis built at the beginning of the twentieth century, and they make excellent family homes. Most people are friendly and, for the first time since I was a boy, I know virtually all my neighbours by name. The street is a cul de sac so the children can play outside in safety as there is no through traffic and, although it slopes steeply at one end, for most of its length it is flat enough for football and tennis. In our first years here, there could be up to twenty children playing out there but there are many fewer of them now, as some families have moved away and many of the remaining children are now, like our three, a little too old to want to play games in the street. The children made good friends here, and they did so very quickly. Of course they had their fights too, but they adapted to living here remarkably well. In our previous home, they'd had a somewhat lonely life but, suddenly, there were lots of children to play with. Almost overnight, Kieran, Paul and Cate changed their accents, so great was the pressure to fit in both on the street and in the school playground. To my ear, this was not a change for the better. I am not terribly fond of the local accent and, besides, the one they lost used to be mine.

Living amongst so many families with children has advantages for parents. When the children were still too young to be left alone, it was very rare for us to be unable to find someone to keep a vague eye on them if we had to go off for an hour or so. We did the same for our neighbours. Cate must have been still under five when she had a fall while trying to climb the gate to her friend Jasmin's garden. She landed head-first on a gravel path, and there was blood all over the place. I knew by then that the blood was not necessarily something to worry about unduly, but I was concerned about the blow to the head and decided that Cate should see a doctor. Marina had taken the boys off somewhere in the car – to look for conkers, as I recall. Jasmin's mother Vee had a young baby to look after and could not leave the house. In any case, she could not stand the sight of blood, and looked so green when she brought Cate home that it was obvious that she could do no more. After a moment of panic, I found another neighbour to drive us to the hospital. We had a long wait in the Accident & Emergency department, but there was no real harm done and Cate was easily patched up. Over the years we've come to know the local A&E well. We've been there with Cate (brass washer worn as ring would not come off finger). We've been there with Kieran (blow to the head during a playground scuffle). We've been there with me (cornea cut by raspberry cane). We've been there with Marina (confused disinfecting solution with rinsing solution when putting in contact lenses). We've not been for a while now, but it did feel at one stage as though visiting the A&E was just another part of our family life.

Most people on the street are remarkably tolerant of the children's games and noise, though we have had the occasional battle over the games of football. Jim, usually a man of astonishing patience, did lose his temper when a football decapitated the blue Himalayan poppies he had grown from seed but that is scarcely surprising, given that it had taken him two years to do so. When the football wars did break out, Kieran was always in the thick of them and his tendency to answer back did not endear him to the adults involved. One neighbour (since deceased) took a serious dislike to him and blamed him for everything. According to her, it was 'always Kieran', but that was only to be expected from a child 'like that', meaning a child who had been adopted.

The house is full of memories now. Pussa had her three kittens in our bedroom. There have been ten Christmas trees in our sitting room. Between us, we have had fifty birthdays here and there have been lots of children's parties in this house. There have been floods in the kitchen because someone left a bath running until it overran and the water seeped through the bathroom floor. There have been loud games in the garden. Snowmen have gradually melted there. We've had bonfires and set off fireworks out there. All three children have, at some point, resolved to spend a warm summer's night in a tent in the garden, but none of them made it to midnight before giving up. Days after we moved in, Paul came downstairs and breathlessly said: 'Cate stuck!' She was indeed. She had put her head through the stair rails and could not get it out. My first reaction was to laugh and I do sometimes still wish that I'd grabbed my camera, but the laughter soon faded. Trying to twist Cate's head did not work, and nor did the application of soap to her neck and ears. She really was stuck, and she became even more stuck as she became more frightened. We made the phone call and a fire engine pulled up aside the house. Three large men in big boots tramped up the stairs, but they could not free Cate either and eventually had to saw through the stair rail. Somewhere in the archives of the county fire service, there is the receipt I signed: 'One small female released.' We asked Cate why she'd done it. 'Paul told me to.' It wasn't quite a repetition of the 'Me show you, Dad' incident with Paul, but it came close.

The children had been very quiet for a long time. Then we heard stifled giggles and footsteps on the stairs. The door to the room where we were sitting was pushed open. 'Exterminate! Exterminate! Exterminate!' 'You will obey! You will obey!' Three Daleks shuffled into the room. Using sheets of paper and about a kilometre of Sellotape, Kieran had turned the three of them into Daleks. It must have taken him well over an hour. No one had helped him.

The previous evening, the three of them had watched Daleks: Invasion Earth 2050 AD (1966, and not a masterpiece of British cinema) on video. Kieran saw it only once, but was able to make very creditable Daleks as a result. Without realising it, he actually improved on the originals: his Daleks could manage stairs with no difficulty at all.

A house was not the only thing we had to find when we moved back to the city after having been away for three years. We needed a school too, and we also had to sort out some kind of childcare. We decided that we would go on having a nanny until Cate, who was now going to nursery in the mornings, began school proper and then think about leaving them with a child minder for a couple of hours after school so that I could finish a full day's work. For the moment we needed a nanny. It was surprisingly easy to find one and the children were soon as at ease with Stephanie as they had been with Angie.

We had intended to visit three local primaries, but the nearest, which was said by neighbours to be the best, refused even to let us look around because it was already oversubscribed. The first school we saw was obviously quite unsuitable. When we saw children sprawling on the floor of an open-plan classroom, we immediately knew that this was not a school for Kieran. He would not have coped with the lack of structure and, left to his own devices, would have done nothing. We then went to look around Greenways Primary. Here, we were shown around by a teacher who talked so much that we could not get a word in but we liked what we saw. The building was shabby but it felt comfortable and lived-in. Only a few children came up to us to show off their work; most simply looked up for a moment and then went back to whatever it was they were doing. We took this to be a sign that they were both contented and sufficiently self-confident not to have to show off to any adult who came along. The nursery class Cate would be in was certainly noisy, but the noises were happy ones.

The school was within easy walking distance from home and it was not an unpleasant walk, but in sociological terms it took us from one world and into another. We would walk up our quiet street and down the next, and then across the footbridge over the railway line. For a couple of years, we were able to walk across an open field, where there were often tethered horses for the children to talk to, to the back entrance to the school. The field is an extension of a broad stretch of open ground known locally just as 'the valley', though that is not what it is called on the map, and it ought to be a good place for children to play. There are ponds and a stream where children could find frogs, sticklebacks and newts in the spring, and where they could watch dragonflies on hot summer days. There are trees and bushes where they could play hide-and-seek, and enough flat ground to play ball games. But almost no children come here because this is a dangerous place. A boy riding his bike here would have it stolen by an older kid from the estate on the edge of the valley, and his watch would be taken too. We never warned our children against going to the valley by themselves; we did not need to because they quickly learned from other kids that this was not a safe place to be alone. Shortly before Cate left Greenways, a girl was raped on the valley, and for weeks afterwards Cate would not go anywhere alone. Like every girl in the school, she was convinced that she would be stolen and frightened that she too would be raped.

Eventually, our route had to change. The level of vandalism directed against the school became so high that security fencing was put up around it and the rear entrance was closed. The children and their teachers now had to work within a perimeter of metal and we had to walk to school through the estate that was its main catchment area. The estate was built in the late 1930s as part of a slum clearance scheme, and it must have looked like paradise to the first families who moved in. Most of the houses are semi-detached and have reasonably large gardens; the layout of the streets is pleasing to the eye, but the estate is no longer anyone's paradise. It is by no means the worst estate in the city, but it is grim. The rate of vandalism is high, and so are the rates of unemployment and crime. There are a lot of single-parent families. Most of Greenways' children come from here, and over half of the school's pupils qualify for free school meals – a classic indicator of poverty. A lot of fathers are away working on the oil rigs. Cate once asked a classmate where her dad was: 'He was naughty and he had to go away.' A school that draws on a catchment area like this has to struggle. A sizable minority of parents with children at Greenways clearly believed that 'teachers are useless' and did nothing to support the school. Most of the vandalism directed against it was the work of disaffected teenagers who were ex-pupils. Everyone knew who they were but there was never enough hard evidence for them to be arrested and charged. In Cate's last year at Greenways, a window in her classroom was broken and a burning petrol-soaked rag was thrown in. The smoke-damage meant that the room could not be used for the rest of the summer term, and most of a year's work was destroyed within minutes.

Despite its many problems, Greenways was a good school. It is true that it has never performed well in academic terms and that it has always been very low down the league tables. In terms of pastoral care, it would, however, be hard to improve upon it. Greenways certainly had a dedicated staff, but the real credit belonged to the head teacher. Miss Barker, who has now retired, was a big woman with a big laugh. She was straightforward and would not take nonsense from anyone, but she also had an extraordinarily anarchic side to her. Marina was once invited to a special morning assembly. Miss Barker entered the hall with something concealed behind her back, walked up to a boy and thrust a chocolate cake in his face. Bedlam ensued. Miss Barker allowed the hysterical screams and laughter to go on for just long enough and then put an end to the misrule within a minute. Only she, the boy concerned and a few teachers had known about her plan to commit assault by chocolate cake. There was, in contrast, nothing anarchic about Miss Barker's deputy, a small, neat woman with the ability to reduce an unruly mob of children to silence with a withering gaze that could have frozen water. She was in reality a kindly soul with a very fine sense of humour, but she could do 'stern' with the best of them.

The teacher we remember best is Miss Hamilton, who taught both Kieran and then Cate in their last years at Greenways. She was young, plain-spoken and stood no nonsense from any of her children. She was also extraordinarily patient, which is always useful when dealing with a boy like Kieran. During his first two years at high school, he went back to see her whenever he could and still speaks of her with great affection. Miss Hamilton was instrumental in setting up the after-hours sports club run by her friend Michelle, a sometime member of the England athletic squad. Kieran, Paul and Cate all took part when they were old enough. Watching Miss Hamilton with her children was a reminder of just how strong the bond between a child and 'Miss' can be. And it works both ways. One hot afternoon, I waited for Cate to come out of her classroom. When the door opened, the children rushed out as they always did but something was different. They were all in tears and Cate ran straight past me without even seeing me. That morning, a boy called Russell had set off for school as usual. As usual, he had to cross a big dual carriageway and at that time in the morning, the traffic is heavy but slow moving. He dodged through the cars as they slowed for the lights and ran into the bus lane. The driver can't even have seen him. Miss Hamilton had taught her class all day, knowing that Russell was dead, and had not said a word until it was time for home. A couple of days later, I asked how she was feeling. 'It's never happened to me before' was all she would say.

As well as a dedicated staff, the school had the support of a devoted and hard-working parents' association known as Friends of Greenways ('FOG' to most of us). FOG raised money and organised events. It collected the computer vouchers from the supermarket, the tokens for books on the crisp packets and anything else that could be collected. We never became active members of FOG – we had enough on our plate – and we drew the line at the bingo and race evenings, but we did go to many of the events it organised. We drank cups of weak tea at summer fairs and nibbled mince pies at Christmas fairs, bought raffle tickets and guessed the weight of the cake, and the number of beans in the jar. When I was at school, we raised money to build a cricket pavilion, but the purpose of this fund-raising was to buy books for the library. We joined in other school activities too. We bought canned vegetables and fruit to contribute to harvest festivals, squatted on low chairs and benches to watch nativity plays in which our children never had big parts because they could not concentrate during rehearsals, and shivered through sports days on damp afternoons in July. One sports day was opened by Michelle, who presented Kieran with an autographed running vest because he had been the star of her sports club. He wouldn't take it off for days and days.

The school looked after our children very well. Although Paul and Cate had problems at school, they were usually well-behaved and caused little or no bother in the classroom. Kieran, on the other hand, was real trouble. He must have been in his second or third year at Greenways, or in other words eight or nine years old, when the phone calls from school began: 'Kieran has removed himself from the school premises and we do not know where he is.' This usually meant that he had been scolded or ticked off about something and had walked out of school, but he never went far. When I went to look for him, I would find him on the field or just outside the school gates. I dragged him back to school a lot of times. And I do mean drag, physically and none too gently, and I had to do it because the teachers had, it seemed, no authority once he had left the school grounds. So I would set off in search of him, furiously angry at having been disturbed again. If I tried to explain to Kieran that I did have a job to do, the response was a shrugged 'So?' Kieran could be disruptive in the classroom too. He was rude and offensive to teachers, support workers and catering staff. He and a mate spent an afternoon disrupting the work of their class by playing the fool and when asked to stop, stormed out of the room and went on to disrupt the entire school's life by running around the playground and banging on the windows. This was, they said, a preparation for the life they were going to live 'when we're street kids'. Kieran could not see that there was a contradiction between wanting to be a street kid and being terrified of being bullied on the way home from school. The school, and especially Miss Barker, were astonishingly generous to Kieran and did not exclude him. Many schools would have done so. Marina's sister-in-law was head of a primary school in the Midlands, and she'd have excluded Kieran without a moment's hesitation.

All of our children have difficulty with school, but it is Cate who has had the most problems. Like all children who have had any involvement with the care system, our three began school with a disadvantage. Children whose lives have been disrupted by loss and constant moves find it hard to settle to anything and often fall behind at school. Part of the problem with Cate was that it has always been so difficult to get her to school in the first place. Getting her out of the door can be like struggling to get a very stubborn cork out of a bottle. There were so many, many mornings when one of us had to fight to get our weeping girl out of the house and into school. Holding her hand and trying to drag her down the street was like tugging at the lead of a puppy that just does not want to go anywhere. Once we got her to Greenways, she made it very hard for us to leave, as she would cling to my hand or leg and beg me not to go. Sometimes she would allow a friend to take her into the classroom, but sometimes a teaching assistant had to prise us apart. At the end of the day, I faced the opposite problem, and could not winkle her out of school. She was always last out of the classroom and she usually had to go back because she had forgotten something. And there was always a job to be done for Miss: a board to be wiped, a chair to put away, papers to tidy. Always. Once she was inside the classroom, Cate was fine. At home, she was content. Getting her from home to school, and then from school to home, was torture because the upheaval of the transition was so frightening to her.

Cate is now fifteen and in year ten at high school, and it is still very difficult to get her to school. There are mornings when she will simply refuse to get out of bed. There are repeated bouts of psychosomatic illness. Then there are the days when she will come down for breakfast fully dressed, only to refuse to leave the house at the last moment. When Cate is in this mood she often attempts to prevent Marina leaving the house for work by standing in the doorway and physically blocking the way. She will stand in front of the car as Marina drives out of the garage. Any physical intervention on my part only makes things worse and leads to an even bigger row. I've learned to keep out of the way as much as possible.

Shortly before we moved here, we had begun to apply for the adoption order that would finally make us parents in the legal sense. Before we could at last become a family like any other, there were forms to be filled in and legal requirements to be met. The move meant that our application had to be transferred to a court in this city, and that led to further delays. There are a lot of parties involved in an adoption. The children were in local authority care, so the local authority had to be represented. There was Viv, and then there were the children's birth fathers. Viv had made it clear that, whilst she would not actually contest the adoption in court, she would not sign the paper 'freeing' the children either. No one knew what the two birth fathers thought and no one was very sure of where they were, though Andy was rumoured to be behind bars. Whether or not either of them had any legal rights was not terribly clear, but Kevin had been married to Viv when Kieran was born and presumably did have paternal rights, whereas Andy almost certainly did not. The legal team of the Social Services Department took the view that we needed a ruling from a judge to determine whether Kevin and Andy had to be consulted or not. After a lengthy delay, we got a date for a hearing and were told that a judge would give his ruling in chambers.

We agreed to meet our social worker at the main entrance to the County Court. To get there, Juliet had had to drive two hours down a busy motorway. We waited and were finally shown into an empty courtroom. Marina once did jury service, but I had never set foot in a court before and felt distinctly uncomfortable.

As we waited, two ushers in flapping black robes passed papers between them. The 'chambers' turned out to be a private office off the main court. The judge was not robed and was just wearing a business suit. We felt as though we were interrupting him. Juliet outlined the situation, explaining that neither father had ever shown much interest in the children, that she had been unable to contact them, and that one was thought to be in prison. It took the judge seconds to give his ruling: 'Then it's nothing to do with them.' That was it. On our way out, I had a glimpse of the mysterious document the ushers had been passing back and forth: the *Daily Telegraph* crossword. Her day's work over, Juliet stoically set off on the two-hour drive home. When we talked about it years later, Marina had no recollection of this episode.

We had been living as a family for three years now and, difficult as our lives were at times, that felt quite natural and normal. We had no doubts: they were our children and they accepted us as their parents. The formal adoption would do little to change our day-to-day lives. So we had explained to the children that we were going to be a forever family, that there would be no more social workers in our lives, that they would have a new surname, and that everything was going to be fine. Kieran had a very clear idea of what was going on, and Paul seemed to have some understanding. Cate did not. Trying again, we told her that the judge was going to turn her into a Houghton. She stared at us and asked 'Will I still be me? Will I still be Cate?' Although Cate did not know it, this was actually not a stupid question as we did have the legal right to give the children new forenames. This, I suppose, is a relic of the old 'clean break/new life' philosophy of adoption, but we did not even consider changing their forenames. They were Kieran, Paul and Cate, and that is who they would always be, but we did change their surnames to Houghton. Marina always uses her own surname, and 'Houghton' seemed to be the simplest solution. It also cleared up a minor problem that had confused a lot of people: for the last three years, we'd been living with three surnames between the five of us.

It was a surprisingly cold July morning. All dressed in our best, we met outside the court: two parents who were apprehensive but basically confident about the outcome of the hearing, three puzzled children, one social worker and one solicitor. Adoption hearings are kept as informal as possible; this time, we were in a courtroom rather than chambers, but the judge was neither robed nor wearing a wig, and we – and an usher – were the only people present. After being introduced to the judge, the children were taken off to another room while the hearing went ahead. Although the hearing was not contested or adversarial, it was nerve-racking and proved not to be as straightforward as we had expected. Our case was outlined. The previous judge's ruling was put on the record. Viv's letter to the court was read out. To be more accurate, the letter that had been written on her behalf by a social worker was read out. She was reluctant to agree to an adoption but hoped that any decision taken would be in the best interest of the children, wanted to remain in contact with them, and expressed the hope that she would be able to send them birthday and Christmas cards, or even little presents. We had discussed this suggestion with Juliet and eventually decided that, whilst we were happy to have 'letter box' contact, we could not accept cards and presents at Christmas or on birthdays. The contact would have to be in the spring or summer; with three birthdays and then Christmas in the space of three weeks, December was quite fraught enough as it was.

The judge now raised an issue that sent cold shivers down our spines. The documents he had before him told him that Viv now had other children and that she appeared to be taking good care of them, though he accepted that she was receiving a lot of help and support from Social Services. He wanted to know why, if that was the case, her first three children were up for adoption and could not be returned to her care. The case put forward on our behalf by Juliet and our lawyer was that, although Viv's life had obviously improved and was not as chaotic as it had been, the children had been taken into care for very good reasons. There was a history of neglect and, in the case of Kieran, sexual abuse. The children had all been at risk and the decision to remove them from Viv's care had been taken in their best interest. They had been living with us for three years, were in a very stable home environment and were making good progress. Staying where they were was very much in their best interest. Besides, Viv had chosen not to contest our application to adopt in any active sense.

The judge nodded. That obstacle out of the way, we were able to go ahead with our formal application. It was granted and the papers were signed. The children were brought back into the room. The mood lightened and the judge suddenly began to look like the grandfather he probably was. Going into his chambers, he reappeared carrying his wig and let all three children try it on. He now explained that he had raised the question of Viv's changed situation simply because he wanted to make sure that everything was cut and dried, as he had seen adoptions unravel over legal points because some minor detail had not been settled, and he did not want to see it happen again. As we all shook hands before leaving, he told us that he had enjoyed his morning's work: 'Granting adoption orders is a much nicer way of spending the morning than banging people up.' Outside the court, our lawyer took photographs of us all with my camera. She was happy. She had had a good morning too. Juliet hugged us all and said good-bye for the last time. The five of us went to celebrate in a pizza restaurant. It was our first meal together as a forever family. We had seen the last of the social workers.

I fell over her. As I opened the front door, I stumbled over a young woman with red hair. She had dropped something as she reached to press the doorbell, bent down to pick it up and disappeared from the field of vision available through the glass panel, and now she was sprawled on our doorstep. When she had regathered her dignity, she produced ID. She was the school's educational welfare officer and wanted to know why Cate's school attendance was so poor. The alarm bells began to ring when her attendance rate dipped below the 50 per cent level. This was three years ago. This term, Cate has, at best, attended school for an average of two or three days a week. She has not been at all for the last fortnight. I've not fallen over any red-headed educational welfare officers of late. I've had no phone calls from school to ask why Cate is not there. I think they've given up on her.

During his first weeks and months at Greenways, Paul was so lost and disoriented that he could not find the drawer his pencils were in, let alone the actual pencils. We assumed that this was because he found it so difficult to adjust to change, and told ourselves that things would get better for him. He had been slow to develop in other ways too: acquiring fine motor skills had been a slow process, and it was a long time before he could tie his laces or hold a pencil so that he could write with it. He always got there in the end so we were not unduly worried and assumed that things would improve over time, but time did not improve things and his concentration was getting worse.

He had such difficulty with reading that we took him to be tested at the Dyslexia Institute. For some two hours, a seven-year-old boy who supposedly could not concentrate for any length of time sat beside a total stranger and did his best to complete a lot of different exercises and tests. He did very well and, although the results were inconclusive, they did demonstrate that Paul was not dyslexic. His learning difficulties meant, on the other hand, that he had a reading age of less than four, the drawing skills of a five-year-old, and the numeracy skills of a six-year-old. By the time he was sixteen, he could read the sports page of the local paper with some fluency but that, and the football results on teletext, was almost all he could read. His oral skills, in contrast, were highly developed by then, and he was both articulate and in possession of a very wide vocabulary. It was the written word that caused the difficulties, and it still does.

His class teacher finally raised the issue with us in his third year at primary school. She suspected that Paul had special needs, or in other words quite severe learning difficulties. She urged us to apply have him 'statemented', or given an official statement of special educational needs. So Paul began a new round of medicals, interviews and tests. He was indeed found to have special needs but no one has really been able to say precisely what they are, as no one has been able to detect any consistent psychological pattern in his behaviour. He has, for example, an excellent short-term memory. Paul is the one we turn to for help when we cannot find our keys, and he usually knows where they are. But he does not have the kind of memory that builds small blocks of knowledge into larger blocks, and he therefore finds it very hard to learn.

Special needs are legally defined as 'learning difficulties or disabilities that make it harder for a child to learn or access education than other children of the same age'. In January 2004, 2.4 per cent of all children in English secondary schools had statements of special need, and Paul was one of them. A further 13.5 per cent had special needs but no statement, and Cate was one of them. The 'special needs' category is so broad as to be almost meaningless. Paul has serious learning difficulties. Cate has learning difficulties and a school phobia. For official purposes, they are in the same category as children who have to live in wheelchairs or who have severe physical disabilities.

In his GCSE year, sixteen-year-old Paul made friends with an eleven-year-old who had just joined the school. This was not in itself surprising as he often plays with younger children and is usually very good with them. With Alan, it was slightly different. Paul described him as being very small for his age and as wearing thick glasses. Alan had special needs and would, in an ideal world, have been at a cosy little special school where he would have had a lot of individual attention. The current emphasis on social inclusion in schools means that special schools are out of favour. They do exist, but efforts are now made to educate as many children as possible in mainstream schools and Alan therefore had to cope with being in a crowded playground where there were a lot of rough lads (and girls). Any bully would see Alan as the ideal victim. Paul decided that he would not let his little friend be a victim: anyone who tried to hurt Alan had to deal with him too. He also mothered the boy. He made sure that his tie was straight and that his shoe laces were properly tied. With a perfectly straight face, he once gave his diagnosis: 'Alan's got special needs. I think his mum's got special needs as well. Always puts his shoes on the wrong feet.'

Paul sees less of Alan these days, now that he is in the sixth form and taking a pre-vocational course that should get him into a Further Education College next year. The course is co-taught by two schools and Paul spends at least half his time at a different school to Alan, but he has grown quite close to Cherie, who is confined to a wheelchair. No one is allowed to tease Cherie when

Paul is around. It in fact sounds as though all the children in the class are very fond of her. They take turns at pushing her wheelchair around the school, but she says Paul pushes it best. He now comes home complaining bitterly about how bad the disabled access is in some parts of the building. A boy with learning difficulties has somehow acquired all the vocabulary of advocacy.

I thought for a while that Paul's obvious and very real empathy with Alan and Cherie might indicate a future for him in health care or even nursing. And then I remembered: he would never pass the exams.

Paul has always been all too aware of his problems. There were many, many days when we could not make him go to school. When he did attend, he would come home from Greenways looking miserable and would eventually sob that he too wanted to score eighteen out of twenty in tests like his friends, but he never did. He would say, 'I can't do that. I'm thick, me.' He would refuse to go to school 'because my head's in a muddle'. At other times, he was reluctant to go to school because he was frightened of his teachers. He was especially terrified of Mrs James: 'She shouts,' he complained. We pointed out that most teachers shout at some point. 'Yes, but she's the shoutiest of them all.' Paul was convinced that she was shouting at him, and not the class as a whole. I mentioned this to Miss Barker, who explained that Mrs James did have a loud voice, mainly because she was a gifted amateur singer who was very good at projection. At a parents' evening, I spoke to Mrs James herself and when I told her that Paul had described her as the shoutiest teacher of all, she howled with laughter because she'd never heard the word before.

As the prospect of high school began to loom closer, we wondered about sending him to a special school and discussed it with the various professionals we were in touch with. We thought that he might benefit from being in a smaller school where he could work at a slower pace and receive more individual attention. The only possibility was an all-boys school on the other side of the city, and we were told that many, if not most, of the boys were there because they presented emotional and behavioural difficulties and that some of them were violent. This was a polite way of describing boys that many people would call junior psychopaths. Paul has learning difficulties but not emotional and behavioural difficulties. He can be violent, but the outbursts of violence almost always occur at home and have more to do with his position as an adopted child than his learning difficulties and special needs. Most of the time, he is quite a gentle soul and he would not have thrived in the harsh environment of a special school. We decided to keep him in mainstream education and prayed that his statement would provide him with some help.

At this time, a statement of special educational needs came with money attached. The statement and the money followed the child throughout his or her school career. The school used the money to buy in additional help, which meant that a child could be taken out of class and given extra individual help with basic subjects like English and maths. It didn't quite work like that in practice. As in most schools, there were more children with special needs, or something approximating to special needs, than there were children with statements. The money was 'shared out' and used to teach them in small groups. At Greenways a lot of this teaching was done by classroom assistants, who were not qualified teachers, who worked part-time and who were poorly paid. The majority of them had children of their own. Classroom assistants get a bad press and are often disparagingly described as a 'mums' army'. We may have just been lucky, but the classroom assistants we have met have been wonderful and they certainly helped Paul. Paul got his statement and the assistance it brought.

Cate has never had a statement of special needs, even though her learning difficulties are at least as great as Paul's. The standards by which special needs are defined have changed and it is now much more difficult to get a statement. Everyone recognises that Cate has learning difficulties, but we have been told again and again that she would not qualify for a statement because her special needs are not, her teachers tell us, 'bad enough'. Her needs therefore have to be catered for inside the existing system. At Greenways, that could be done without too much difficulty, but secondary school was a nightmare from the very beginning because so few allowances could be made. Cate was expected to cope with being in a class of thirty, with changing rooms and teachers for every lesson, and with a pace of life she was just not accustomed to. Not surprisingly, she could not do it. After a lot of negotiation with school, she has been 'disallowed' from a number of subjects and now studies only the most basic topics; she no longer does a modern language or geography, for example. Whenever possible, she is taken out of class and does individual work with learning mentors who concentrate on improving her literacy and numeracy skills. She is making progress, but it is a slow and arduous process for her, and she will probably experience a lot of frustration in years to come. Cate says, for example, that she would like to become a vet, and we've not had the heart to point out that getting into veterinary school is more difficult than getting into medical school.

If she is asked why she will not go to school, Cate will say that she is poorly, that she is tired, that she is frightened of a bully or this or that teacher, or that she is embarrassed about her period starting. She will sometimes say that she doesn't see the point of going. She will say that she is frightened of being 'nicked' or abducted on her way to or from school. And very occasionally, she will give her real reason. She knows that something dreadful will happen to either Marina or me while she is away from home. A psychoanalyst would say that this is a disguised expression of unconscious hostile wishes directed at us. Cate is afraid that her wishes will come true and therefore refuses to go out: if she is at home, they cannot come true. It is a possible explanation, and it may be the right one. It may also mask something more frightening still: what will happen to Cate if something happens to us? And something did happen to Cate: her birth mother gave her away and then her foster-mother gave her away. She does not want it to happen again.

Our children have always found the fact that I work at home very comforting. I can understand this because my mother did not work outside the home, though she certainly worked hard enough inside it, and because I very rarely had to go home to an empty house. When I did, I hated it. There are days when Cate will not come home if she knows the house is empty; she will go to a friend's and phone again and again until she knows that there is someone at home. This is a big old house, and it makes noises, creaks and talks to itself. I sometimes find myself starting at some unexpected noise I can't explain. It is usually caused by one of the cats. Anyone who thinks cats move silently has never heard Pussa lumbering down the stairs and sounding as though she is wearing football boots. One rather alarming noise proved to be Sammy the guinea-pig sucking and sucking in a forlorn attempt to get a drink out of an empty water bottle. This could be a spooky house for any child. In Cate's fantasy, it is not, I suspect, just a temporarily empty house: it is a house that Marina and I have left.

Working at home has many advantages and I normally enjoy it. The disadvantage is that the children know that I am at home, and so does the school. It is all too easy for a worried teacher to ask the receptionist to phone me to say that Cate has a headache and feels ill, or that Paul is sick and wants to come home. It would be much more difficult for her to try to contact Marina at work because she is often in meetings. She also has a PA who is very good at telling diplomatic lies and saying that she is 'out of the office'. I've gone to school to pick up a 'sick' child many times. If the phone rings during school hours, I always feel the same stab of apprehension, but on most occasions, the illness has been nothing that could not have been cured by a quiet hour in the medical room. Coming home ill from school has very rarely been an obstacle to playing in the street a couple of hours later.

The real disadvantage of being at home is the feeling that I have to be there. There are days when I bitterly resent that feeling. I do not want to go home for three, even though I have no particular desire to be anywhere specific: I just do not want to go home, but it is very rare for me not to be there when the children come back from school. Somehow their fears or, to be more specific, Cate's fears – Paul does not have this problem to the same extent – echo or reawaken fears of my own. I discussed this with my psychotherapist more than once. She had commented, not without a hint of mild irritation, that I sometimes spent more time talking about the children than about myself. She was quite right, but we worked out that this was probably because there are times when I no longer know where I end and where they begin. I recognise myself in Cate. When my father was hospitalised after his accident I did not want to go to school. I had to be taken by a teacher who lived near us, and she led me by the hand. Otherwise, I would not have gone. I vaguely recall someone telling me that I had to be the man of the house now. It is the sort of thing that is said in the circumstances, and it was well-intentioned but it was also a foolish thing to say. Boys of five-and-a-half cannot look after themselves, let alone their mothers and sisters. There is an element of this in Cate's behaviour: she is afraid of what will happen if I am not here, and she wants to be here to look after me. There is another reason why I ought to be more sympathetic to her problems than I am: there have been, and there are, times when I couldn't bring myself to go out. I've never been afraid of anything specific, but I have felt very uncomfortable about leaving the house. I've often wondered how Cate would react if I told her 'I can't go out either', but I've never said it.

We did not witness what happened, but we assume that it began with the kind of squabble that is so commonplace that no one takes a lot of notice. Kieran got into an argument with a boy from over the street who was two or three years younger than him, and much more slightly built. Words turned to scuffling and then blows. Kieran, who was wearing his heavy school shoes, knocked the boy to the ground and began kicking him in the ribs and stomach. One of the other children on the street must have called the lad's parents because the first we heard of all this was when we were told that he had been taken to hospital. The boy's mother spent anxious hours waiting in A&E. We had to go regularly to ask his father if there was any news of his condition, and it was an uncomfortably long time before there was any. He had not suffered any serious injuries but he was quite badly bruised. The imprint left by the sole of Kieran's shoes was clearly visible on his body and suggested that Kieran had stamped on him too.

A fight between two boys is hardly a major event, and the kids involved usually make friends quickly enough. But we found this incident very disturbing. The age difference and the heavy shoes meant that Kieran could have inflicted some serious injuries, and there was every indication that he intended to do so. We already knew that he had very little control over his impulses, and that he was capable of lashing out in anger, but what really disturbed us was his complete lack of remorse. He did not feel sorry for what he had done and clearly did not feel that he was in the wrong. He no doubt believed that it was the other boy's fault, and that 'he made me do it'. Cate often says that of Paul – 'It was him that started it' – even though we saw her strike the first blow. This kind of logic is what might be expected of a very young child but Kieran was ten.

When I spoke angrily to him, he thought I was going back to the argument we'd been having over a half-finished jigsaw that he had threatened to break up. That I might be angry – and frightened – about the damage he had inflicted on another boy just did not occur to him. The consequences of what he might have done did not matter. We were gradually beginning to realise that we were not just dealing with a boy whose behaviour was 'naughty' or 'bad', but that what we had on our hands was a boy with some quite severe problems and whose behaviour was becoming more and more disturbed. We became caught up in the potentially dangerous game of amateur psychological diagnosis. The way Kieran could so obviously divorce his actions from their consequences even made us begin to wonder if we were dealing with some kind of psychopath. He certainly admitted to hitting the boy, but seemed to have no sense that he was responsible for sending him to hospital. It was impossible to speak to Kieran in such a way as to get him to realise that he had done something seriously wrong. There seemed to be no emotional reality to him and he seemed quite incapable of empathising with anyone.

We needed help. A call to the Fostering and Adoption Unit got us nowhere, as whoever it was we spoke to had no idea of what 'post-adoption support' might possibly mean. It would be another three years before that began to change. It must have been Marina who contacted our doctor as I have no memory of meeting her at this point. We were referred to a consultant and eventually got an appointment with the Department of Child and Family Psychiatry at the local hospital.

The hospital is a large teaching institution and occupies a sprawling site on the edge of the city. The original buildings, which are now used as offices, are fine examples of Victorian hospital architecture but the hospital itself consists of a collection of ugly 1960s towers and more recent blocks. This was once one of the most densely populated places in the country, and the site was originally covered in cramped, working-class terraced housing. Part of the hospital is surrounded by a high wall and the remnants of an old terrace still stand just inside it. Most of the terraced houses are used as stores, but two of them are home to the Department of Child and Family Psychiatry. That it is in some of the oldest buildings in the entire hospital complex says a lot about the position that this branch of psychiatry occupies in the medical hierarchy. There is nothing new or shiny here, and not a lot of money has been spent on the buildings. Psychiatry is not a glamorous specialism and has none of the prestige that surrounds, say, transplant surgery. Child and family psychiatry is less glamorous still.

The air in the waiting room tasted stale. The few magazines and books were old and tattered, and the toys had seen better days. This was not a happy place. And the thick plate glass that divided the receptionist from visitors was a reminder that any psychiatric unit can be a dangerous place. Our first meeting was with a consultant – a likable lady who has since retired. We explained the situation and described what was happening to us, and how worried we were about Kieran's behaviour. We explained that getting the children out to school in the mornings was becoming more and more difficult. We feared that we were starting to lose control, that something was going seriously wrong in and for our family. Yes, we had struck our children in anger and frustration. We had never used violence as a form of discipline or punishment, because we did not believe in it and also because we knew from experience that it did not work. But yes, we had hit them. All five us kept getting involved in rows that were growing worse almost by the day, and it felt as though there was a potential for real violence. Someone could get hurt. The consultant listened quietly. Her view was that the best option appeared to be some family sessions to begin with. We made another appointment.

The appointment was with a young junior doctor. He seemed to know what he was doing, and we rather took to him. The five of us sat in an anonymous room and introduced ourselves. Then Marina took the children off into the play corner while I talked to

Dr Johnson. It had been explained to us that this session was being videoed from behind a two-way mirror; the video would be used for both diagnostic and teaching purposes. I didn't really mind but it must have added a little edginess to the situation. Dr Johnson's initial diagnosis was that we were basically a 'competent family', but that we were teetering on the edge of becoming an 'incompetent family', which sounded very close to the truth. He also thought that we were all suffering from separation anxiety. We were afraid of being apart, probably because we felt we were in danger of losing one another, and that in itself was making it difficult for us to be together. This was not easy to take on board: surely the problem was that we were finding it hard to live together? It would take me, in particular, a very long time to realise that Dr Johnson was perfectly right about this, if not about everything.

Most forms of family therapy are based upon the thesis that a member of a family who is presenting symptoms of some disorder is not so much an individual as a member of a group that is having difficulties. The family group functions as a system of relations between individuals, and it can break down. Relations within the family may need to be reshaped or modified. A common assumption is that the relationship between the parents is the most likely cause of the problems: a bad relationship between husband and wife can obviously affect the way their children behave. This is not necessarily the 'fault' of any one individual; individual members of the family are probably reflecting or reproducing the difficulties experienced by a small group that is greater than the sum of its parts. The therapy has to take that into account. Individual work may well be necessary, but so too is work with the family group. The model for family therapy is, of course, the 'normal' family: father and mother, plus birth children. The model was not designed with adoptive families in mind, and I should imagine that adoption was not discussed in any detail during Dr Johnson's training. Any child that is adopted is likely, almost by definition, to have been damaged in some way; in other words, a disruptive factor has been introduced into what might otherwise have been a perfectly competent family. If the adopters already have children when they adopt, which is by no means uncommon, the new addition to the family may be the factor that disrupts it. We had adopted three damaged and very disruptive children and our forever family had been subjected to terrible stresses from the very beginning. 'Teetering on the edge of becoming an incompetent family' was a huge understatement.

There was something that we could neither see nor understand at this stage. Dr Johnson could not see or understand it either because he was not trained to deal with the adoptive parents of traumatised children. We were all suffering from separation anxiety, but there was something else. Marina and I had adopted a five-year-old boy who had suffered the trauma of abuse, and a three-year-old boy and a fifteen-month-old girl who had suffered the trauma of abandonment and loss. In doing so, we had in effect adopted a trauma, or even suffered some form of secondary traumatisation. When we saw Kieran in his 'fuck me' posture in the bathroom, we were drawn into a traumatic situation. Every new upheaval took us back to that situation and, thanks to a process of identification, to Kieran's trauma. When we responded with anger to behaviour that resulted, ultimately, from his trauma, we made it worse.

We had very few sessions with Dr Johnson: two, perhaps three. We had not realised that he was coming to the end of one of the six-month rotations that make the life of a junior doctor so difficult. After only a few weeks, he moved on to another post. For the moment, there was no one who could replace him. We watched another lifeboat disappear into the distance. But at least we were thrown a small lifebuoy. It would, we were told, be possible for Kieran to have a course of individual therapy. I was never terribly clear about this new therapist's background, but I think she was originally a psychiatric social worker. The sessions were weekly and lasted for an hour. I would collect Kieran from Greenways, try to dodge other children's questions about where he was going, and take him to that little house. On our way, we bought sandwiches and a drink from the canteen run by the Women's Royal Voluntary

Service. Kieran disappeared into another part of the building with Rosie and I sat in the stale waiting room. I tried to read, but always found it hard to concentrate. I often went outside for a cigarette, but even that distraction was denied me when the building's security was improved. It was now impossible to open the door from the outside and I could scarcely go out and then interrupt the receptionist again by ringing the bell when I wanted to get back in. When Kieran's session was over, I took him back to school. A lot of my day was gone by now, and I resented it.

We had little sense of what went on in the sessions, and respected Kieran's right to confidentiality. It is not a good idea for a parent to get too closely involved in this kind of thing, as they are part of the problem. We do know that Rosie's main tool was art therapy. Kieran was encouraged to paint as a way of exploring his emotional world. He did not think much of the idea, but did accept that it was better than 'just playing', as he had with his first therapist. All therapy assumes that an inner world can be understood and eventually modified thanks to the controlled use of some means of expression, which may be verbal, visual, musical or even theatrical, that allows 'inner' to be translated into 'outer'. Over time, Kieran's paintings did change significantly as the large areas of black in the first paintings became smaller, and the colour fields grew larger. This was, it was thought, a major improvement: as the negative thoughts took up less space, there was more room for positive and vividly coloured thoughts and feelings. His behaviour at home also began to improve.

The therapy was not entirely satisfactory. A few sessions had to be cancelled and there was a gap of several weeks when Rosie broke her arm playing netball ('for the first and last time'), but the real disappointment came at the end. We, or perhaps it was just Marina, were supposed to have one last session to review what had happened and what progress had been made. It never took place. We have never been told why it did not and we still feel that something was left incomplete. We were, on the other hand, assured that we could come back to the unit for help at any time: 'Just phone to make an appointment.' In retrospect, I am not entirely convinced that these sessions did any real good. It is true that Kieran's behaviour did improve, but only for a while. There were, I now think, a number of problems that were never really addressed, let alone resolved. All our children are very good at 'talking the talk' and have a chameleon-like ability to take on the colour of their environment. They can react as they are expected to react and are very skilled at disguising the symptoms of what is really wrong. I have no doubt that Kieran appeared to be a responsive patient who was making good progress: that is what he was supposed to be. It may not have been what he was. Years later, Cate was referred to a psychotherapy group for school-refusers. One day a week for ten weeks, she went for intensive assessment sessions. To our amazement, a team of experienced specialists found nothing wrong with her and refused to take her into therapy. We were living with a girl who would not go to school, but they never even met that girl because she was so adept at concealing her problems and difficulties.

None of the specialists we had consulted to date actually came up with an explicit diagnosis of what Kieran's problems were and of where the causes lay. I think there was still a suspicion that the real problems were in the heads of his parents. Almost inevitably, it is the mother who is held to be at fault: she wanted it all, and now she can't cope or, more crudely still, it's all in her mind. When we were eventually given a diagnosis that actually fits our children's problems (and ours), it was astoundingly simple, though its implications are by no means simple. Their main problem is that they suffer, like so many adopted children, from attachment disorder. 'Attachment' means what is often called 'bonding'. A baby or young child in a difficult or deprived situation finds it impossible to form a normal attachment with its mother, and all subsequent relationships will be damaged as a result. If mum is not there, the baby literally cannot become attached to her. It is almost impossible to replace or reproduce a relationship that never existed in the first place. Children who have not been allowed to form that relationship find it impossible to get beyond the belief that there is no one they can trust. In the case of a boy who had suffered serious neglect and then sexual abuse, trust does not exist. For months after his initial placement with us, Kieran could not call me 'Dad'. Marina quickly became 'Mum', but I was just 'John' for a long time. That was not easy to live with but it was quite understandable. There had been two significant men in Kieran's early life. One abandoned him, and the other abused him. How was he to know that I wasn't going to do the same?

Attachment disorder has many implications. One is that one-to-one therapy rarely works: attachment-disordered children cannot establish the trust – which must be absolute – on which it is based. They can, on the other hand, simulate trust with astonishing realism. Neither Dr Johnson nor Rosie sensed that this might be a possibility. That is no criticism of them. The only criticism is that they had not been trained to diagnose attachment disorder, and had no experience of working with adopted children and adoptive families. It was to be over four years before we even heard the words 'attachment disorder'; we are still learning what they mean. We are learning by the day, and it is a very, very hard lesson.

I took the three of them to see *The Blues Brothers* live at the local theatre. We'd seen the film more than once but we didn't know what we were in for. I feared for the worst when it started with some corny stage-business. Someone in the audience had to supply a screwdriver to finish building the set. And then came the announcement that the police would not allow the show to go ahead. We were going to play bingo instead. The ushers began to hand out bingo cards and pencils. Kieran just sighed. Paul looked as though a tasty lollipop had just been snatched from his hand. 'Boring, Dad,' whispered Cate. Then the houselights went down and the eight-piece band kicked into action. The horns soared over the dirty riff from the organ and guitar as Jake and Ellwood were lowered on ropes from the flies. After a quick blast of Otis Redding's 'Can't Turn You Loose', they hurtled into the intro to Solomon Burke's 'Everybody Needs Somebody to Love'. Within seconds, Kieran was on his feet, together with half the audience.

The theatre can hold over twelve hundred people, and it must have been at least two-thirds full. A lot of the audience had come in costume. We were sitting almost next to two sub-teenage Blues Brothers sporting shades, black suits and pork-pie hats. There is little enough narrative in the film; tonight there was almost none. It was just a peg to hang the songs on. And the songs were all it took. I don't think the children had ever heard a real performance by a live band before, and they had certainly never experienced the huge emotional power of live soul music, but they knew how to respond to it. They danced, clapped their hands and yelled with *pure pleasure. We became part of something that has a life of its own: an audience on its feet and in synch with a band in full flight. I had often been to the theatre to see opera and have felt it throb with emotion, but I'd never felt the building rock.*

This was the six o'clock performance; God alone knows what the nine o'clock show was like. An hour and a half later, the audience poured out on to the street, still intoxicated. Women in pork-pie hats sang to policemen. Men in shades and black suits danced. Three young children sang as they skipped down the street. 'Everybody needs somebody . . . Everybody needs somebody . . . To love . . . Everybody needs somebody to love . . .' Marina was away from home that week. I still wish she had been there with us.

IV

Slowly but inexorably, as the days grew longer and the evenings became lighter and as Kieran span out of control, it turned into the worst of summers.

He had occasionally stolen from us in the past, but the thefts now became a serious problem and a major source of tension. He stole mainly from me and I experienced the thefts as a form of aggression. It began with the dinner money for school. I'd got in the habit of leaving it out before I went up to bed, as that left one less little task for the morning. But now it was disappearing and I could no longer leave my wallet on the mantelpiece, as I had done for so long. If I did, there would be ten pounds missing when I next opened it. If I said anything to him, Kieran would deny having taken anything. This happened so often that I began to doubt my own reason, to think that I must have been mistaken, and to wonder if I had had the money in the first place. I would try to think back : 'I went to the bank yesterday, spent so much on food for tonight, bought a packet of cigarettes, spent so much here, so much there . . .' But the sums never added up. There was always more money missing than I had spent. I now had to lock any money I had away in a drawer, and then I had to put a lock on the door to my room. Trust had begun to leave our home.

I must have started thinking about holidays because I went to check on how much foreign currency I had. As both Marina and I go abroad from time to time, we usually do not bother to change any currency we bring back and just put it on one side for the next trip. The drawer was empty. At first, I thought that I must have been mistaken and that there had been no currency there after all, but I then worked out that there had indeed been roughly the equivalent of £200. When I mentioned this to Marina, she immediately went to check the drawer where she kept her passport and currency. That money was gone too. Kieran had obviously taken it. This was not the opportunism of a boy who sees money and takes it on impulse. In order to find the currency I'd been keeping, Kieran had had to go through each of the twelve drawers of a filing cabinet. In order to find the money in Marina's room, he had had to search every drawer in a big partner's desk. These thefts had taken time, planning and determination. When I accused him of stealing Kieran tried to deny everything and claimed that he had no idea what I was talking about, but he eventually did admit to taking the foreign currency. He had taken it to the bank, changed it and spent it all, mainly on treats for his friends. Incredibly, the bank had changed money for a fourteen-year-old without asking any questions and without requiring him to produce any identification, but by the time we discovered the theft it was far too late to make a complaint.

We now had endless rows over the stealing and they were increasingly brutal. I would scream at Kieran in rage, with my face inches away from his face. He screamed back. The 'soft bastard' I got instead of 'good night' was the least of it. I found it harder and harder to let the anger go or to calm down. I kept stoking the arguments and could not or would not let things drop. I could not step back from the rows, and kept stepping back into the nasty circle of anger we had created and were now re-creating. I would storm out of the room or out of the house, and then storm back to begin the row all over again. I could not stop myself and it was as though I was, in some ghastly sense, actually enjoying this.

Kieran apologised from time to time, but his behaviour did not change as a result. In his calmer moments, he would try to explain why he was stealing but he could never come up with a real explanation. He did admit that he 'felt bad' afterwards, but also said that he felt nothing at the time. His explanations changed nothing, and nor did anything I said. If I told Kieran that I had only so much money, and that if he went on stealing like this we would reach a point where there was none, he just shrugged. He laughed when I told him that now that he had begun stealing from me, he would begin to steal from other people too, and that one day he would spot a five-pound note on a table in a friend's house and take it when he thought no one was looking. What I did not understand was that, for Kieran, there would have been no point in stealing from other people, as this was not really about money, or not just about money. The repeated thefts hurt, and they were meant to hurt; Kieran had worked out that they were a way of wounding me.

He found other ways to hurt Marina. On the mantelpiece in her study, there was a model sailing ship he had built from a kit we had given him. The boy who had been able to turn himself and his siblings into Daleks had a real talent for making models and took a lot of trouble over them. We were proud of his skill and told him so. In the course of yet another bad row, Kieran picked up the ship. He was very, very angry, but he did not just throw it to the floor. That would have been too easy. Slowly, carefully and with great cruelty, he broke the ship he had built into small pieces in front of Marina. He got what he wanted when she finally burst into tears. All our children, like so many adopted children, are very good at hurting us and they know just how to set about doing so. Kieran had it down to a fine art.

Stealing was an act of aggression, but that was not all it was. Kieran stole because he wanted. He did not want anything in particular as such. He just wanted, endlessly, emptily and painfully. He was trying to fill a void that had always been there. At times he had tried to fill it with food, and now he was trying to fill it with the money he stole. I think in retrospect that he also stole to justify a feeling of guilt; he stole because he felt bad, and to prove that he was bad. That is why so many of the thefts looked as though they were intended to be discovered. Kieran was certainly no career criminal in the making; on the contrary, he was a very poor thief. Picking up an unopened packet of cigarettes, I would notice that the cellophane wrapping had been tampered with. When I opened the packet, I would find that two or three cigarettes were missing. Kieran had opened the packet very carefully, removed the cigarettes, closed the packet again, and then tried to smooth down the cellophane to make it look as though it had never been touched. He may not have realised it at a conscious level, but he wanted to let me know that he had stolen the cigarettes, and wanted to be found out. It was the same pattern we had seen, but not understood, in the Kieran who had first been placed with us. He was behaving in such a way that he would be punished for what he had done. He was still the bad baby who had been given away by Viv over ten years ago, and he was desperate to prove to himself and others that he was bad. And we reacted just as he wanted us to react: we became angry with him, and responded with rage to the provocation of a child who was determined to make us reject him. We were caught up in a game he was controlling and we were playing by his rules.

This is a game no one can win. Everyone loses and everyone hurts. We understood nothing of all this. We thought we were dealing with a boy who was naughty, out of control or even delinquent. We thought that we were trying and failing to be good parents. There was no one to tell us that when children have been as badly hurt as our three had been hurt, they hurt those who try to love them. It has taken us years to learn the cruel lesson: for many children who have been adopted from care, 'normal' parenting will not work. We did not know that. And so it all became worse and worse as we all ran towards the edge of the cliff.

Mealtimes became another focus for conflict. Kieran could never turn up on time, even though he knew perfectly well when we ate. Either Marina or I would go to look for him. We would bring home a boy who was both angry and resentful, and that ensured that the meal got off to a bad start. Arguments broke out and we shouted at each other. The children fought with each other, and we joined in. My usual complaint was 'If I can spend half the morning making your lunch, the least you can do is turn up on time to eat it!' I threw meals I'd made into the bin because I'd put too much of myself into them to be able to take what I saw as more rejection, but also because I wanted a row too.

I was over-reacting and constantly making things worse for all of us. A more relaxed attitude would have helped, but I could not relax in this emotional climate. It was all the worse in that I did not want the sort of family in which everyone just comes and goes and eats snacks as and when they wish. I wanted us to eat togeth-er. It didn't seem too much to want. To add to the tension, Kieran now developed a nasty new habit. On coming into or leaving the kitchen where we ate – and it is not a large kitchen – Kieran would make sure that he had to push his way past Cate. A quick nip or a knuckle twisted in the small of the back was all it took to make her cry. 'I didn't do nothing. Why are you having a go at me? Fuck off.'

The evenings were as bad, if not worse, and 'Off out' was a phrase we came to dread. 'Out' could usually mean one of a small number of houses on the street, but we rarely knew which house Kieran had gone to and we never knew when he would come home. In an attempt to compromise, we would agree on a time, but Kieran never kept his side of the bargain. If he said he would be back at nine, we would be looking for him at ten; if he said he would be home at ten, we would be knocking on neighbours' doors at eleven. The parents of his friends often did not know if he was there or not, as these are such big houses that it is easy for two or three kids to disappear unnoticed into an upstairs room.

In some ways, it was of course a relief to have Kieran out of the house. We could at least sit quietly and watch television with Cate and Paul before getting them ready for bed. It had been a long time since we had been able to do that with Kieran in the same room. When Cate and Paul had gone to bed or just to their rooms, we did not have to do anything in particular but we felt unable to relax, and as the evening wore on, we began to feel increasingly tense as we watched the clock and waited for Kieran to come home, knowing only too well that he would be late again. Eventually, we would have to go out to look for him.

Kieran just could not see that there was a problem: where he went and when he came home was his business, and nothing to do with us. He did not understand when we tried to tell him that parents have both a right and a duty to know where their fourteen-year-olds are. A boy who occasionally comes home late is not a problem, but Kieran was coming in late so often that it became a recurrent problem. It was another source of conflict on top of the stealing, the problems over meals, the bullying of Cate and everything else. Perhaps we were asking too much and making too much fuss over what might in other circumstances have looked like fairly minor issues, but Marina and I had now been living for nine years in a state of hyper-vigilance and rising tension. We had reached the point where there was no such thing as a minor problem.

Then there was school. Kieran had had problems with school ever since he began to walk out of Greenways, but the main issue was now homework, as Kieran was in Year Ten and should have been beginning to prepare for GCSEs. The school told us that he should be doing about one and half hours of homework every evening, and other parents confirmed that this was what their Year Ten children were doing. Kieran was doing virtually no homework. As a result, his performance at school began to deteriorate badly. Until now, he had been able to wing it and get by on little work because he was a bright lad. That worked on a day-to-day basis, but everything went wrong now that he should have been thinking and planning ahead. Preparing for GCSEs is a long, slow business and it means having at least some vision of the future, but Kieran had no such vision because there was no future in his world. There was only the now in which he wanted so much, and which he refused to spend on homework.

There were always excuses. Kieran would insist that no homework had been set, but the 'none set' entry in the planner had been scrawled in Kieran's hand. At this point, our communications with school began to break down. It was Kieran's head of year who told me never to believe the 'no homework set' entries in the planner, but Kieran's form teacher saw those entries when he checked the planner and signed it to indicate that all was as it should be. He never questioned the number of 'no homework' entries. Kieran would also argue that he could not do his homework because he did not have the Encarta computerised encyclopaedia. The fact that the elderly computer I was using could not play CD-ROMs just went to prove what crap parents we were: everyone he knew had Encarta. Kieran finally succeeded in convincing himself that there was no need to do homework, or even that no one did homework. Proving this was simple. If he found that one friend on the street was doing some work, he could easily find another who was not. By moving on from one house and friend to another, he could always find at least one friend who was not doing homework when he called, and he used that fact to convince himself that there was a world in which no one did any homework at all. The reality of school did not fit in with this imaginary world and a new pattern developed. Kieran would fail to hand in his homework, and then fail to hand it in again when he was given a second chance. He would be given detention, fail to show up for detention, and then be excluded from school for three days. That was what he wanted: he could watch videos all day and then vanish 'off out' when the other kids got home from school. We had so many rows over this that Marina and I just gave up. We gave up arguing about homework. And I gave up trying to stop him watching videos or TV during the day.

When he was at school, Kieran was becoming increasingly disruptive. He was insolent to teachers and swore at dinner ladies. If he did not feel like going to a particular class, he simply hid somewhere or left the premises, and as a result he began to alienate those teachers who might otherwise have supported him. He lost an important ally when he lied to one of the gym teachers about why he had not turned up for class. He was caught smoking on a few occasions; he'd found a new way to use his dinner money, and a new reason to steal money. I began to get the phone calls again: 'Kieran has left the school premises.' I began to dread the sound of the phone ringing, but I always agreed to go and look for him. At first, he repeated the old pattern of hanging around just outside the school gate, but he then began to truant for whole days. One day, I found him hiding at the bottom of the garden. He'd probably been there all morning and, if I had not gone outside at about eleven and seen him, could well have stayed there for the rest of the school day. His explanation was that someone had been picking on him and that he'd run away in fear, so I marched him back to school and demanded to speak to someone. The big Irish guy who took him for rugby turned up and listened to the whole story. He liked Kieran and was sympathetic, and told him that if he was being bullied, he should go to a teacher and leave him or her to sort things out. One of the many good things about this school is that it does not deny that bullying does take place; a school that claims that there is no bullying is a school that is lying. At the time I believed Kieran's story and so, as far as I could tell, did his rugby teacher. It later dawned on me that he was in fact an unlikely candidate for bullying. He had been bullied in the past, but he was a big lad now. He was quite popular, had good friends at school and was quite capable of looking after himself. He was making it up as he went along.

There were other ways of avoiding school. Kieran could be so ill or so tired that it was physically impossible for him to go. If he was tired, it was because he had crept downstairs while we were asleep and had watched videos for half the night. If he was ill, the symptoms were invariably psychosomatic. Kieran has never had Cate's truly remarkable talent for developing psychosomatic illnesses, but he could certainly present enough symptoms to look convincingly off-colour. It had become easier to lie to school than to have yet one more row about getting him there, so we would phone in to say he was ill, knowing full well that he was not. I hated having to start the day by telling lies, but I don't think that telling the truth would have done us much good either. During one of these bouts of so-called illness, Kieran waited until I briefly left my study to make a cup of coffee, sneaked in and lifted twenty pounds from my wallet. I at once saw what he had done – the wallet had obviously been moved – and flew at him and told him he was a lying little shit of a thief. Another ugly row began, but Kieran eventually came to me and silently handed me two ten-pound notes. He'd forgotten that he had taken a twenty-pound note.

We were watching something that was as sad as it was frightening. No one would ever have described the fourteen-year-old Kieran as 'academic', but he had talent and potential. He could have done it, but he made us sit and watch as he wasted his talent and abilities. It was a painful sight, and we could do nothing. It was not just his intellectual abilities that were being wasted. Kieran was very good at sport, had played both rugby and football for his school, and would have been a much better player if he had listened to what his games teachers said to him. I am still not convinced that he realised at this stage that football is in fact a team game and not just an opportunity to show off. He really seemed to think that his ability to run rings about younger boys on the street meant that he was going to be the next Alan Shearer. He did, on the other hand, have enough genuine talent to have a successful trial with a local youth team that could have given him a good training. We were pleased for him, proud of him and encouraged him to make the effort that would be needed. For a while he glowed, but it did not last. He turned out for no more than two or three training sessions. 'Too tired.' 'Don't feel well.' 'Can't be bothered.' 'Off out, instead.' There were always more immediate pleasures on offer.

I had overslept and was only half-awake when I sensed that Kieran had come into the bedroom. Very quietly, he came over to my side of the bed. Sleepily, I asked him what he was doing. 'Looking for a hairbrush.' He then turned and left the room. Kieran's hair was so short that it needed sandpapering rather than brushing. He knew perfectly well that there was no hairbrush on the bedside table. He also knew that there would be money in the pocket of my jeans, which were on the floor next to the bed.

Kieran's rejection of school was a rejection of us. Both Marina and I place enormous value on education, and we are acutely aware that we would have got nowhere without it. We did our best to explain to Kieran that it mattered, that his teachers were not talking crap when they insisted that homework mattered, but it was as futile as trying to interest the cats in higher mathematics. We love books, so Kieran would not read. I think it was as simple as that: we said it mattered, so it did not matter. What did we know about anything? Kieran may not have said it in so many words, but he was making it quite clear that we were not the parents he wanted. We were offering him love and intimacy but it was not us he wanted them from. We were the only adults who had tried consistently to love him and he did not want us to. The boy who wanted so much for us to do things together 'as a family' and complained so loudly that we never did so was also the boy who did all he could to ruin family outings. Kieran was perpetually angry with us, but we were also the target for a much older and more violent anger; at fourteen, Kieran was still an angry baby, and a baby's anger is extremely destructive. We were the only people he could be angry with and we were on the receiving end of an anger that was also directed at his birth mother. He also decided that, given that we were not the parents he wanted, he could find others.

He did not have to look very far. Kieran had by now become quite friendly with a family who lived a few doors away. Marina and I knew them in the way that anyone knows their neighbours but that was as far as it went. Alan was slightly younger than Kieran but they often played together. Alan's sister Lisa was a year or two older than Kieran. She was a very pretty girl, and really did look something in her short skirts and thick tights. Kieran probably was attracted to her, but the real draw was her father Peter and, to a lesser degree, her mother Judith. Peter and Judith were good to Kieran and liked having him around their children and their home. They found him charming, well-behaved and pleasant to be with. Everyone did, because Marina and I were the only ones who saw the other Kieran. Kieran admired Peter almost to the point of hero-worship: Peter had built his brick garage single-handed, could tune video recorders, liked computer games, drove a 4x4 and played a good round of golf. He was in the process of buying a house to let, and knew how to do the rewiring himself. Kieran loved going with him to help out on odd jobs. Peter was obviously all the things I was not. I've never wanted to build a brick garage. Peter represented the father Kieran thought he wanted, and, at a fantasy level, the father he had lost.

Most, if not all, children enjoy the fantasy that their actual parents are not their real parents. A little girl dreams she is a princess who is being brought up by paupers, and a boy knows that he is really the heir to a great fortune, even though his parents are surviving on social security benefits. For an adopted child, all this is much more complicated because there was (and often still is) a different real parent. In Peter, Kieran had found someone who was very different to me. It must have been easy to jump to the conclusion that this was what his real dad must have been like. To complete the picture, Peter was adopted as a baby. It was almost too perfect.

It was Peter and Judith who introduced Kieran to the world of car-boot sales. They used to set off early on Sunday mornings to go to various sales around the city, and when Kieran asked if he could go with them we saw no reason to say no. Car-boot sales proved more attractive than training sessions and that was the end of the football. Part of the appeal was no doubt that neither Marina nor I see the point of car-boot sales and have no interest in buying other people's junk when we have quite enough of our own. That was further proof of just how boring we were. We teased Kieran about the sales, telling him that the police enjoyed them too because they allowed them to recover so much stolen property. We asked him if he really believed that so many guys really owned three power drills, 'never been used, still in the box'. We also warned him about the goods on sale: dodgy computer games and pirate videos that do not play properly. We did not really object to his new obsession, but we were sad about the football. We were dubious about what he might come back with but we knew that he was in the company of two responsible adults and would come to no harm.

But then we woke one Sunday morning to find a window open in a downstairs room. We had not, as we at first thought, been burgled. The alarm was still on but there was no sign of Kieran. When he finally returned hours later, we wanted an explanation. For once, Kieran was quite forthcoming. He had got up at four, climbed out of the window to meet a friend in the street and had gone with him to a big car-boot sale on the other side of the city. It must have taken them at least an hour to get there on foot. At four in the morning, a fourteen-year-old and a twelve-year-old had set off to walk through the most notorious of the city's estates to go to a car-boot sale. On that estate and at that hour of the morning, the local vampires are still walking the streets. Anyone with a brain who had to drive through the place at that time would lock the car doors.

Kieran's companion that morning was Ryan. They first met the day we moved into the street and quickly became good friends. At one point, Ryan was spending so much time at our house that his father half-seriously offered to have his child allowance signed over to us. Both Marina and I became fond of Ryan, who was, we thought, a very endearing boy who was lively and full of fun, if a bit of a handful too. As he grew older, we began to have our doubts about a boy who had always been impulsive, strong-willed and very independent, as it was now becoming increasingly obvious that his 'independence' meant that he just did not recognise the existence of rules, let alone the need to obey them. It was quite simple: what Ryan wanted to do, Ryan did. It did not help that Ryan's parents were the last of the hippies, and that whatever he did was excused on the grounds that he was 'just experimenting'. Kieran and Ryan were a dangerous combination. One of Ryan's experiments involved the theft of half a bottle of rum from our kitchen, and I have every reason to believe that Kieran was the laboratory assistant on that occasion. Ryan was also a confused boy, and he had good reason to be confused. The guy who organised our local neighbourhood watch jokingly asked him if he had noticed anything suspicious of late. Ryan replied that he had indeed seen something suspicious: his mum kissing a man who was not his dad. The marriage did not last for much longer after that. Ryan and his family – now in pieces – moved away and we lost touch. We subsequently heard on the grapevine that his experimental drug-dealing had led to his permanent exclusion from one school, and then from a second.

On the day that we found that Kieran had taken all our foreign currency, we had to go to Comet for something and took the children with us. We had been talking about buying a stereo for the lounge and stopped to look at what was available. Kieran wanted us to buy one on the spot and just could not accept that I did not feel like spending a lot of money only hours after discovering that he had stolen over £200 from us. For Kieran, it was as though that had never happened. A few weeks later, we relented and went back to Comet. We had convinced ourselves that the children were old enough to be trusted and we were tired of having no music in the lounge. The stereo we bought was neither sophisticated nor expensive, but it did have a turntable and we wanted to listen to some of the piles of records that were gathering dust in various cupboards. We were able to listen to just one record when we got home. When Marina went to put something on the next day, she found a broken stereo. The stylus had been bent to an angle of forty-five degrees and the drive belt had been broken. What had happened was obvious. Ryan's older brother had a set of decks, and Kieran had seen him 'scratching'. He had tried to imitate him without realising that professional decks are very robust and that they use a different drive-system. Anyone could have been forgiven for not knowing that, and if Kieran had admitted to having made a stupid mistake, it would all have been forgotten about soon enough. But Kieran insisted that he had done nothing, that he didn't know what we were talking about, and claimed that Paul or Cate must have been messing around. Kieran could not see that his lies were more unconvincing than ever. Paul knew nothing about stereos, and Cate was interested in the Spice Girls, not hip-hop and scratching. Marina and I were really beginning to feel the strain. Kieran was almost impossible to live with and the minor problems were occurring so regularly that we were being driven mad.

Kieran was also becoming friendly with someone we should have mistrusted from the very beginning. Mark was the son of the delightful couple who lived directly opposite us. They had both divorced their first partners in order to marry and had a total of six children between them, but we only knew the three who were still living at home. The two younger boys were fine and no trouble to anyone, but everyone thought that Mark was trouble. He was in his early twenties and claimed to be an alcoholic. I don't know if that was strictly true, but he was certainly drunk a lot of the time. He was living at home because another job had fallen through and he had nowhere else to go; like all Mark's jobs, it had lasted for only a couple of months and he had been sacked for being late and turning up drunk. His story was that he had come back to live with his parents because he wanted to get away from his old friends, who would get him back on the drugs and drink he was trying to avoid. It was much more likely that his friends had moved on and could no longer be bothered with him. Whatever the real explanation, he was now hanging out with the kids on the street. Kieran was fourteen. Alan was, I think, about thirteen, and Lisa fifteen or sixteen. Ryan was twelve. Mark's story impressed them greatly. Older and tarnished idols are always appealing to impressionable youngsters, and Mark was certainly tarnished. Kieran really fell for him.

The little group began to congregate on the street and at the bottom of our garden. Mark would appear with a carrier bag containing cans of beer. Odd bottles of wine began to disappear from the cellar. I had rows about this with Kieran, but I always suspected that it was often a case of 'Go and get us a bottle, Kieran. They'll never notice.' As we've never seen the point of drawing up long lists of forbidden fruit, we'd been offering Kieran the odd glass of wine or beer. He rarely drank them, and did not really like the taste of alcohol, and I never really believed that the empty bottle of Bacardi we found in Kieran's room had been polished off by him. No adult on the street liked or trusted Mark and even his long-suffering parents found it hard to put up with him. Lisa's father certainly did not want him sniffing around his daughter. She was, her dad thought, a sensible girl, but it looked to me as though she was enjoying the attention. Kieran found this upsetting because he was jealous. Late one evening, he arrived home in something of a panic. Lisa's parents were out and he'd been in the house with her and Alan. Mark turned up with some drunken mate and more or less forced his way in. Kieran was beginning to panic: 'Mark's trying to touch up Lisa! You have to stop him! He's touching her up! Stop him!' I went to speak to Mark, taking his father with me. Eventually, we persuaded him to walk away. Even dads who are soft bastards have their uses.

Marina and I were now beginning to have our own rows, and they were always about Kieran and how to deal with him. I felt that he was being allowed to get away with murder and was taking over our lives. I wanted more strictness or at least some discipline, but had no idea of how to obtain either. I wanted Kieran to realise that he was making all our lives very difficult, and wasting a lot of his own, and I wanted him to develop some sense or vision of the future he wanted for himself. I was tired of being stolen from, tired of being sworn at, tired of waiting up, tired of all the fights, tired of being angry. Basically, I was tired of living with Kieran. Marina was, if not more tolerant, at least more prepared to go on trying to negotiate with him. Her attachment to Kieran had probably always been greater, or more visceral, than mine.

She was not willing to let go of the boy who could now call her 'bitch' to her face. I was starting to feel that I could do so and might have to do so. Kieran and I had now come to blows more than once. It is all very blurred now, but I remember one particular argument in which I was screaming in his face and making as though to hit him. It would not have been the first time. I'd never hit anyone in my adult life, but I could strike our fourteen-year-old son. On this occasion he reacted by kicking me hard in the stomach. Marina had to pull us apart.

Paul and Cate watched and listened as all this swirled around them. They heard the noisy rows and the insults that were traded: 'You little bastard' . . . 'Soft bastard' . . . 'Bitch' . . . 'Cunt.' They saw the fights at mealtimes and watched me throw away the meals I had spent so long making. They saw me throw things and then walk out of the house. They saw Marina bursting into tears again and again. They saw us fighting. They saw and heard things they should never have seen or heard. They were disturbed and frightened, and we were so caught up in our difficulties with Kieran that we scarcely noticed.

At times, I began to think that there was only one solution: I would have to leave. My relationship with Kieran was disintegrating, and I began to blame myself for that. I began to believe that I must be the source of all the problems, and to convince myself that, if I were not there, they would not be there either.

We were the only people who saw all this. Others saw our three charming children. Peter and Judith saw a Kieran who was friendly and polite, and who interacted well with them. His teachers were beginning to see a rather different boy, but they certainly did not know the Kieran we knew. We did not talk to anyone of the difficulties we were having with Kieran, except in the vaguest of terms. No one would have believed us. Kieran reserved his aggression for us, so no one else saw it. Our neighbours may well have thought that we were over-reacting when we went looking for him night after night but no one said anything and we never hinted at what was really going on. There are all sorts of hells hidden behind suburban doors, and we were living in one of them. We simply kept the door shut and hoped that no one would hear the shouting and the screaming.

There was, we thought, one hope: we could go back to the Department of Family and Child Psychiatry we had consulted when Kieran beat up the boy on the street. When we rang up, we were told that we could not have an appointment without a formal referral from our family doctor. No one was going to help or rescue us.

Time was passing and the holidays would soon be upon us – first the school holidays and then our family holiday, which we had already booked. I don't know which I was dreading most. School holidays were always a respite in one sense, as not having to worry about getting the children off to school meant that there was one less thing to fight over. But with Kieran going off the rails, there seemed little prospect of any reprieve and it seemed more likely that six weeks of school holidays would just give him more time to spend with Mark, and more time to get into trouble. The idea of a family holiday appalled me because I did not want to spend hours in the car with the children, because I did not want to make an overnight ferry crossing to France with the children, and because I did not want to spend three weeks in a rented house with the children. In particular I did not want to do any of those things with Kieran, and I said so, often, loudly and in anger. Kieran made it quite clear that he did not want to go on holiday with me either.

I told Marina that she could go if she liked, but that she would have to have the three of them on her own. Eventually I relented and said I would go after all because I had, with a lot of difficulty, convinced myself that going away might be a way of breaking the destructive cycle and that I might be able to make it up with Kieran. The holiday would give us a new start, and when we got back we could set to work on the garden together. It needed a lot of attention: the bushes needed cutting back, and the big rocks around the central bed needed moving. I planned to use them to build a rockery behind the pond.

Two or three weeks before we were due to go on holiday, Marina and I were having a quiet end-of-the-day drink when Kieran suddenly erupted into the room where we were sitting, sweaty, wide-eyed and breathless. I don't remember where the other two children were. He was clearly in a very agitated state and may have been drinking, though we both have such a poor sense of smell that we could not be sure. He at last calmed down enough to begin to tell us why he was so upset: he'd been sharing secrets with Lisa. At first he refused to share her secret with us but then let slip that her mum was leaving her dad for someone else. Kieran's secret was that he had been abused by Andy. We are quite certain that he had never before mentioned this to anyone outside the family (other than professionals), so he must have had a lot of trust in Lisa. And then he began to talk about Andy, which was something he had not done for a very long time. He said he could not understand why he had been abused but he knew what he was going to do about it. When he was old enough, he was going to find Andy. And kill him. He was going to get a big sharp knife and stab him through the heart. Stab him in the head. Stab him in the eyes. Stab him in the stomach. Stab him dead. Stab him dead. His eyes glittered with rage as he made stabbing gestures.

We held him and tried to calm him: 'There's nothing to be ashamed of. It wasn't your fault. There's nothing to be afraid of. You're safe here with us.' It became a mantra – on and on, over and over again. 'Nothing to be ashamed of. Nothing to be afraid of.' The mantra worked and he calmed down. He suddenly became very, very tired and just flopped.

We shared Kieran's anger and many others would have shared it too. None of the professionals who had been involved with Kieran's case would have condoned the death he wanted to inflict on Andy, but few of them would have mourned him for very long. We were proud that Kieran had felt strong enough and trusting enough to tell his friend about what had happened to him because it seemed to indicate a new maturity on his part. We did not often see the Kieran who could trust us enough to come to us for help and comfort, and we at times wondered if he still existed. It was nice to have him back. We could sympathise with his total inability to understand what had been done to him so long ago because we didn't really understand it either. There was no way for us even to begin to explain to a fourteen-year-old boy why an adult he trusted had buggered him and put him in hospital. We did not have the words to explain it. A therapist or child psychiatrist may have known the right words to say. We did not. We could not undo the harm that had been done to Kieran and we had no words to explain it. All we could do was offer the consolation of our little mantra: 'There's nothing to be ashamed of. There's nothing to be afraid of. You're safe.'

I came down for breakfast to find Marina in tears. She looked at me: 'Kieran has been abusing Cate.' All I could say was: 'That's that, then.'

It was day three of our holiday in Brittany, and we had eighteen days to go. Kieran and Cate had disappeared together on the evening we arrived, and Marina had gone looking for them. She eventually found them in a room on the top floor of the house we were renting. At the end of the room there was a sort of walk-in cupboard, and that was where Marina found a startled Kieran trying to do up his jeans, and a Cate who was naked from the waist down. Always quick to lie, Kieran said that they had been making a den. Some time later, when she was alone with her, Marina asked Cate what they had been doing: 'Sex.'

For two days, Marina said nothing to me about this. She was afraid of how I might react, afraid that I might be violent and attack Kieran. Given how tense and angry my relationship with him had become, it was not an unreasonable fear. But there was no violence and I'm not even sure that what I felt could be described as anger. We did have fights. We did scream at each other. I did threaten to walk away and go home; I even began to pack at one point. The anger and the fights were about the usual things: the stealing, the rudeness, the refusal to cooperate, the bullying of Paul and Cate, the refusal (or inability) to enjoy anything and the contriving to ensure that no one else did either. They weren't about this.

Marina's discovery of the abuse left me feeling numb, shocked and afraid for the future, but not angry. After such a difficult summer, I really had hoped that this would be a time to reach out to Kieran, a time to make a new start. And now, there was just a terrifying blankness that lay on the far side of anger. This was not the start of anything; this was an end.

We were a long way from home and there was no one we could turn to in France. We did briefly discuss going home at once, but getting a car and five passengers on to the Plymouth ferry at short notice at the height of the holiday season would, as we well knew, have been almost impossible, as the crossings are fully booked months in advance. We could have driven to Calais and taken the shuttle but we didn't, telling ourselves that we needed a holiday, and that the children needed it too, and that we had worked hard all year for it. All that was true up to a point, but the real reason we stayed was that we were afraid to go home because we knew perfectly well what we had to do: we had to report the abuse to Social Services and to the police. We also knew what was going to happen: that it was over, and we were going to have to lose our son so as to protect our daughter. We knew that this was going to be the last family holiday for the five of us.

We tried so hard. And we did have some good times that summer. We swam on a beach where the sand quickly gave way to rock, in achingly cold clear water, and came out into hot sun. We swam in warm, shallow water on another beach. Paul and Cate learned to gather cockles at low tide and we cooked them in white wine for supper. Paul caught guppies in a bucket. At dusk, I took Cate for walks to see the bats flying and we watched glow-worms in the dark. On wet afternoons, I even managed to do jigsaw puzzles with Kieran. The house we were staying in was adjacent to a pig farm owned by our landlady and, like anyone who stayed in her gîte, we were treated to the grand tour. We held piglets, and were surprised to find how warm they are, how fast they breathe and how fast their hearts beat. As luck would have it, we'd bought pork chops for supper that night. No one could eat them. Cate loved the little pigs, and even saved one from being chased on to the road by the farm dog. After that, she and

Madame were fast friends. When we left, Madame gave Cate plaster-of-Paris figurines of pigs, and they still sit on her bedside table.

And we had hellish times. If Cate went into the sea, Kieran would splash her very aggressively; if she began to build a sandcastle, his football would accidentally knock it down. Never easy, car journeys became nightmares, as Paul and Cate fought almost constantly, and as Kieran slyly stirred things up even more. We had obviously not said anything to Paul about what we had discovered, but he could sense the tension, knew that something was seriously wrong and therefore began to behave very badly. As he walked back to the car one damp afternoon, he took out his frustration by kicking the bodywork and leaving big dents in it. People watched in disbelief. We could read their minds: 'Mad English. Can't control their own children.' 'That boy deserves a smack.' There was no way they could know that they were watching a family implode and disintegrate. On one journey, the fighting in the back of the car became so bad that Marina could not drive safely and had to pull over. Paul and Cate leaped out and started chasing each other. Kieran sat there looking smugly satisfied, and then joined in. I set off to walk back to the house, but then realised I couldn't actually walk the twenty-five kilometres. Totally out of control, the children were now screaming as they ran around, yards away from an unfenced road where the traffic moved very fast. They were so close to death and all I could do was scream at them in anger. All Marina could do was weep. We couldn't help each other.

We survived the remaining eighteen days of our holiday. As we had lost all trust in Kieran, he could not be left alone with his sister, who moved into our bedroom with us. Paul quickly joined the three of us. I could not leave money anywhere; even if I put it at the bottom of a suitcase, notes still disappeared. Cigarettes disappeared too, but any attempt to challenge Kieran over their theft was met with sullen defiance; the cigarette ends we found in his bedroom were nothing to do with him and he had no idea how they got there. He swore that he hadn't taken 100 francs from my wallet. He did not spend the money he took in France, but as soon as we were on the boat he began to feed a lot of money into the video games. It was only when we got home that we found the packs of batteries and the aerosols of deodorant that he'd lifted from the supermarket we visited most days.

We could not talk to Kieran. We just could not speak of what had happened on holiday. Besides, there would have been no point. Kieran would have stared us in the eye and denied everything. He would not have admitted a thing. We could detect no sign of any shame, remorse or sorrow. It would be a long time before he could feel any of those things, and even longer before he could begin to express them. For the moment, he probably felt very little. He had the ability to split his life into compartments that had almost nothing to do with each other. He could steal from us, know that he had stolen from us, know that we knew, and still expect us to behave as though nothing had happened as he moved from one compartment of his life to another. If he did apologise, he did so only in words, and it would not stop him from stealing again. It must have been the same when he was abusing Cate. He just did it.

There was little Marina and I could say to each other either. We couldn't really find any words. We turned on each other as I took refuge in alcohol and became angry when Marina told me that I was drinking too much. I told her I didn't care that I was drinking too much and I didn't care that she did not like it. There were evenings when I refused to eat with my wife and children. I could not sit down at a table with Kieran, and so I did not. I refused to go on excursions with my family and left Marina to cope as best she could; and she coped much better than I would have done. We seemed to be able to do very little to help each other. We had no idea of how to begin to help Cate, or even of what help she needed. We didn't even know exactly what had been done to her.

It took time to work it out. We pieced it together from what little Kieran and Cate could tell us. The incident in France was not a one-off occurrence. The abuse had been going on for about four years, and we had noticed nothing. It had taken place in Kieran's bedroom, following invitations to 'come and play on my computer', invitations we had taken as a signal that Kieran could be kind to his little sister after all. Cate had said nothing to us; she may have been frightened, and Kieran may have threatened her in some way. She may even have derived some pleasure from these incidents. Sexual pleasure is, at least in part, a reflex response to a stimulus and we have little control over it. That is one of the reasons why it is so easy for the abuser to say to a victim: 'You enjoy it really. You know you do.'

Our vigilance had let us down, and we were flooded with guilt because we felt that we should have known. We have spent a lot of time trying to understand why we did not know or see what was going on, and we are still trying. We still look for clues in our memories of the past. At about the time when Kieran was seeing Rosie at the hospital, Cate went through a phase we found disturbing. As we watched television together in the evening, she would sprawl on the sofa, dressed only in a short nightie; as she was wearing no knickers, nothing was left to the imagination as it rode up over her splayed legs. We did not make much of this, but just teased Cate a little, tried to make a joke of it and told her to put some clothes on. It was not until much later that we began to wonder. Was this when the abuse began? Was Cate's body language trying to tell us something she could not say? Had the work Kieran was doing with Rosie somehow stirred up the demons inside and brought them back to life? I don't suppose we will ever know, but I keep asking the questions.

We got home in one piece, though I'm not sure how. We got back late at night. It must have been after eleven, but Kieran's first reaction was to announce that he was 'off out', and we had to stand in his way and physically prevent him from leaving the house. As far as he was concerned everything was back to normal, but his sense of normality was now so warped that he thought nothing of turning up on someone's doorstep at that hour. Nothing had changed and he did not need to change either. He must have known somewhere inside himself that what he had done would have consequences, but that seemed to have no effect.

There was one thing we had to do: we had to inform Social Services as soon as we could. We had no choice in the matter, and what had happened was something we could not keep to ourselves.

The worst thing about this period – and the long time that followed – was that there was no one we could talk to. We dealt with the various professionals we encountered as best we could but that provided no real outlet for our feelings. At times we felt as though we were trying to cope with a bereavement, but there was no corpse and no way of mourning. As we both knew, death is difficult to deal with and to come to terms with, but it can be done. We'd both done it. There are social protocols for dealing with the death of a parent, inadequate as they may be. There are ways of talking about death and most of us are familiar with them, and although it is difficult and painful we can usually do it. There are no social protocols for dealing with what we now had to live with, none at all. Sibling sexual abuse is not something to be discussed over a meal or a drink with friends, and it was a long time before we could say anything to even our dearest and closest friends. We were being forced to look at something that scarcely has a name. We had discovered that we had been living for years with a son who was abusing our daughter. Only a short while longer, and we could well have been coping with an incestuous pregnancy.

Suddenly, all the horrors associated with the children's past, and especially Kieran's past, were flooding back into our lives. We had never been naive enough to believe that they were gone forever, or that they could be safely forgotten about. But this was something no one could have expected or predicted. We were going to have to lose our eldest child, and there were moments when I never wanted to see him again. We were going to have to deal with another sexually abused child. We probably could not have found it at the time, but there is a name for what we were experiencing: trauma, meaning an encounter with some terrifying reality that is beyond anyone's control. Everything began to merge into one great vision of horror: the thought of Kieran being abused, the memory of Kieran inviting abuse in our old bathroom, and the image of a half-naked girl and a boy zipping up his jeans. This was our forever family.

I think I can say that we are both strong people, or at least we are a strong couple with a lot of inner strength, but I don't think that any couple can survive a trauma like this on their own. There are not the mental resources, not the strength, not the sheer bloody toughness. We were angry, furious, badly wounded, terribly afraid and facing despair. We were flooded with guilt because we felt that we should have been able to prevent what had happened and that we should have been watching more closely and carefully. We had let our vigilance slip, and it was our fault that our beautiful son had hurt our beautiful daughter. We felt that our family would just disintegrate, that we would lose them all, that everything was gone. If we could not prevent this, what else couldn't we prevent? We'd failed. We'd failed Kieran, Paul and Cate. We'd failed ourselves. And in the midst of this welter of conflicting emotions that changed from minute to minute as anger turned to tears, pain to rage, and shame to fear, we were alone.

V

Andrea was the social worker who had been allocated to our case, and one of the first questions she asked us after introducing herself was, 'What can you do to protect Cate?' As questions go, this was a very stupid one. We were frozen, hypnotised by the fact that our adoption of Kieran had ended in disaster and, whilst we did not know what was going to happen next, we did know that the damage that had been done could never be repaired and that the five of us were not going to be a forever family. Marina and I were on our knees, frightened, and had no idea of what we should do. We wanted help, and we had a social worker asking us how we could protect Cate just as we were trying to come to terms with the fact that this was precisely what we had been failing to do for the last few years.

I can't really remember what we finally said but I think I mumbled that I could sleep on the landing outside Cate's door, which is a good indication of just how disoriented I was. As I remember it, for the next month Cate slept with her mother and I camped in my study. It wasn't an uncomfortable solution but it was not a very pleasant one either. But that is not Marina's memory: she remembers moving into Cate's room with her, sharing the narrow bed at first and then sleeping on the floor. She reminds me that we couldn't put Cate in our bed because she was bed-wetting so much. Either my memory is correct, or Marina's is.

We should have taken Andrea's question as a warning that, for the moment, nothing was going to be done and that we had to protect Cate because no one else would. An adult perpetrator would have been immediately removed from our home by the police. As Kieran was a minor, that was not going to happen and we were going to be left with perpetrator and victim – our son and our daughter – living under the same roof. It was not until much, much later that we worked out why we were left in this position for over a month; it looked as though there were no established guidelines for dealing with a case like this. No one we spoke to knew what they were doing. Over the last four years, social workers, teachers and educational welfare officers have all asked us what we could do, and it has always been their way of asking us what they should do. Again and again, so-called professionals have asked us to tell them how to do their jobs.

The grim realisation that there was no policy for dealing with boys in Kieran's position now fits into a much broader and darker picture. Like anyone else, Marina and I had initially acquired what little knowledge we had of sexual abuse from media reports and then, as we thought about adoption and eventually became adoptive parents, from more specialist sources. We thought we knew quite a lot. We knew about Kieran's abuse, and thought that we had dealt with it, and that it was part of a past that had gone. It had now returned, bringing its horrors with it, and ushering in a future that looked very bleak and held many uncertainties. It was almost immediately obvious that there would be no spontaneous offers of help. No one was coming forward to offer Cate any form of counselling or support. No one was going to give us advice on what we should say to her and Paul. No one was rushing up to us to tell us what we, as parents, should be doing to try to confront our own feelings of failure and guilt. When we first phoned Social Services and 'grassed' on Kieran, as he would have put it, we had assumed that we would find that some kind of system was already in place for cases like this one. We were wrong. All we had was a baffled social worker.

Kieran now contrived to make matters even worse than they were. He came back late one evening and, when we asked where he had been, calmly told us: 'Baby-sitting with Lisa.' In reality,

Lisa was more than capable of looking after herself and Kieran posed no threat to a baby he did not know, but he had put himself in a dangerously compromising position. We could just see the headlines: 'Boy accused of abusing sister left in charge of baby.' It may have been a panic reaction, but we felt we had no option but to report this to Social Services, and this time the response was immediate. Another social worker briefly visited us and immediately rushed off to warn Lisa's parents that she should not be left alone with Kieran. Nothing was said about just what trouble he was in, and they were left to imagine the worst. Peter and Judith asked to see us and we agreed to talk to them, but we had to do so alone, because the worker who had spoken to them had vanished as quickly as she had appeared. We tried to reassure them that Kieran did not pose any threat to the sixteen-year-old Lisa or her brother, but we were not prepared to explain that he might be a threat to younger and more vulnerable children. We could not tell them what had happened to bring about this crisis; we and our children had to go on living on this street and we did not want any gossip.

Later that month, we were visited by two women police officers, and it was almost funny to see that the old division of labour was still in place and that dealing with child abuse was obviously 'a woman's job'. It was also quite grotesque. Kieran was at school and we had to talk about what he had done with the police, and then wait for him to come from school for his tea as though nothing was the matter. Trying very hard to pretend we knew what we were saying and doing, we 'discussed the situation' with the officers. They thought it likely that Kieran would have to be questioned, that Cate would have to make a statement on video, and that Paul would have to be formally asked if he had been abused too. When he was subsequently asked that question by a social worker, he simply stared at her and said: 'No.' At this point, the officers did not think that Kieran would be charged with any offence or would have to go to court. We began to swing from one extreme to another. We hoped Kieran would just be given a caution and at the same time we wanted him inside some kind of secure unit. We wanted him to be helped and we wanted him to be punished. We never wanted to see him again and we didn't want to lose him. We wanted to protect him too, but I gradually began to want to have him arrested. I did not welcome the thought of Kieran being taken into custody, but I half-sensed that being arrested might be the start of a process that would provide the help he needed.

Cate was examined by a female paediatrician in the presence of her mother. When the report came, it was inconclusive. There had been sexual activity but precisely what had occurred remained unclear, as the physical evidence was 'consistent with but not diagnostic of' penetrative sex. Cate was also interviewed in a video suite at the local police station. Marina went with her because a child of nine cannot be interviewed unless a parent or carer is present. I don't know the details of what Cate said and have never thought it appropriate to ask too many questions. Some things probably are best left to the professionals.

Mine is not an easy position. I've never had any problem when it comes to talking about sexuality with Cate. When she began to menstruate at the age of about ten, she readily talked about her periods and she still asks me to buy her pads from the chemist's. When it comes to the abuse and its aftermath, things get much more difficult. I was very aware of being the man closest to her, but I was uneasy about asking questions and was uncertain how she might respond. Kieran learned as a very young child that he could not trust men. It was not impossible that Cate might draw the same conclusion and decide that I was not to be trusted. But she was still the same girl and, when one professional after another asked me if the abuse had changed my perception of my daughter, I was always able to say that it had not. I have never seen a sexually-abused child coming down the stairs in the morning. I simply see Cate, just as I simply see Kieran.

And then the blow came. Kieran was going to be charged with indecent assault, and could count himself lucky he was not facing a charge of rape. He was going be arrested and would have to appear in court. We still do not know if the police officers we spoke to had been lying to us, or at least misleading us, when they said it was unlikely that Kieran would face criminal charges. We still wonder if that was a ploy to encourage us to cooperate, which we would have done anyway. We do not know if the decision to press charges was taken by the lawyers of the Crown Prosecution Service, and if the police were overruled by them. No one explained anything to us, but it was probably the age of the children, and the age difference between them, that decided the issue. If Cate and Kieran had been, say, three years younger or if there had been only a year between them, things would have been different. Marina and I would probably have dismissed what had gone on between them as mere sex play. It is, after all, not uncommon for siblings and half-siblings to play sexualised games, and what became abuse may well have actually begun as a game. We might well have been upset, but we would have felt no need to go to Social Services, and even if we had gone to the police, I don't think charges would have been brought. As it was, Kieran was fourteen and a half, and Cate ten and a half. When a boy is sexually active with a half-sister who is four years his junior, 'abuse' really is the only appropriate word. He was too old to be playing sex games.

A lot of scurrying about was going on in Social Services' grubby warren of offices. It was now clear that Kieran could not go on living at home and would have to be taken into the care of the local authority. Alternative accommodation had to be found for him and we would have to sign away our parental rights. Thought had to be given to Kieran's education, and both Greenways Primary and Kieran's high school had to be put in the picture. Andrea and her colleagues organised a planning meeting at what they called the local One-Stop Centre. We had no real idea that such places existed, and no idea of what went on there. This centre was a converted school, and was by no means unpleasant once we got inside; it was the razor wire that topped the security fences that was off-putting. Social Services and Housing both had offices here, and the centre also housed a library that was open for only a few hours a week. What had once been the school's hall was now used by a luncheon club, and the smell of cold mashed potato had seeped into everything. The planning meeting was attended by social workers, more social workers, youth workers and teachers. We had met only a few of them, and we never saw most of them again.

Plans were being drawn up and accommodation for Kieran had been identified. He was being taken into remand foster-care, and after he had appeared in court he would be returned to his carers until he was sentenced, at which point everything would have to reviewed, as remand placements are, by definition, for children between ten and seventeen who are facing trial or awaiting sentencing. Remand foster-carers, who are paid by Social Services, are very difficult to recruit and even more difficult to retain. Their role is to ensure that children and young people who have been remanded into local government care while they await trial enjoy at least a semblance of life in a family home, and all the evidence suggests that the remand-care system does reduce the rate of re-offending, and that it is preferable to institutional care. It is not, on the other hand, perfect. The 'family homes' in question are homes in which carers share their houses with children facing charges of theft, burglary, serious assault and many worse things. Remand carers soon learn that, if they leave even a small amount of money unattended in a room, it will vanish; they also learn to lock the doors to their bedrooms and to any other spaces they wish to keep private. They cannot trust the children they are looking after, and the children do not trust them. Children in remand foster care often have to share bedrooms and they quickly learn that their personal possessions are at risk and that they cannot trust their room mates. Kieran had a lot of experience of stealing from us; before long, he would have a lot of experience of being stolen from.

One afternoon, Marina and I went back to the One-Stop Centre and its smell of cold mashed potato and, after a long talk with Andrea, signed the papers that allowed Kieran to be taken into care. This was the end. In legal terms, we were no longer his parents. Kieran was going to be cared for by a rather elderly couple who were, we were told by Andrea and other professionals, 'very good and very experienced'. While all these arrangements were being made, Kieran was still living at home and Marina was still camped out in Cate's room. Everything was moving much too slowly for comfort, but it was only at our insistence that Kieran was at last removed from our home. We actually had to phone Social Services to protest that we could not be expected to go on living with Kieran and Cate under the same roof, and to say in so many words that we wanted Kieran to be taken away immediately. And then we tried to back down and put the whole process into reverse. We wanted Kieran to go and we did not want him to go. He was finally removed on the day after my birthday. Before he was driven away by Andrea, Kieran stole all the money he could find in Marina's purse and wallet, and then smashed the mirrors he'd been so pleased with when we bought them for his bedroom.

The accommodation was on the other side of the city. We felt ambivalent about this because, whilst we certainly did not want Kieran living on the doorstep, we did want fairly easy contact with him. Then there was the issue of school. Kieran was already having difficulties with school, and a move would have been disastrous because it would have completely unsettled him. For the moment, the school was – to our surprise – willing to keep him on and prepared to make an effort with him. Social Services made arrangements for Kieran to be taken to and from school every day by taxi, presumably at considerable cost. We experienced enormous relief when Kieran was removed from our home, and we felt deeply ashamed about feeling so relieved. But the relief was genuine: there were no more anxious evenings waiting for him to come home and we did not have to worry about the drunken Mark hanging around, because Paul was still far too young to be of interest to him. We knew that Cate was now safe and would come to no harm, and could concentrate on her and Paul. They were both very bewildered and needed a period of calm.

A few days later, we drove out to see Kieran in his new accommodation. He was not exactly overjoyed but did not seem unduly unhappy to see us either. The house was perfectly comfortable, and he was sharing a reasonably large room with another boy of roughly his age. His carers, Bob and Anne, seemed pleasant enough and welcomed us into their home. They explained that they were fairly strict with the children they looked after, that school and homework were the main priorities, and that Kieran would not be given much money because most of the allowance he received from Social Services would be saved and used to finance outings at the weekend. He would have very little time to himself, and would not often be allowed to go out unsupervised, though he might be able to take the dog for walks now and then. Bob and Anne made it perfectly clear that their neighbours neither liked nor trusted the children they looked after. They did not blame them for that, or for regarding them and their charges with some suspicion. Our 'very good and very experienced' remand carers soon began, however, to look distinctly spooky in some respects. They – and especially she – clearly thought that sexual abuse was not a serious matter. Kieran had struck Cate, and that, in Anne's view, was much worse than indecently assaulting her. Bob and Anne's grown-up son Anthony was often at the house, and they obviously believed that he could do no wrong. They constantly talked about his achievements in front of Kieran, and may as well have told him outright that he would never be as good as Anthony was.

I was also beginning to wonder about the nature of our social worker's relationship with the real world. Andrea drove me out for a review meeting at Bob and Anne's and lectured me all the way there, telling me that we were wrong to let the children have televisions in their bedrooms and that watching selected programmes was something that we should have been doing together. I had no idea why she was talking to me like this, but I did not like it at all. I had not, in fact, liked the idea of televisions in the bedrooms at first, but we eventually gave in, mainly because every other child we met had one. When I pointed this out to Andrea, she would not listen and just repeated what she had already said. This woman was an experienced social worker, yet she seemed not to know that many children of Kieran's age have bedrooms resembling a large branch of Dixons or Comet. Televisions are the least of it. My initial irritation with Andrea was so great that I quite failed to notice the incongruity of what she was saying: we were on our way to discuss the future of a boy who had committed a serious sexual offence, and our social worker wanted to talk about the evils of television.

Kieran seemed to settle into the bizarrely Dickensian regime of life with Bob and Anne. He did his homework, watched the soaps in the evening and even read some books. He took the dog for walks and laughed as he watched it try to catch rabbits. He went to school and back by taxi every day. He came to us for lunch most Sundays, though this was always a time of great tension. He obviously could not be left alone with Cate and he in fact showed little sign of wanting to be with her. He wanted to play with his friends, just as though nothing had happened. Marina saw much more of him than I did and took him out for lunch now and then, but they were joyless meals. I did not join them and I had the perfect excuse of being unable to leave Cate and Paul by themselves. I did not really want to see Kieran, and I certainly did not want to be alone with him. The five of us went bowling a couple of times but the tensions were so high that it was a miserable experience. From time to time, we all went together to the cinema, which at least meant that we did not have to talk. I was finding it quite impossible even to begin to say anything at all to Kieran about what he had done and why he had had to be taken from home; I just did not have the words. Marina was more successful at this than me, and was able to talk to him when they were alone together. Strangely enough, they both found it easier to talk in the car: a conversation in a moving car does not involve any eye contact.

We were, we thought, quite happy about the placement itself, even though we were increasingly aware that there was something strange about it, and just assumed that Bob and Anne knew what they were doing. Kieran soon began to test the limits, as was only to be expected, not least because he was so dangerously bored with the life he was being forced to lead. He began to be rude, insulting and uncooperative. The taxi took him to the school gates each morning, but he did not always make it from the gate to the classroom. Acquaintances began to report seeing him in town or near the house during school hours. Kieran was like that: he would accept confinement and restrictions for a while, push at the limits to test them and, when they did not give, explode. The pressure was beginning to build up, and without realising what they were doing, Anne and Bob were stoking it.

A date was set for a first court appearance. We found a lawyer to represent Kieran; we were firmly convinced that he should not be in a courtroom without a legal representative at his side, but we also needed someone to guide us through the maze. We were right to engage a lawyer, and she was remarkably efficient and objective. It was she who advised us that, as Kieran's birthday was coming up shortly after the initial hearing, it was important to get a plea of guilty on the record before he turned fifteen. That would make it a lot easier to guarantee that the case would be heard by a youth court, and it would also mean that a custodial sentence was not an option available to the court.

On a damp morning, we met Kieran, his remand carers and his lawyer outside the court building. The hearing was set for ten. The youth court was all polished stone and blonde wood, an impressive building, but also one that was designed to intimidate. The individual court rooms open off a long hallway that serves as a waiting area. People were clustered around the doors to the courts, trying to learn where different cases were being heard. We now learned a first lesson: the court system does not understand time in the same way as the rest of the world. A hearing may well have been set for ten, but that is not necessarily when it will take place. Ten o'clock is when the court complex opens its doors. Which case will be heard first depends upon nothing more rational than a lawyer's ability to grab the attention of the clerk of the court and to convince him that his or her case should take priority. A good lawyer may succeed in having the case heard shortly after ten. If that does not work, a hearing 'set for ten' may not take place until the court reconvenes after lunch, in which case it will be in competition with every case held over from the morning session and all those due to be heard at two. We had been lucky enough to find a good lawyer.

Kieran's initial court appearance did not last long. The lawyer spoke for him and all he had to do was to confirm his name and enter a plea of guilty to the specimen charges of indecent assault over a period of four years. All Marina and I had to do was to identify ourselves in order to explain why we were in court. I was surprised at how low key and matter-of-fact it all was, how calm and quiet, and I hadn't realised that there is no public gallery in a youth court. Kieran was clearly very frightened – as well he might be – but he did not lose his self control and made, we thought, a good impression. A date was set for a further hearing. It was explained to Kieran that it was his responsibility to attend, and that a warrant would be issued for his arrest if he failed to do so. The clerk formally thanked 'mum and dad' for having attended. When Kieran entered a plea of guilty, he was acting on the advice of his solicitor. It was sound advice. His plea meant that the court would probably look more kindly on him. It also had wider implications: it meant that Cate would not have to give evidence or be cross-examined. I assume that she would have been able to give evidence on video or from behind a screen, but it would still have been a dreadful ordeal for a little girl. And if Kieran had decided to plead not guilty, it is more than likely that Marina and I would have been called as hostile witnesses. Marina would have had to tell the court what she saw that day in France.

It was as we left court that I noticed what I had not seen before. A lot of the youngsters waiting around were accompanied only by people who were obviously social workers. Others were quite alone. Not every 'mum and dad' attended their child's court appearances. And that was why we had been thanked: simply for being there.

All our children have December birthdays, and Kieran's comes first. We'd been exchanging confused messages with Anne and Bob all week and had reached the point where I no longer had any idea of what we were doing. Either we were taking Kieran out for a meal – as we usually do on birthdays – or we were having a meal at their home but, as we set out, I didn't know which. As it turned out, we were eating at Anne and Bob's, and they really had made an effort. The table was already laid with good things to eat, and Anne had obviously dressed up for the occasion. Even so, it was a very strained evening and no one could relax. It was impossible to talk to Kieran in any real sense. From time to time, Anthony appeared in the background. Anne referred to him again and again, telling Kieran that, if he kept on working well at school, he might do as well as Anthony. Having to listen to all this was difficult enough, but I really did have to bite my tongue when Anne yet again made it obvious that she did not believe sexual abuse to be a serious offence. All this was said in front of Cate, but fortunately she was too preoccupied with playing with the dog to take a lot of notice. The evening dragged painfully on.

We left as soon as we could do so without being rude. Leaving Kieran behind hurt, but we had no choice now. He was caught up in a system we could not influence, and this set-up was part of it. Both Marina and I were furious with Anne but we kept quiet because we didn't want to say anything in front of Paul and Cate. The trivialisation of Kieran's offending behaviour was agonising. We were trying at once to mourn Kieran, to go on loving him without condoning what he had done, and to keep our family together; we did not take kindly to being told that it was a lot of fuss over nothing.

Two weeks later, Marina drove out on Christmas morning to collect Kieran while I cooked lunch. He spent most of the day with us and Marina took him back to Bob and Anne's in the early evening. Cate went with them because she wanted to see the dog again. They got home much later than I had expected, and Marina was not in a good state when she came in. She had intended just to pop in to discuss when we could pick up Kieran to take him out on Paul's birthday, which was in just a few days, but had become embroiled in a long conversation with Anne. Anne had just received a letter informing her that an appointment had been made for Kieran to see a forensic psychiatrist for a pre-hearing assessment. She had had previous dealings with this psychiatrist in connection with another boy, and described her as 'useless'. In her view, the entire prosecution was a farce staged by social workers who were obsessed by sex and saw it everywhere. If she had to take Kieran to his appointment, she would go in and 'lie for him'. She told Marina that everything should just have been swept under the carpet, and then turned on Kieran, and complained about his attitude, his behaviour and the untidy state of his bedroom. Cate was again playing with the dog in a corner, and could hear every word. Members of Anne's family were also present. Kieran was fidgeting nervously and beginning to look upset. Anne snapped at him to sit still. When Marina objected that Kieran might be finding all this a little difficult, she was told that it would come out in public in court, so what did it matter? She at last found an opportunity to leave, gave Kieran a hug, gathered up Cate and walked out, hurt, worried and furious.

The four of us went to pick up Kieran because we were going to go out for a special Chinese meal to celebrate Paul's birthday. As we pulled up outside the house, we could hear the dog barking. It took Bob a long time to open the door to us. He seemed to be on the defensive, and all he said at first was: 'He's not here.' Anne was not there either. She'd 'gone away for a few days'. Bob went on to say that Kieran had walked out on Christmas night, and that he had no idea of where he might be. The police had been informed and were looking for him. As we grabbed Kieran's few belongings from his shared bedroom, Bob mumbled that it was all very sad, but perhaps it was for the best. Somewhere else would be found for Kieran, and perhaps we wouldn't have so far to travel. Perhaps he and Anne would now get a boy who could keep the room tidy. He said that more than once. We walked out, got back into the car and went straight home. Paul did not get his Chinese meal.

All this occurred two days after Christmas so it was only in the New Year that the different versions of what had happened emerged. Everyone agreed that there had been a row. According to Bob's version of events, Kieran had been very rude to Anne, had reacted violently when warned about his language and behaviour, and had stormed out in a rage. Andrew, who was the other boy they were looking after, went with him. This was by no means an implausible scenario. Kieran later provided an alternative version in which he had become involved in a row with Anne. He lost his temper and told Anne that he was sick of hearing about Anthony, and that he hated both him and his 'bastard parents'. Bob and Anne told him to get out of the house. Andrew had walked out too, and the two of them had gone to Andrew's mother, who had taken them in, which meant that she was, technically, breaking the law. Kieran told anyone who would listen that he never wanted to see Bob and Anne again, and refused to go back to them. This too is a plausible scenario, but there are no reliable narrators in either story.

That was Kieran's introduction to being fifteen years old and to finding himself trapped in the remand-care system and the court system. And it was our introduction to having a fifteen-year-old boy caught up in those systems. A young boy on remand – and officially very much at risk – had been able to walk out into the night. His carers had let him go, and may in fact have thrown him out. There is no denying that Kieran could be impossibly difficult and could react violently when he felt himself threatened. We knew all about that, but we could not understand why no one told us what had happened. No remand carer, no social worker, and no police officer had contacted us, yet it could so easily have ended up as another of those news items: 'Boy in care of Social Services missing/found dead.' The possibilities were as endless as they were unthinkable. We were beginning to realise that we were quite powerless; we had no rights and no one had any obligation to consult us or to keep us informed. If we wanted to go on being involved in Kieran's life, we would have to fight to ensure that we were. We could have given up, and there were moments when we almost did. A lot of parents do, and that is why so many children attend court alone.

Kieran was found emergency accommodation while Social Services tried to sort out a new long-term placement. Marina and I were not really in a position to make a complaint about the way Bob and Anne had behaved, as we had not actually witnessed the scene on Christmas night and had only Kieran's account to go on. We did write to Social Services to express our concerns and worries about Bob and Anne, but I cannot find any reply to our letter in our files. Kieran was very angry indeed and insisted that he was going to make a formal complaint, though he cannot have had much idea about how to go about it and I don't think he would have had much of a chance. He was on remand and facing some nasty charges; they were 'very good and very experienced' remand carers. To the best of my knowledge, they still are.

At the initial hearing Kieran had entered a plea of guilty, had been granted police bail and had been remanded into the care of Social Services. A date had been set for the hearing at which a sentence would be passed. In the meantime, a pre-sentence report had, under the terms of the Criminal Justice Act, to be drawn up by a member of the Youth Offending Team, whose remit was to 'prevent offending by children and young people'. Magistrates sitting on the bench look all-powerful and all-knowing but most of them are not professionals, have no legal training, and usually act on the advice of a specialist clerk. A pre-sentencing report prepared by an expert can have a great influence on how they deal with the case, and on the sentence they hand down. The YOT worker was Bernard, who contacted us and came to the house to explain the role he would be playing. A quietly-spoken man, he looked almost like a caricature of his type, with his cropped hair, boots, jeans and bomber jacket, but he proved to be very effective and professional.

Bernard explained that he would be basing his pre-sentencing report on two lengthy interviews with Kieran, and one with Marina and myself. He would also be making a risk assessment to determine whether or not Kieran posed a threat to himself or anyone else. He had already spoken to our social worker, and one of his colleagues had talked to the school. He had seen the documentation drawn up by the Crown Prosecution Service. He had also had sight of a long report written by a psychiatrist based in another city. This had been commissioned at the suggestion of the lawyer representing Kieran, and was based on a structured clinical interview with Kieran, an interview with Marina and a discussion with Bernard. It was poor Marina who undertook the wretched task of driving Kieran to his appointment with the psychiatrist. Kieran said almost nothing until he saw the road sign saying 'Psychiatric Hospital' and then began to grumble that he wasn't a nutter and had no business in such a place.

From what I gather from Marina and from what was said in court, the interview dealt with Kieran's past life, with his account of his abuse of Cate and with his feelings about it. He was, the psychiatrist thought, a fairly typical juvenile perpetrator and had abused Cate, rather than another child, simply because he had such easy access to her. He had told her that the abuse would probably have stopped anyway, 'When I get a girlfriend.' When that was reported to me, my immediate thought was: 'God help the poor girlfriend.' The psychiatrist found Kieran quite cooperative except when she raised issues he did not want to address. Asked what he would wish for if he were granted three magic wishes, Kieran said that he wanted to be a successful sportsman and be happy for the rest of his life. His choice of partner for life on a desert island would be Marina or his girlfriend ('if I had one'). If he could have gone back and changed his life, he would not have been adopted, and would have had a birth mother who could give him a good start in life. As I might have expected, he expressed a lot of hostility towards me. He complained that I tried to hold conversations with him that were way over his head, and would do nothing practical with him. He added that I was a heavy smoker and that I was not well. Asked if he was worried about me, he looked sad but said nothing. Kieran's behaviour was, in the consultant's view, almost certainly the result of his early experience of sexual abuse. For the moment, at least, he had to be considered a threat to vulnerable others, especially girls, and there was also a possibility that he would become a threat to women as he grew older. She recommended that he be referred to a specialist team: he would be a challenge to anyone but an experienced therapist. Treatment on a residential or community basis should be considered. Any team working with Kieran would also have to work closely with us.

Bernard's report was broadly similar. He was very struck by the fact that Kieran had expressed little or no empathy with his sister-victim and by how much he concentrated on his own losses and fears for the future. He thought Kieran did pose some risk to the community and to other children and agreed with the psychiatrist about the need for intensive therapeutic work. In his view, the most appropriate sentence would be a supervision order that would oblige him to work on addressing his offending behaviour with help from the Youth Offending Team and specialist social workers. In private, Bernard told us that he was quite confident that the court would agree with his findings and suggestions. The one real uncertainty that remained was the issue of where Kieran would be accommodated after sentencing. It was by no means certain that he would be able to remain in a remand foster placement. The words 'children's home' were uttered in the course of one meeting, and everyone present flinched. Kieran would have been surrounded by vulnerable younger children and might have been a potential threat to them. He was also in a very vulnerable position himself. Every effort would, it was agreed, have to be made to keep him in his current remand-care placement but no one was in a position to make promises.

As the time for the court hearing drew nearer, we learned that it had been adjourned. This did not bother Kieran: he thought it would buy him more time in his new foster-placement. He was settling down now and beginning to take a liking to his carers, but they had not been able to change the pattern of his behaviour. As he had done at home, he happily ignored curfews and broke promises about when he would be back in the evening. He was also ignoring his bail terms and refusing to keep away from the street where we live. Unfortunately, the new placement was, for a fit lad, within easy walking distance of our house. Only days before he was due to attend court, Kieran turned up unannounced on the doorstep. Cate let him into the house. Fortunately, I was at home too and was able to tell him to leave. He could easily have turned up when I was out.

We then received a letter from the local police informing us that Kieran had been found in the company of a group of teenagers who were making a nuisance of themselves. The police were cracking down on anti-social behaviour and on groups of kids that were becoming large and rowdy; there had been a lot of vandalism of late and their patience was wearing thin. Kieran had been part of this group for some time, and that had worried us. They gathered in a car park behind a local branch of Comet. It was a good place for mischief, as they could not be seen from the main street. The off-licence immediately opposite was a convenient source of cigarettes and alcohol and its owners did not seem to be too particular about asking for proof of age. This was also a potentially dangerous spot: a steep ramp to the side of the car park leads down to the railway station, and some of the trains come through at high speed. Some of the kids used to skateboard down that ramp on to the platform.

I suspect that many of the kids were doing little more than hanging out, flirting and drinking a bit, and that most of them were probably not involved in the vandalising of telephone boxes that was so common, though a few of them undoubtedly were.

We were not the only parents in the street to receive that letter. A couple over the road had it too. By chance, I met the father in the street one day and he happened to mention receiving the letter and told me that, whenever time his son went out in the evening, he felt sick with worry until he knew that the boy was back in the house. We tried but failed to convince Kieran that he was not in the same position as the rest of the group he was associating with. At worst, the others risked a parentally-accompanied visit to a police station and a caution. Kieran was due to come before a court and risked a great deal more, as he could be charged with breaching his bail conditions. We were also concerned that the letter had come to us. Our house was no longer Kieran's home, and it should have gone to his foster-carers. He clearly thought that this was still his home and had given our address to the police. He could, in theory, have been charged with giving a false address. Perhaps he actually thought that he would be able to come home after his court hearing.

One day in February, we waited in the corridor of the Youth Court again. We were an odd bunch: two parents who no longer had any real parental rights, one boy who did not really know what was happening to him, one remand carer, one lawyer and one YOT worker who had seen it all before. Three of us were nervous and frightened; the others were there as professionals and were perfectly calm. We went in to face the bench of magistrates. Kieran's plea of guilty meant that there would be no adversarial trial and that the main purpose of the hearing would be to determine his future. There was very little for Marina or I to do or say once we had confirmed who we were. Bernard and Kieran's lawyer did most of the talking. They described the background to the case, the nature of the offences and the context in which they were committed. Bernard summarised his report and made his recommendations. The forensic psychiatric report was put before the court. Bernard was quite confident that we would get the result we wanted and tried to reassure us that the outcome would be a supervision order. We had allowed ourselves to be convinced, but our stomachs turned when the magistrates suddenly went into a huddle and began to whisper to one another. They consulted the Clerk of the Court several times and then went back to their deliberations. Although we had been given to understand that a custodial sentence was not an option available to the court, we are still convinced that that is what they were discussing.

Kieran stood in silence as the sentence was handed down. He was given a supervision order for a period of two years, which was quite a heavy sentence as supervision orders can be made for a maximum of three years. He was ordered to attend a sex offenders' programme as part of his supervision. He could not have unsupervised meetings with his sister, and could not enter our street without our express agreement and approval. Compliance with the terms of the order and attendance at all meetings was obligatory, and he had to turn up on time, and neither drunk nor under the influence of drugs. Failure to comply was an offence. He could be brought back to court and re-sentenced. Kieran was also placed on the sex offenders' register for a period of two and a half years. He was told to report to the police station immediately. Failure to do so was another offence. The police had to be informed of any change of address; failing to give proper notification was also an offence. Kieran was to be accommodated by the local authority, meaning that he would stay in his remand placement until he was eighteen.

I am not sure of what Kieran thought of all this. He was no doubt relieved that it was all over and glad that he could go on living where he was. He was also very angry. Over a month later, he had yet to register with the police. Being 'placed on the sex offenders' register' does not quite mean what it seems to mean. The offender has to physically go to a police station, explain to the desk sergeant why he is there and actually sign the register in person. Kieran refused to go. Marina offered to take him on two separate occasions; the offer was met with angry hostility. By refusing to go to the station, Kieran was again putting himself at risk. A time limit had been set, and he was running out of time. I think it was a social worker who finally got him to sign, but I do not know how she persuaded him to do so. Throughout all this, Kieran expressed no regrets and no remorse, probably because he could not establish any link between his actions and their consequences. We were back to the old problem. He had been told to stay out of the street and its immediate vicinity. But why should he? It was his patch and no one could stop him being there. Nothing was his fault. We had thrown him out of his home, and now we were trying to keep him away. That was our fault, and Cate's fault. It was nothing to do with him.

Marina and I were relieved that the sentence was what we'd been given to expect. Kieran would see Bernard and a specialist social worker on a regular basis and would, we hoped, gradually be able to come to some understanding of why he was in his present situation. He would be encouraged and helped to accept that he had committed a crime, and to accept responsibility for what he had done. We began to feel more hopeful, if not exactly optimistic, but we also had some misgivings. The forensic psychiatrist we had consulted had spoken in her report of specialist residential placements for young men who sexually harm others. The placements provided a direct therapeutic input as well as education and high levels of supervision. It sounded almost ideal: a combination of therapy, education and structured supervision was, we thought, just what Kieran needed. We had been dazzled, and we were being very naive. We had been dazzled because we thought we had been pointed in the right direction; we were being naive because we did not realise that, by mentioning it to Bernard and suggesting that this might be the solution we were all looking for, we were treading on his toes. Like all professions, social and youth work has its professional rivalries and its demarcation disputes. Bernard was a professional with a lot of experience behind him. Understandably, he wanted to keep the case on his own patch and it must have seemed to him that we were questioning his competence. In our dazzled naivety, we had simply assumed that a consultant forensic psychiatrist would know best. We were also being naive in another way: we actually believed that our local authority would send Kieran to an independent institution in a different city, not realising that a week in a place like that would cost thousands. And we were talking about long-term therapy; the money was just not there.

The first reports that filtered back to us were not good. Kieran was refusing to engage with or to commit himself to the therapy he was supposed to be having. He was uncooperative, was trying to control the situation and was being rude to Bernard and his support worker because he did not want to be in therapy and believed he did not need it. He was given warning after warning by Bernard and we tried to talk to him whenever we saw him, but it did no good. Bernard had – and needed – immense reserves of patience and settled down to a long and difficult task. He knew that the work he was trying to do with Kieran had to be based upon trust, and that Kieran found it hard to trust anyone, but he also knew what would happen if Kieran went on like this. We knew too, and so did Kieran, but he chose to take no notice. In the short term, the only option open to Bernard was to 'breach' Kieran – that is, take him back to court for breaching the terms of his supervision order. This happened more than once. On one occasion, Kieran was fined a small amount and told that, if necessary, he could pay instalments by postal order. Kieran began to mutter that he knew nothing about postal orders and then lost it. Looking directly at the magistrates, he finally spat out: 'I don't know anything about this. I don't know where to get a postal order. It's all right for you, you do this everyday and you understand how it all works. I don't fucking know how it fucking works . . .' Our hearts sank, and Bernard put his head in his hands. Speaking very slowly, and with great anger, the senior magistrate told Kieran that, if he said one more word, he would be held in contempt and put in the cells.

Throughout all this, we had to get on with our lives as best we could. We had two children to care for, to get to school in the morning and to feed. We had a household to run. Marina had a job to go to every day, and I had to go on with my own work. Until now, Paul and Cate had been difficult at times but they had never been impossible to deal with. Their behaviour was now beginning to deteriorate badly and their squabbles were turning violent. It was more and more difficult to get them into school, and there were more and more mornings when we just could not do so. They were confused and frightened. They did not know what was happening, and had no way of understanding what was going on. Marina and I were their only source of help, and we were failing them. Our arguments were turning into vicious quarrels. I did not know how long I could go on coping with this or living like this. The house was full of feelings of anger, guilt and fear, and was no longer a good place to live. Everything was beginning to unravel. There were days when it felt that we were in pieces all over the floor, waiting for someone to walk over and crush us into even smaller pieces.

Paul, in particular, was devastated by Kieran's departure. For a long time, the two boys had been virtually inseparable, though the two-year age difference was beginning to make itself felt at about the time when Kieran was taken into care and he was growing away from his brother. We had tried our best to explain to Paul what had happened, using language he could understand, but I don't think he really had much idea. In any case, he had his own explanation: Marina and I had had Kieran taken away, but it was really Cate who had driven him out. It was all her fault, and he hated her for having Kieran taken away. Cate, for her part, thought that she was to blame and carried a terrible burden of guilt. She presumably also felt guilty about the abuse itself, as it is quite common for the victims to conclude that they brought it on themselves. Reaching the point where they can say 'It was not my fault' is an important therapeutic milestone, and Cate was nowhere near that point. She was in the terrible position of knowing that she had been abused by her elder brother, and also knowing that she still loved him. All this swirling anger and guilt was made even worse by the children's realisation that, if Kieran could be sent away or got rid of, so could they. Cate and Paul's behaviour began to deteriorate badly because they were trying to answer a question: 'How badly could we behave and still not be sent away? How badly do we have to behave before we are sent away?'

Looking back, I cannot begin to imagine how we got through this period. I certainly cannot remember. It is true that we were gradually beginning to find the support we needed and had needed long before the real descent into hell began. We were in regular touch with our social worker, but she was as out of her depth as we were. We were still in contact with Kieran and saw him quite often. He would come for lunch on Sundays, but those meals were never happy occasions. Kieran could not be left alone with Cate, and we watched him like a hawk. Still refusing to accept that things had changed for ever, Kieran would have lunch with us and then disappear 'off out' to his mates' houses, and he was gone for the rest of the day. We still had to go to look for him when it was time for him to leave, just as we had had to do for the whole of the previous summer. Things were no easier when he did stay in the house. On a number of occasions, we found him rolling around the floor of his bedroom with younger friends he had invited in. They were wrestling. Kieran had always enjoyed the wrestling on TV and had always tried to imitate what he saw. We did not like this, but had convinced ourselves that it was basically harmless. Since our discovery of his abuse of Cate, we began to see the wrestling in a much more sinister light. It now seemed to have sexual overtones, perhaps because we had failed to see real sexual abuse and were now seeing potential abuse everywhere. The only way forward was to space out Kieran's visits and to see him much less often. We scaled it down to once a fortnight. Slowly, reluctantly and very fearfully, we began to let Kieran go. We could not hold him any longer.

Although we were now receiving professional help, we were on our own in most respects. It had been a long time since we had had a real social life, and now we had none at all. We scarcely went out. Marina obviously saw her work colleagues every day, but I saw nobody. There was no one we could talk to, as we had not told any of our friends about what had happened. And we had certainly not told our families. We lived alone with our terrible knowledge of what happens when sexual abuse occurs inside a family, and with our fear that our family was going to fall apart. We were not a family teetering on the edge of incompetence; we were a family teetering on the brink of disintegration, but it was all we had, and we clung to each other fiercely. We did not always like ourselves or each other but there was no one else.

We could not have done it without help. Andrea, who had originally been assigned to our case, had now moved on to a new job. Daniel, who was her replacement, worked on a part-time basis and was also acting as Kieran's social worker. His main function was to liaise between him and us, but he had very little experience of working with adopted children or adoptive families, and still less of dealing with the aftermath of adoptions that had ended as catastrophically as our adoption of Kieran.

Tall, slim and elegant, Sandra sat on the sofa in our battered-looking lounge and listened in almost complete silence for at least an hour as we went through the whole sorry saga. And then she simply said: 'Poor Marina. Poor John.' We could have kissed her. Sandra works for the Post-Adoption Support Unit of the Department of Social Services. At this time, Sandra was half of the entire Post-Adoption Support Unit, and she worked part-time. The unit had been in existence for little more than a year. After the incident in which Kieran kicked the young lad in the street, we had tried to find help by ringing Social Services to ask about post-adoption services. The response was discouraging: 'Post? Oh, you mean "after". No, there's nothing like that.' The only post-adoption service on offer was a letter-box contact system that allowed adopted children to remain in touch with, or trace, their birth parents. The general assumption was that adoption was the solution to a problem, and not the source of a whole new set of problems. It was the happy ending that would make everything better. All this has changed in the last few years, and local authorities now have a duty to provide post-adoption support.

It was Sandra who arranged the initial meeting with Vanessa and Catherine. Vanessa is an adult psychotherapist, and Catherine an art therapist; both come from a social work background, but they have worked on adoption issues for a long time now. Both women are very experienced and highly skilled, and I know that, without their help and support, this family would no longer be together. I don't know just where we would all be, but I am certain that we would be in five different places. Although Vanessa and Catherine work together a lot and joke that they are interchangeable, they are very different. Vanessa is the younger of the two. Although Vanessa is very warm and at times very funny, she is also the more brusque of the two, and an hour with her can be a bruising experience. During one of our first sessions, we told her about the senior social worker who, a few weeks into our placement, had told us that Viv had given us a great 'gift'. Vanessa snorted: 'Some gift! Three mad children!' That hurt and stung. Catherine is quieter but just as intense. We subsequently met a mother who had seen them both for a long time, and who had finally given up on Vanessa because 'she was so abrasive'. She went on seeing Catherine, and commented: 'She's nice and easy, and we just chat.' Catherine may seem gentler and more relaxed than Vanessa, but she does not just chat; she listens with enormous concentration and misses nothing. I once came across her speaking to a very young child in the waiting room, big dark eyes concentrating hard on the child's face and reading its every detail. She was not even aware that I was in the room, and she was effectively quite alone with that child.

I remember little of our first meetings. That is not surprising; at this point, I was seeing my GP on a weekly basis and, in retrospect, my memories of consultations with her blur into memories of those we were having with Vanessa and Catherine. Initially Vanessa and Catherine saw us together, once a week for one hour; four years later, we are still seeing Vanessa, but only once a month. Most of the early sessions were devoted to describing what had happened and what state we were in. And we were in a terrible state: traumatised, battered, afraid, ashamed, angry and hurt. We did not know which way was up and which way was down. We had learned that we could not trust the social work system, and we were not sure that there was anyone we could trust. The first task facing Vanessa and Catherine was to get us to trust them, and they did. That is not the same thing as being kind to us or being gentle with us. As we struggled so hard to find the words to describe what we were going through, one of us remarked that what we had to do now was to protect and care for our two children, and to do what we could to look after Kieran's interests. That brought out Vanessa's more abrasive side. She quickly told us in terms that were none too gentle that that was not our first priority; our job was to look after ourselves and each other, because if we could not do that we would be in no position to look after anyone. Vanessa knows her way around the system and is very well informed about what help is available, but she does not work with children; she is there for their parents. That is how she sees her job: she is there to help people in our position survive a hellish experience. She was there to keep us out of the psychiatric hospital, and she has done it.

With Vanessa and Catherine, and then with Vanessa alone, we embarked on a long and often painful exploration of our experience. We have described – so, so many times – all we have been through ever since we took the decision to look into adoption. We've gone back to the beginning and asked ourselves again why we decided to adopt, discussed what we thought it would be like and compared our dreams with the reality we've had to live with. We've remembered things, reconstructed them and taken them apart again. We've gradually begun to understand things, and to understand ourselves. We've said things we thought we could never say. We have expressed terrible feelings about all our children, and felt the dreadful liberation that comes from being able to say: 'I hate Kieran because of what he did to Cate.'

After four years of working with Vanessa we are still hard at it. It is not easy to describe precisely what her role is, or just what we are doing with her. The sessions are obviously therapeutic, but we are not really 'in therapy' with Vanessa, as a lot of the advice she gives us has been very direct and concrete, and because she often strays away from the clinical neutrality one would expect of a personal therapist, and is much more open about herself than she would be in a more clinical setting. Vanessa has criticised us, and the way we have handled things, in ways a therapist would not. No personal therapist would turn to me and say in so many words, 'John, stop looking at me like that with those big blue eyes of yours, I'm not going to rescue you.' Vanessa has allowed, or enabled, Marina and I to have arguments and near-rows in her presence. Sometimes she is a referee-cum-interpreter; sometimes it feels as though she is joining in the argument. We get angry with her, and I've told her I'm angry with her. She helped us to see where things began to go wrong, and why they did so. It can be hard for us to confront our own feelings when they are so confused. It has been hard to admit to and voice our deep fears for the future and to speak of the fears that still haunt us from the past. We could not have done it unaided.

VI

A few weeks after Kieran had been taken into care and shortly before we first met Vanessa and Catherine, I did something I should have done much earlier and went to see our family doctor. I did not find this easy, as it meant admitting to myself that I was losing control of my own life. I was smoking and drinking far too much, and felt that I had no patience with the children. My moods could change suddenly and violently, and I had lost the ability to concentrate on anything. I felt tired all the time and kept falling asleep; I had lost interest in sex and was finding it very difficult to show Marina any affection at all. I wasn't enjoying anything and I did not like myself. Nothing seemed to have any substance and tomorrow did not exist. It took Dr G minutes to make the obvious diagnosis: I was depressed. I suppose I already knew that, but having a name for what I was feeling was in itself a help. It is not only dragons in the night that have to be named before they can be tamed. Dr G then asked me how my home life was, and I tried to explain just how bad things were, and why everything had gone so wrong. This was the first time that I had been able to tell anyone but a social worker what had happened. The only response was a hissed 'Oh my God.'

My first consultation with Dr G lasted for the standard five minutes. 'Make an appointment to see me next week, and ask for a double session,' she told me as I left. Ten minutes is a very long time for a doctor to devote to one patient and I was almost pitifully grateful. For the next couple of months or so, my visits to Dr G were weekly events. I had been diagnosed as suffering from clinical depression, which may well have been the result of a long-term predisposition, but I was also living in a situation of extreme tension and needed specialist help. There are various ways of dealing with depression. Antidepressants are prescribed on a huge scale but, as Dr G explained to me from the very outset, they do not provide an automatic cure for depression. They are not the 'happy pills' of myth; there are no 'happy pills', or at least not on the legitimate pharmaceutical market. The alternative is some form of psychotherapy, or one of the many 'talking cures'. Dr G set about trying to find specialist help and referred my case to various agencies. In the meantime, she again told me that antidepressants might help. I was reluctant to take them, and explained that I was afraid that I might become dependent upon them. She told me that I was confusing antidepressants with the old tranquillisers, some of which are highly addictive, and that the new drugs were not addictive and posed no danger. I was still reluctant, and it was only after considerable persuasion from Vanessa and Catherine that I finally asked for the prescription. Vanessa's argument was brutally pragmatic: 'If you have a headache, you take aspirin, don't you? You're depressed, so why not try antidepressants? Most, if not all, of the adoptive parents I know are on them.' I was prescribed Cipromil.

I went off with my prescription to the nearest chemist. The assistant took it and came back a moment later. 'I'm sorry. We're out of stock for the moment. Can you come back tomorrow?' I went on to the local branch of Boots, and met with the same response there. It was a perfectly ordinary morning in an ordinary suburb, and two pharmacies could not fill a prescription for antidepressants. It was almost laughable: 'Drugs famine hits eastern suburb of city.' My tale of woe amused Dr G but it did not surprise her. It is estimated that one in five adults will suffer from depression at some point. I had become one of the twenty-six million consumers of antidepressants in Britain, and demand had outstripped supply. I do not really understand the science involved here, but I do know that, whilst the Cipromil did not take away or cure my depression, it did make it easier to live with it, especially when the dose increased from 10mg to 20 and then 40mg a day. I began to feel slightly disconnected or removed from things and could therefore handle them better. My moods became less volatile, I was able to be more patient, and I lost my temper less frequently. I was able to work better. Cipromil can apparently have a fearsome number of adverse side-effects. I suffered none of them, but the manufacturers' product data sheets did not list the one side-effect I did suffer: every time I swallowed one of the little white pills, it reminded me that I was still depressed.

I was perpetually exhausted and there were long days when I could not do anything. I was living in a cold dark place, and I found it hard to emerge from it. There were mornings when I got up, drank my breakfast coffee, got the children into school, said goodbye to Marina when she left for work, did half the crossword and then went back to sleep for a couple of hours, woke up, tried to finish the crossword, and went back to sleep again. There were days when I did little more than sit and feel sorry for myself. I found it harder and harder to look after myself, and often couldn't be bothered to wash or comb my hair properly; what I wore or what I looked like didn't matter because I wasn't going anywhere. At times, I almost deliberately retreated into my dark place because I felt safe there; no one could touch me there, and I didn't want to be touched. At the same time, I desperately wanted the love of Marina and the children but could scarcely talk to them. People suffering from depression turn in on themselves, become very selfish and put themselves beyond help. I don't think I ever touched rock bottom – wherever that may be – but I did go a long way down. At times, I would think to myself that things could be worse, which was probably true, but that was also a way of saying, 'This will get worse.' Yet even before the drug kicked in, I managed to keep going in some ways. The children never missed school because I was too down to take them, and I was always able to cook an evening meal for the four of us. I certainly neglected Marina and the children but I went on trying to look after them.

My depression was in part a reaction to the dreadful situation in which I was living, but there was a sense in which it had ceased to be about anything and had become a way of being and living. People suffering from depression often speak, as I do, of being in a cold place, of coming too close to the edge or of falling into a pit or void. These are not metaphors or symbols. I was in that place. People do get too close to the edge, and they do fall. Like everyone else, I have often said 'I'm depressed' when all I really meant was 'I'm sad today' or 'I'm feeling a bit low.' This was different. In retrospect, I can see that the discovery of Kieran's abuse of Cate was a severe trauma, an encounter with something that I perceived as a serious threat. Marina had suffered the same trauma and was living with the same stress, but her reaction was much less extreme. She too was diagnosed as suffering from depression and did take antidepressants for a while, though she is still not convinced that she really needed them. Perhaps she is simply more resilient than me. I think that having to go to work must have helped too. Marina had to interact with other people and respond to them. I didn't. Working alone and at home, I had no outlet. I was alone with what I was living through. And yes, there probably was a degree of self-indulgence about all this. At times, I think I did enjoy letting go and giving in. I think I did enjoy my depression. With hindsight, I think that there were two sides to it: an underlying tendency towards depression, and a depressive reaction triggered by the trauma of having lived for so long with such damaged children and then discovering Kieran's abuse of Cate.

Dr G did at last find a possible source of specialist help and referred me to a community mental health counsellor. I had eight sessions of psychotherapy with her and I did benefit from it, but it was not really enough. Perhaps she was not the right counsellor, or perhaps I was not the right patient. Perhaps the setting – a borrowed consulting room in a doctor's surgery – was wrong. I don't know, but what did become clear was that I would do well to find a more intensive form of therapy. I had already been thinking along those lines, and Vanessa had also suggested that it might be a good idea. Marina and I were making progress with her but we were doing so as a couple, and there were times when I felt that I was being marginalised, or even excluded, by Marina and Vanessa. They were highly articulate women who got on well and had a lot in common, and there were times when I could not get a word in edgeways. It felt as though I had no voice, or none that could be heard. I was a parent, and was having difficulty in being a parent. I was also an individual, and I was having difficulty in being an individual. I was finding it hard to be me. So this time, the therapy had to be for me.

A few minutes before eleven one Thursday morning, I sat nervously in the waiting room of a charitable trust that offered psychotherapy and counselling. A young woman came into the room, smiled, asked me to confirm my name and invited me to follow her up a flight of stairs and down a corridor. She then let me into a quiet room and shut the door behind her. I had just met Jan. I went on seeing her for nineteen months. All Jan knew when we first met was the information contained in the report prepared by the therapist who had carried out my assessment interview a few weeks earlier. I now went through the whole story again. There was little or no reaction from Jan, but she did admit to knowing next to nothing about adoption. She knows a lot more now.

The room was small, quite bare and decorated in neutral colours. There were two armchairs facing one another and little else; this was not psychoanalysis, and I was not going to have to lie on a couch and talk about my dreams to an analyst I could not see. We sat facing each other over a small table with a little vase of flowers on it, together with an open box of tissues and a travel clock so placed that I could not see its face. There was a picture on the wall but I never looked at it, even though I always look at pictures on walls. This was our clinical space and I immediately felt very safe and knew that anything could be contained inside this space and by this woman. There was no time inside that room, or perhaps it would be truer to say that time became elastic. It could pass very slowly, and it could pass very quickly. Fifty minutes could be over in a flash, but fifty minutes could also last for ever. I knew that nothing could intrude, and that no phone and no doorbell would ring. We were alone and we had all the time in the world. I do not know who 'matched' us or why they did so, but I immediately sensed that I'd found the therapist I needed: she just felt right.

The ground rules were simple and easily explained. Within certain limits, I could decide what fee I should be paying, and it could always be renegotiated. For the 'analyst's hour' of fifty minutes, Jan and this room were mine; neither the room, the eleven-o'clock slot, nor Jan could be reassigned to anyone else. If she went away on holiday or was ill, I did not pay; if I missed a session, I paid for it, and if I turned up late, I paid for the full session. Unless Jan thought I represented a danger to myself or others, everything I said in that room would remain completely confidential: nothing was off limits and I could say anything. It took a while for this to sink in. Being able to say anything meant having to say something, unless of course I opted to say nothing at all. There would be very little prompting from Jan, and very few direct interpretations of what I said (her memorable 'What I think you're trying to say, John, is that you feel like crap' was very much the exception to the rule). I once made the mistake of asking Jan what state she thought I was in. She deliberately avoided the question and then, half way through our next session, told me I had answered it myself. She did not need to say anything else.

Jan was brilliant. She listened well and was very good at maintaining eye contact. She was also good at making me look at her and at following and imitating my body language. And above all, she had a great ability to remain neutral. 'Neutrality' does not mean indifference. The gentle questions – 'How does that make you feel?', 'What do you think this means?' – were accompanied by a slight but delightful smile and it was impossible not to respond. Jan was always sympathetic but if I began to cry, I had to reach for the box of tissues because she never passed it to me. This was a way of telling me that I could cry and did not have to wipe the tears away, but it was also a way of saying that no one else would wipe them away, that I had to do it myself. There were times when Jan abandoned, or perhaps pretended to abandon, her stance of clinical neutrality. There were flickers of annoyance when I seemed to her to be talking about the children rather than myself. It finally became apparent that there was a reason for this, and we worked out that there were times when I didn't know where their problems ended and where mine began. Sometimes, I didn't know where the children ended and where I began.

Of course I fell in love with her. Not immediately, but I did. She was a beautiful woman, slightly shorter than me and considerably younger, with dyed blonde hair, enormous blue eyes and an almost perfectly heart-shaped face. I've often found Vanessa rather more attractive than I should, but this was a very different experience, and I began to have sexual fantasies about Jan. No doubt she was well aware of what was going on and of what I was feeling; that was part of her job. I did fall in love with Jan, but I also wanted her to remain remote. If, as she leaned forward, her top revealed just too much of her cleavage, I felt uncomfortable and had to look away. I was very glad that Jan always wore trousers or jeans. I saw her outside the context in which we met on only two occasions. As I stood finishing a cigarette on the other side of the street one Thursday, I watched her enter the building with a colleague but I scarcely recognised her at first because she looked so ordinary: Jan was just a young woman in a denim jacket. Only days before our last session, I thought I glimpsed Jan in the local shopping centre. I was sure it was her, but she had two young children with her and that surprised me, even though I knew by then that she had children. The moment was over before I could even think of speaking to her.

Jan later confirmed that I could well have seen her in that place and at that time, but gave no hint that she might have seen me. That was probably just as well; actually acknowledging one another and speaking could, I suspect, have been very embarrassing. Both these occasions were disappointing and disillusioning because I did not want Jan to be just a pretty young woman in a nice denim jacket, and because I did not want her to be a mother and a wife. Just before one of the rare interruptions to my regular sessions, I remarked to Marina that I wouldn't be seeing Jan for two weeks as she was going to Cyprus for her holidays and added

'Sounds nice' or something to that effect. 'Yes, I know you'd like to go with her.' I had been talking a lot about Jan, and I had been doing so in very affectionate terms, and Marina's barbed comment hurt. Of course it would have been wonderful to go to Cyprus with Jan, but not with the Jan in the denim jacket who went shopping with her children and who went on holiday with them and her husband. I wanted to go with the Jan who never went anywhere and whom I met only in that room.

I can compare my experience of working with Jan to only one thing. A few years earlier, I had been diagnosed as having cataracts on both eyes. The removal of cataracts is a simple procedure carried out under local anaesthetic at a day clinic: an incision is made at the top of the eye, and the lens is removed and replaced with an artificial one in an operation that takes under half an hour. For surgeons who perform the operation seven or eight times in the course of a morning's clinic, all this is routine. For the patient, for whom the operation is at most a twice in a lifetime experience, it is terrifying. Anaesthetic drops were placed in the corner of my eye at regular intervals. Before long, I could feel almost nothing, and then nothing at all. After what felt like a very long time, I was wheeled away to have the final anaesthetic on my way into theatre. This time, the anaesthetic was administered by injection and I lay there flat on my back, looking up at the anaesthetist, thinking, 'This nice woman is going to put a needle into my eye.' And then she did. I felt only a pinprick. The main thing I remember about the operation is that glorious colours flooded through my eye as the lens was removed. At some point in the course of that morning, I had ceased to be afraid of what was going to happen. The atmosphere in the small ward was such that it was impossible to be afraid. The drops were administered by two staff nurses, and I would happily have followed the pair of them into a blazing building, absolutely confident that they would save me from all harm.

They were taking care of me by holding me. And for nineteen months, that is what Jan did. The experience of being held like

174

this, and of being able to have total trust in someone who is in so many ways a stranger, is profoundly moving, and that is because, somewhere, it awakens a memory: we have already been held. The vast majority of us were held when we were babies, and being held as an adult is a deeply regressive experience.

A mother who holds her baby supports it without dominating it. Holding protects the child from psychological harm, takes account of its physical sensitivity, provides care and facilitates the minute day-to-day changes inherent in the child's growth and development. It is only when the child is being held that spontaneous communication can take place. In a clinical context, it is the holding environment that makes it possible to go back to fundamental and dangerous issues without being hurt by them. That is what Vanessa was doing for the two of us. That is what Jan was doing for me: she could allow me to look at painful things because she could absorb the pain and the fear. She obviously did not do this alone, and she too was being held by her supervisor or analyst. I somehow knew that, but the safe holding environment neutralised that knowledge. We were alone and I was safe, and that was all that mattered. As adults, we do not normally need to be held in this way. We can cope for most of the time but when we are weak, hurt or scared, we may need to be held. We hold our babies and children, our wives, husbands and lovers, and in time of need we hold our friends. Although we would not have actually used the word at the time, Marina and I spontaneously held Kieran when he became so distraught after sharing secrets with his friend Lisa.

'Holding' can also mean something very different. It is possible to 'hold' a child who is having a tantrum. The parent pins the child's arms and immobilises her; the child screams and struggles but is prevented from moving. This is a containment strategy: the fear and anger are contained, just as the child is held and immobilised. The strategy has to be implemented with great determination, and there can be no letting go. Eventually, the child will go limp and then fall into a deep sleep but it may be necessary to hold her for hours before that happens. Vanessa explained the technique and then demonstrated it, and I was promptly immobilised by a woman who joked that she was the city's first street-fighting psychotherapist. This might, she suggested, be one way of dealing with Paul's increasingly frequent outbursts of violence and anger.

We tried. Marina pinned his arms while I immobilised his legs and, before we knew it, we were all in a heap on the floor. Paul was not very big at this stage – he was just over eleven – but he was strong and what wasn't bone in his body was hard muscle. He fought hard. We tried to hold on. Again and again, I had to grab a leg before he could wriggle free. I began to get frightened: this was degenerating into a fight and I was afraid that someone was going to get hurt. Marina was doing much better with Paul's arms than I was doing with his legs. She just held on, and she held tight. I think I managed to keep this up for an hour, perhaps an hour and a half at most, but at one point I couldn't go on and gave up. Marina held on and did eventually succeed in calming Paul. I'd had to give up; I couldn't hold him in that way and I felt defeated. Perhaps mothers are better at holding than fathers.

After nine months or so, I decided to come off the antidepressants. I genuinely felt better and thought I was growing stronger. After talking to Dr G, I gradually reduced the dose and then stopped taking the Cipromil altogether. It was a disaster. Within a couple of days, all the old problems were back: I was irritable, experiencing violent mood swings and feeling both powerless and hopeless. I had no patience with Paul and Cate, and I actually burst into tears when a favourite character left a soap opera I enjoyed watching. I felt quite defeated, and more depressed than ever by my inability to get by without the antidepressants. I was soon back on 40mg a day. It was only after months of work with Jan that I felt strong enough to try again. Once more, I gradually reduced the dosage and then stopped taking the white pills. Nothing happened and I had no adverse reactions: I'd done it. I wouldn't have been able to do it without Jan. In one of her rare direct comments, she told me that I'd taken an important step forward.

And, perhaps without either of us realising it at the time, it was the prelude to an even more important step. A holiday was coming up soon and there would be a natural break in the therapy. Did I think it might be time to think about bringing things to an end? Jan had asked me this before, and I had always said no, but something had changed this time. I knew what she was going to say as she began to speak, and had been on the point of saying precisely the same thing. Some say that there is always an element of telepathy in psychotherapy. I don't know about that, but there is certainly a lot of unconscious communication involved, and there are moments when the two people involved are thinking as one. We had both sensed that the therapy was drawing to a natural end.

Ending a course of psychotherapeutic treatment is a delicate matter. My sessions with Jan could not be just broken off or brought to a sudden end, and we had to work towards an ending and set a date for our last session. Once established, that date could not be changed because Jan had a long waiting list, and it would not be possible to squeeze in an extra session. Most of the remaining sessions went on as before: I talked about my present situation and we tried to find in my responses to it patterns that had been established long, long ago. At this point, we were working very, very well together. We laughed a lot. Some Thursdays, the end of the hour felt like a brutal interruption: we could have gone on. And for the first time, I broke the pattern by missing a session. I suddenly had to go to Paris on business and was genuinely convinced that I could not fit in what I had to do and see Jan in the same week. I missed what would have been the 'last but third' session.

As it turned out, what I had to do in Paris took no time at all, so I spent most of the week on holiday. At eleven on that Thursday morning in Paris, I was well aware of where I would otherwise have been at that time and I thought of Jan, but not for long. We'd been right; it was time to bring it to an end. The last session was tricky but strangely serene. For the first time, I was able to tell Jan to her face how fond I had become of her, how much I would miss, not just our sessions together, but her. I wasn't telling her anything she didn't know, and I knew it. But I had to say it, and perhaps that was the moment when it ended. I still don't know if it was the right thing to do, but I took her a present, and she seemed genuinely pleased. And then we said goodbye. We didn't even shake hands and it was only when I got out into the street that I burst into tears.

Antidepressants do not cure depression and I am not convinced that nineteen months of psychotherapy can cure it either. I am not sure that anything cures depression. The cold dark place is still there and I do crawl back into it from time to time. Those days return, but then they go away again. There are still times when I can't do anything. Living with our children can still reduce me to the deepest despair. That has not changed; what has changed is the way I deal with it, and the way I understand it. With Jan, I went back a long way into a past – some of it real, some of it fantasy – that I cannot change. But I think I can understand it, or at least a lot of it.

When I first went to the counselling service, I was asked to fill in a diagnostic questionnaire that included a question about 'suicidal feelings'. A few weeks after my last session with Jan I was asked to fill in a very similar questionnaire about how I felt now. If they were collated, the two would give some indication of what changes there have been in my mental life. I hesitated over how to answer the first 'suicide' question and finally settled for 'occasional suicidal feelings'. That was about as honest as I could be. I've never deliberately self-harmed, cut, overdosed or planned to kill myself. At this point, Vanessa would rightly pick up my use – and over-use – of alcohol. She calls it 'self-medication' and tells me that men in particular often use it in a misguided attempt to deal with depression. If the self-administration of an anaesthetic is 'medication', she is no doubt correct, but the so-called self-medication has never been suicidal in its intent. I was never really afraid that I would kill myself; I was afraid that I would leave home.

In the build-up to that worst of summers when we discovered that Kieran had been abusing Cate, the arguments Marina and I were having became more and more savage, and eventually ceased to be 'about' anything other than hurting each other. And we were bloody good at it. Again and again, I complained that she was 'never at home'; Marina works long hours and often does not get home before early evening. I was increasingly pissed off with having three children around from three o'clock onwards, and I blamed Marina for my own failure to control my frustration: it was all her fault because she was always at work. I told her that the first psychiatrist we had taken Kieran to see had been right: she'd wanted it all, was finding out that she couldn't cope with it all, and expected me to cope with it all instead. And then I reached the point where I told her I just could not go on living with Kieran. She would have to choose: him or me. She made the obvious choice. I said I would move out and find a little flat. There is a lot of rental accommodation in this city and it wouldn't have been impossible to find something. I screamed at Marina: 'No. I don't want to sell the fucking house and take half the fucking proceeds. I don't fucking want anything from you. I don't fucking want anything.' And I didn't.

All I wanted to do was to go, but I soon realised that rented accommodation was more expensive than I had thought, and that I probably couldn't afford it. The financial imbalance of our relationship – Marina makes much more money than I do – now became part of the increasingly vicious argument. 'Are you just staying because you couldn't afford to leave?' 'Yes.' It must have been then that I began to lose my grip. I didn't want to live in some flat or bedsit; I just wanted to walk away. I nearly became one of the 30,000 persons who are reported missing to the Salvation Army every year.

I just wanted to go, walk away and go on walking until I could feel nothing. I thought and dreamed of heading north on foot, of leaving the city, walking into the hills and not coming back. Disappearing into the high hills of Scotland or somewhere began to look like an attractive prospect. I could do it. I'm not claiming that I could cross Rannoch Moor alone on a dark, wet night, but I certainly know how to cross rough country in reasonable weather. I've done it often enough in the past, and I would become fitter as I went. My boots were not new, but they were comfortable and still had several hundred miles in them. They would take me far enough. And then I changed my mind about where to go. No, not north and not into the cold. South, across France into Spain and perhaps even Morocco. I would travel on foot and alone, and there would be no coming back. I looked at equipment catalogues and made a list: bivouac tent, new sleeping bag . . . It wasn't a very long list. It must have been when I started to look at the catalogues that I came to my senses. This would have been a walk to self-destruction, and would have taken me on the scenic route to suicide by some other name. I would have found a lonely death somewhere in the mountains. After a lot of thought and a lot of work with Vanessa and especially Jan, I realised that I had never really wanted to kill myself. There was a suicidal dimension to all this, but that was not the important thing; there was something more, something deeper. I didn't know it at the time, but I had touched upon my deepest fear of all. It took a lot of time to find out just what it was.

Suicide may well result from despair, but it is an incredibly aggressive act. The aggression is directed at the survivors and it tells them: 'You've driven me to this, and you will regret it for the rest of your lives. If I kill myself, it will always be your fault.' I felt that aggression, and I expressed it. I was aggressively cruel towards Marina, telling her that she wanted it all, and could have it all, but not with me. I told her she'd have to get used to the idea of being a single parent and trying to keep her precious job. A pathetically tearful Marina asked what would happen if I met someone else. I told her that there was no one else: no other woman, and no man either. I didn't want anyone else; I just didn't want what we had. The flip side of this was my belief that I was the problem. And if I was the problem, I should go. 'You'd be better off without me.' The arguments went on and on. They got worse and my threat still hung in the air. And then late one evening something happened. We were both exhausted, had had a lot to drink (I had, at least), and were intent upon hurting each other. And I suddenly screamed at Marina: 'I'm not the fucking problem! Kieran is the fucking problem!'

I was right, and this was an important insight but it would take us a long time to realise that. At the time, it felt like an admission of defeat and I hated myself for saying it. We have now met a number of adoptive families and we have read about many more. When things begin to get this difficult, most, if not all of them, reach the 'him/her or me' moment. And in some cases, someone does take the irrevocable step. Someone does leave, and it is usually the father. When this happens, the damaged child wins, and splits its parents, but the parent who walks is colluding with the child. I don't know of any agency that is bold enough to put it so baldly, but advice to prospective adopters should include the warning: 'What you are about to do may destroy your marriage or relationship.'

Adoption can stir up very primitive emotions, and primitive emotions are destructive in the extreme. One of them is jealousy. A very young Paul sat on Marina's lap at breakfast; her dressing gown had fallen open and he stared at her exposed breasts: 'Me like them, Mum.' We laughed and it was funny. The trouble was that I liked Marina's breasts too. Fathers are jealous when their partners become mothers rather than lovers, and when the baby becomes the primary figure. Adoptive fathers are not, in most cases, jealous of babies. They are jealous of children who are much older, but who are still living with the emotions of very young children. Adoptive parents do not have to deal only with the classic Oedipal problems; they deal with Oedipal problems that come in distorted forms and often at inappropriate ages. We often complain (and sometimes joke) that our problem is that we are living with three-year-olds in teenaged bodies. In some public space, Paul watched a brother and sister beginning to fight. They pinched and insulted each other. They threw things at each other and began to chase each other. One caught the other and a real fight began. Had their parents not finally intervened, real damage could well have been done. Paul looked at Cate: 'They're as bad as we are.' He was quite right, but he was ten and those children were less than half his age.

I have often felt that I am being pushed out, that I am being excluded from my own family and that there is just no room for me. There has often been no room for me to sit on the sofa to watch television, and certainly no room for me to sit next to Marina. For a long time, Cate would quite literally force herself between us. As we walked down the street, Cate would push between me and Marina in an attempt to claim Marina for herself. If I walked ahead of her, she would tread on my heels. If I walked behind her, she would stop suddenly so that I bumped into her, and then scream at me that I had done it on purpose. Holding Marina's hand or putting my arm around her was impossible because Cate would try to prise us apart. She went on doing this until she was thirteen or fourteen. This was not just adolescent queasiness about displays of inter-parental affection, though she has often expressed that disgust in perfectly normal teenage terms. When that happens, we can just laugh and tell her that is what parents are there for: to embarrass their children. Cate never gets the joke. For a long time, she behaved as a very young child or even a baby would behave; she literally wanted to come between Marina and myself and wanted Marina for herself. She wanted in a desperate, primitive way that tolerates no argument, no reasoning and no compromise. She wanted in the way that Kieran wanted more food and more money because, long ago, there had never been enough. She wanted in the way that a baby wants, and she wanted what a baby wants: she wanted her mother because she was the one with the breasts. At other times, she did want me. I remember how we were about to cross a field in the course of a family walk when a very large dog came bounding towards us. It was a Pyrenean mountain dog and, if it had stood on its hind legs, it would have been taller than me. Cate cautiously moved behind me, and clung to my thigh. This was odd in two ways: she is not normally afraid of dogs, and she usually turns to Marina for protection. But this was a very large dog indeed. Cate was acting on the basis of what every little girl knows: daddy can protect me from all the big dogs in the world.

I didn't leave and I won't leave. I knew there was nothing else, and nowhere else. I cannot live without Marina and our children, and I do not want to. Even at the darkest moments, there has always been Cate's smile and Paul's laughter. They were there when we went through all the fumbling discussions about whether this was the right placement for Kieran and feared that the entire adoption would end in tragedy. They were there when I span elaborate fantasies about walking to Morocco or wherever else it was going to be.

I do go away though, and so does Marina. From time to time, we both have to travel for professional reasons but we also run away, usually to Paris. Sadly, we can't run away together and will probably have to wait for another couple of years before we can do so. I stay alone in quiet little hotels. It is lonely, but there are times when a lonely hotel room can be a very good place to be because there are no demands on me there. I also like having my breakfast made for me. I don't do very much when I'm in Paris. I go to exhibitions and to the cinema, walk for miles across my favourite city, and I sit in cafés by myself and eat alone. It feels very good for five or six days, and then the homesickness sets in and I can't wait to get back to Marina and our children. The first time I went away by myself, I suddenly realised that it really is possible to miss changing shitty nappies. When I'm away, I phone home every evening, but this is often a duty rather than a pleasure. Sitting in a room hundreds of miles away and listening to the children screaming at each other is not fun. They fight over who gets to talk to me first and scream at each other to shut up; sometimes I just hear them continuing the fight they were caught up in when the phone rang. When they settle, it does get better. Cate will inevitably ask me if I have eaten and, if I haven't, where I am going to eat and what I am going to eat, because that is her way of worrying about me and telling me to look after myself. Paul will tell me the football results, in great and grim detail, because that is what he is interested in.

As we learned long ago, there is a price to be paid for running away. Just a few weeks after the children were placed with us, Marina was invited to become part of a council-organised delegation to our twin town in France. She came back with lovely gifts: a wooden train for Cate, a spinning top for Paul and a fabulous Pinocchio puppet for Kieran. Cate played happily enough with the train, but Paul kicked his spinning top and then jumped on it; it was still pretty but it didn't spin any more. He was angry with Marina but he couldn't kick her, so he kicked her gift. And as he knew it would, that hurt her a great deal; she ended up in tears on the night she came home with presents for her children. Over the next days, Kieran very carefully drew a picture of his puppet. The result was a fine drawing. We made a great fuss of him, and framed his drawing. Later, we noticed something strangely disturbing about it; it was very neat and very accurate, but all the limbs were disconnected from the body, and the body from the head. Kieran had literally dismembered Pinocchio.

Years later, we still get punished for going away. There will be a night of violent fighting and obscene abuse, either on the evening before either of us goes away, or on the evening we come back. Cate, in particular, will scream that we can't go. On one occasion, she grabbed my suitcase, stuffed it with anything she could and then flung it out of the front door. When I went to get it, she locked me out. The next day, I had to leave by midmorning to catch my flight. Cate had refused to go to school and when the taxi came, I had to leave her alone in the house, knowing that she would be alone for at least four hours before Paul got home from school, and that the two of them would be alone together until Marina came come from work three hours after that. I've rarely had such a dreadful trip out to the airport because I knew Cate thought I had gone for good. If Marina or I stay with friends or colleagues when we are away, another factor comes into play. If I mention a woman, or if Marina mentions a man, Cate immediately assumes that we are having affairs. Explaining that the man or woman concerned is happily married and has grown-up children does nothing to shake her conviction. The reassurance, and the knowledge, that we do not have affairs and that we always come home cannot take away the fear. For Cate, every relationship is so fragile that it could be destroyed at any moment. And then there will be no forever family.

Being alone at home with the children for a week or so is not easy. Getting them out to school, feeding them and generally looking after them is hard work and it can be very tiring. Refereeing the fights over who gets to speak to Marina on the phone first is unpleasant. But having them to myself is also deeply satisfying. Sometimes, but by no means always, they are very relaxed when Marina is away from home. Whatever the ostensible reason for them, many of the fights are about who has Marina. When she is not there, they can't fight over her and they can relax a little. But we are all so glad when she comes home.

The children do not like us to go away, but they don't like going away either. Even sleepovers at a friend's home can be difficult, and Marina and I are regularly punished for letting them spend the night away or for allowing friends to stay, even though they beg for it to happen. Every year, the school organises a trip to an adventure-holiday centre in southern France for children in Year Ten and they do terrifying things like canoeing, white-water rafting and abseiling. Kieran coped with his trip quite well, but Paul found it very hard when his turn came. He certainly enjoyed himself and came home with tales of high adventure. He also came home very angry indeed, and took it out on both us and Cate. The angry Paul had not been on an exciting holiday; he had been sent away from home by parents who didn't want him. We've never had the opportunity to see how Cate might have reacted to one of these trips as she was not at school when the relevant letters and application forms were handed out, and therefore could not go. I don't think she would have wanted to.

As, slowly and with a lot of help, I began to emerge from the worst of my depression, the world did begin to change around me. It was a lot warmer and lighter, and my wife looked more beautiful than she had done for a long time. The children's laughter rang louder and their smiles were broader. I was beginning to be able to enjoy the things I like, or used to like, and to concentrate on the things that make me happy. Being unhappy and suffering depression are not the same thing. For much of the time, I had not been desperately unhappy, or even particularly sad. But depression eats away at happiness, and that had prevented me from seeing what made me happy. I stood on the patio that overlooks the garden at the back of the house one morning. We live almost at the top of a hill and the view from here is extensive; the sky is big and we can watch the weather fronts moving in from the west. It was a windy day, and the sky was a dull pewter colour. The sun was low. Suddenly, a crow appeared; it was probably one of the pair I see at the end of the street most mornings. The wind caught it from below and tossed it, the sun caught its belly and the underside of its wings and, for just one brief second, the jet black of a crow turned to a silver flash in the sky. I gasped with pleasure. A few weeks earlier, I would not have seen that beauty. Or if I had, it would not have affected me in the same way. It would have been a crow being tossed in the wind, and nothing more: just one more black crow. For a brief moment that day, it was much more than a crow. It was as though I had seen my own depression turning into its opposite – black become silver – and flying away.

It does not take a lot to make me happy. I like opera, exhibitions and serious music as well as the great blues-jazz-gospel-soul mother-lode, but many of the things I love and enjoy are very simple. That is why I watch the birds in the garden. The blue tits, robins, wrens, occasional long-tailed tits and odd goldcrests I see are neither rare nor exotic but they give me great delight, and so do the frogs in our little pond. Watching birds and animals like this is a very ordinary pleasure for anyone who is lucky enough to have a garden. And I hope so much that I will always have it and enjoy it because I pity anyone who cannot enjoy the sight of a robin or wren. We ought to be able to enjoy these things simply because they are wonderful. Years ago, I took the children to London Zoo on a bitterly cold day. I almost had to drag them away because they could not believe that an elephant was so big, or that a tiger was so powerful yet could move with such grace, and even Kieran kept asking me if the animals were 'really real'. Paul, who was still quite young – nine, perhaps ten – was desperate to see a lion. He'd heard about the king of the jungle at school and insisted he wanted to see him. The lion did not want to play along: it was cold and he wanted to stay inside. I thought Paul's day was going to end in disappointment but we went back to the lion enclosure to give it one last try. A lion stalked into the enclosure, stared at us, yawned and went back inside. It didn't matter. Paul had seen his king of the jungle, and he was wonderful. What Paul saw in his king of the jungle was what I saw when my black crow turned silver.

As the depression moved away, other pleasures became greater too. One of the great things about working mainly from home is that I can listen to a lot of music during the day. Not all of it is to the rest of the family's taste, but I can play it loud when I have the house to myself. And now it began to sound much richer and deeper. The blues sounded bluer, the soul was more soulful, and Miles Davis's muted trumpet was more ethereal than ever. I'd never stopped listening to music but I'd almost stopped hearing it properly. In what must have been one of my very last sessions with Jan, I tried to describe how I was feeling. I never found this easy but I did try to do it. I tried very hard and, hesitantly, I came up with the image I needed. It may well have been trite, but it was also very accurate. I suddenly thought of the film *Billy Elliot*, which we'd recently seen on television. It is very sentimental but has undeniable power: the boy from the pit village becomes the ballet dancer he has always wanted to be. In the last scene, he waits in the wings. (The actual footage is, I think, of the all-male version of *Swan Lake* performed at Covent Garden.) Billy stands in the wings in his feathered costume, concentrating, and with every muscle tensed. On cue, all the coiled power is unleashed and he leaps through the air and on to the stage. The excitement and the feeling of release are incredible. And, talking to Jan that Thursday morning, I just knew that I could leap too. I could fly through the air. I was back.

I do not pretend that I am in a state of perfect mental health, always assuming that such a state exists. There are bad moments and bad days. There are times when I find it almost impossible to deal with the children, times when I do not even like them and when I do not like myself either. Every now and then, the colours begin to fade again and things begin to lose their taste. Sometimes I can fight the return of my depression, but often I do not even try to. I know that it won't last and that it will pass, so there is no need to fight it. My depression is an old acquaintance now, and I'm no longer afraid of it.

Anyone in therapy is extremely vulnerable. Like anyone else in my position, I was vulnerable, open to suggestion and probably ready to be influenced by a woman in whom I had placed enormous trust. Strange memories and associations do emerge during therapy, and I did begin to remember things differently and in a different order. Things I had not thought about for years sometimes took on a new importance. I don't think I learned anything 'new' about myself or my life during the many hours I spent with Jan, but I did learn to tell my story differently, and to understand it differently. There were sessions when I was so overwhelmed by what was going on in my day-to-day life that I could not talk about anything else. Jan put up with an awful lot of complaints from me, but she could use some of them to nudge me into talking about my childhood and family circumstances. She could also ask some very searching questions that demanded painful answers. On the whole, I think that my childhood was happy and secure. There are many good memories, but there are bad ones too. I've always known that I was very badly affected by my father's accident and subsequent hospitalisation. I almost lost him and I've always known that. I've always known that I am still a little boy who is afraid that, one day, dad will not come home from work. I find it difficult to talk about that fear but I can do it. I also know that I am still the forty-year-old who found it hard to accept that his father has died. I console myself by reminding myself that parents never really die: they live on inside our heads.

What is harder to come to terms with is that there is also someone inside my head who has always been dead. My sister is fourteen years older than me, and we had a brother who was born and died seven years before I was born. Whether he lived for days or weeks is something that I have never known. Somehow, I have always known about our brother but I have absolutely no memory of actually being told about him. We knew about what had happened, but did not talk about it. At the heart of our safe little family, there was a silence about a death and the silence of death: we could not talk about a dead baby. Talking through all this with Jan and thinking about what I was now going through, I suddenly saw with terrible clarity that my mother must have been depressed for almost forty years and that she probably never completed the terrible work of mourning. For a woman of my mother's age and background, the word 'depression' would either have been non-existent or quite meaningless, and it would not have meant much to our family doctor either. At best, he might have been able to prescribe a tonic of his own devising. But the symptoms of depression were there, and I can recognise them now. My mother was kind and loving, but rarely showed anyone any physical affection, and often seemed to have little or no interest in the outside world. She was often ill, and took to her bed with what was said to be 'flu'.

I know relatively little about the circumstances of my own birth, but I do know that my mother spent time in a convalescent home quite a long way from where we lived. So did I; there is a photo of me in a pram and there is thick snow on the ground. I was born at the beginning of October and, even in a bad year, it does not snow heavily that early, so the pair of us must have been in that place for a long time, perhaps for months. In one of the cupboards in our little terraced house, there were some large tins that once contained powdered baby milk; we used them to store rice (it was pudding rice; long-grain and basmati lay far in my future). The powdered milk had been for me, and I suspect that I was not breast-fed, or that if I was, not for long. I suspect that it was not only a brother that was missing; part of my relationship with my mother was missing too. There was always something that had never been there, just as there was something that had never been there for the children. This was the point where my problems and difficulties merged into theirs.

I was a safe child in a supportive home, and with good parents. But I grew up with a deep fear of loss. I almost lost my father and feared that I would lose him. I grew up knowing that my mother had lost a baby, that my father had lost a son, that my sister had lost a brother, and that I too had lost a brother even before I was born. My wife lost her mother as a young girl and was, as she probably experienced it at the time, sent away from her home. Our children have suffered repeated losses. Kieran, Paul and Cate lost their mother, and then their foster-carers. There is a lot of loss in this family and we all have difficulty in coping with it. I grew up convinced that, outside the little circle of security, there was great danger. People died out there. People who went outside sometimes never came back. That is what Cate fears when we walk out of the door.

It is not just a fear. These children have been abandoned, and they know that it could happen again. We have all suffered loss, and we all fear the same thing. We are all afraid that the loss will be repeated. And because we all share the same fear, we communicate and pick up each other's emotions very easily. We are in almost constant communication, but it is the fear of loss and the threat of loss that we communicate to one another. I have always been afraid that someone would not come back, that I would be abandoned. I have always been afraid that the circle of security would not hold. And if, as I sometimes thought, I was the one who was going to break the circle, I had to leave and hope that it would hold without me. I would walk away and, somewhere along the way, I would die. No one comes back, do they?

I was afraid of being abandoned, and so I became afraid that I would abandon my family. I've never been afraid that Marina would leave me; there have been times when I have been afraid that I would leave her. That has always been the heart of my darkness.

VII

Kieran had now been in his remand-care placement for over six months, but he was still drifting dangerously out of control. There was a particularly disturbing incident when he somehow heard that a family living opposite us was having a party. Their older boy had been a good friend for a long time, and Kieran was determined to go to the party. He turned up, and found that he was not welcome at what proved to be a quiet family gathering and not the all-singing, all-dancing, all-drinking affair he had been expecting. After being politely asked to leave, Kieran turned up at our back door, possibly slightly drunk, possibly stoned and definitely in an ugly mood. When we refused to let him into the house, he hurled a dustbin lid through the garage window and then punched his fist through the glass, cutting himself badly. We were frightened of what he might do next and both Paul and Cate were becoming hysterical, so we locked the doors and called the police, who turned up very quickly; the local policy on domestic violence of any kind is one of zero tolerance, and calls reporting it are prioritised. Kieran tried to hide in the garden and then attempted to resist arrest, but within seconds he was on his back and being handcuffed.

One of the officers later explained that they do not – and dare not – take chances in circumstances like this because they might be in danger and don't see a young boy, but a potential assailant. No charges were brought, but Kieran spent the night in the cells.

Daniel, who was our current social worker, appeared to be unable or unwilling to do anything about Kieran's refusal or inability to comply with his supervision order, and left us to cope with his reappearances as best we could. They became so frequent that we tried to contact the police officers who had arrested Kieran after the party, but they were hard to reach and whenever we phoned the station, we were told that they were out, off shift or just not available. For reasons that were never really made clear to us, we were not allowed to get in touch with them directly, but they did finally respond to a message we left by calling at the house. It was eleven at night: they had just come on shift, but we were just going to bed. The discussion lasted for an hour and was perfectly pointless. They explained that they could do nothing to stop Kieran hanging around the end of the street; they could arrest him only if he was actually seen on the street itself. They also made it clear that breaches of a supervision order were a matter for the Youth Offending Team and not them.

Living with incidents like this, and anticipating more incidents of the same kind, was very tiring and stressful. We wanted to go on seeing Kieran on our terms and in controlled circumstances, but we felt that, as things stood, we were being harassed and that Kieran was controlling our lives from a distance. We began to dread going out in case we bumped into Kieran yet again. Living with Cate and Paul was difficult enough and we simply could not cope with Kieran's invasive presence too. Another problem was looming as Cate was now in her last year at Greenways school and was due to start high school in the autumn. This meant that she would be at the same school as Paul and Kieran. We had already raised the issue with a teacher who knew Kieran well and he had admitted that the school would not be able to guarantee Cate's safety if she was in the same building as Kieran. I don't suppose that he believed that he might have to deal with a full-scale sexual assault on school premises – he was just covering his back – but this did complicate the issue as we were not prepared to send Cate to a different school.

She was already very nervous about making the transition to

high school, and greatly reassured to know that a lot of the girls and boys she knew from Greenways would be going with her. The prospect of going to a strange school with very few children she knew would have terrified her. In any case, she had done nothing wrong and there was no reason why she should be the one who was inconvenienced. The only solution was to get Kieran into a different school and to leave him to face the consequences of his own actions. We knew that he would find this hard to take because, although he was not making much academic progress, he had a lot of friends in the school and losing them would be painful. We also knew that it would be very difficult for him to fit into a new school. Marina and I now experienced a major failure of nerve, and could not bring ourselves to tell Kieran what was going to happen. We went back to the teacher for help and advice. We thought he would be the best person to approach as we had come to know him quite well over the years and trusted him. He agreed to tell Kieran the bad news on our behalf. We knew that we had now given Kieran another reason to hate us.

It went on like this for months until we were desperate to get away. We began to look forward to our summer holiday, anticipating that it would, for all the usual reasons, be as tricky as our holidays had always been, but also telling ourselves that at least we would not have to worry about Kieran for three weeks. We had decided that, this year, we would go camping rather than rent a house and we had bought a big three-bedroomed tent with more than enough room for four. We'd not been camping since our first holiday abroad, and that had been over seven years ago. That year, we'd been on a site in Normandy where everything from tent to tin-opener was provided and where children's entertainment was laid on. We have two dominant memories of that holiday: Kieran flying into a temper and trying to run away from us with no clothes on ('Another nudist,' remarked a blasé campsite owner) and the look of malicious glee on the boys' faces as they described how they'd caught the children's courier who played the part of Captain Blood in a game of pirates and thrown him into the muddy lake. We were looking forward to being under canvas again, but this year it was going to be very different. We were going to a site on the Atlantic coast, just north of Bordeaux. Marina and I had good memories of the short time we had spent in the area years and years ago, and we knew that good weather was almost guaranteed and that fabulous food and wine were easily available. We would be using our own gear, which would mean roughing it to some extent; we would be able to cook only basic meals on the little gas stove, but we would be able to supplement them with stuff from the on-site take-away shop. We would also be able to feast on oysters, seafood and all the ready-cooked delights of French supermarkets.

We were right to assume that the journey across France would be as awful as always, but I have pleasant memories of the holiday itself, which probably just means that I've filtered out the worst bits. It was a good campsite, set amongst tall pines and with a small pool beside the bar; the weather held for most of our stay, and the tent easily survived the one major storm we did have. Its three separate sleeping compartments were wonderfully cosy, and Paul and Cate nested in them as though they were little birds. They did fight intermittently and at times viciously, but they also made friends, including a blind boy whom they gently led by the hand around the site. Neither Cate nor Paul had ever encountered a blind person before, but they were patient and kind with him, and stood perfectly still and smiled as he ran his hands over their faces so that he could 'see' them with his fingertips. There were other English families on the site, but not many, and most of the children Paul and Cate played with did not speak English – the blind boy, for instance, was Dutch. But with the mysterious ability that only they seem to possess, all the children contrived to communicate amongst themselves without a common language. Paul, Cate and their new friends found a toad and carried it very gently to one of the few damp places they could find.

Not all the local wildlife was as docile as the toad and Paul in particular had some scary encounters with hornets and other large things that flew and looked as though they might sting badly. Like Cate, he was just beginning to display a fear of insects that has now developed into something that verges on a true phobia, and he is terrified of spiders in particular. Even now, as he comes up to eighteen, the sight of a spider on the bathroom wall can make him quiver with fear and revert to the voice of a five-year-old: 'Me don't like spiders. Me don't like spiders. Get rid of the spider. It's watching with its big eyes. It wants to get me.' I am now an expert on the capture and safe release of large spiders.

A lot of the time, we did little and settled into a lazy routine. As always on holiday, we slept a lot and slept late, in part simply because we were living in the open air. We developed big appetites and ate hearty, if simple, meals. And we went to the beach. We all enjoy the water and all our children can swim well. France's Atlantic beaches are as dangerous as they are beautiful; the waves are enormous and one of the resorts nearest to our campsite regularly hosts international surfing competitions. This is not a place for paddling, with lifeguards watching from a look-out post on the top of the dunes and Land Rovers patrolling the beach. An area is cordoned off for swimming and anyone who strays beyond it is quickly called back, as dangerous rip tides can sweep the unwary out to sea. It was not really possible to swim but we could play in the waves. If we waded out until the sea was up to my thighs, great waves would break over our heads and the undertow would grab at our feet, making it hard to stay upright. Playing in the water like this meant holding the children's hands tight and clinging on when they were knocked off their feet. They loved it. If we wanted to swim properly, we had to go to the pine-fringed brackish lakes that lie on the landward side of the great coastal dunes. Here, the water was warm and shallow but the children did not like the feel of the muddy lake bed under their feet and much preferred the exhilaration of the sea. They did, on the other hand, enjoy looking for frogs on the edge of the water.

We were very glad to be away from Kieran, but we were also vaguely worried about what he might be getting up to. A few days into the holiday, Marina phoned to see how he was getting on. She was told by his carers that they had not seen him for five days; the police had been informed but no one knew where he was. We held our breath. A couple of days later, we rang again and learned that the police had found Kieran. The details were a little vague, but it was known that he and some of his friends had been living in our house for five or six days. We were told that there was no sign of forced entry, so we assumed that he must have taken one of the spare keys on his last visit. The police had, we were told, 'secured the house' (meaning that they'd made sure the front door was locked) and there were no signs that any serious damage had been done, but everything was in a terrible mess, with wine bottles, beer cans and cigarette ends everywhere. We assumed the worst and had visions of going home to a wrecked house in which some hard partying had been going on.

The remainder of the holiday was uncomfortable, as we were too anxious to relax completely and too worried about what we might find to have any positive feelings about going home. We did enjoy our holiday, but there was always that sense of foreboding in the background. The journey back was horrendous. Paul and Cate fought most of the way, hitting each other and trying to throw each other's things out of the car window. They had either overheard us talking, or had just sensed that something was wrong, and were as anxious as we were. They are extraordinarily sensitive to changes of mood and atmosphere, but their response to them is always the same – they become angry and they fight. The last stage of the journey home involved driving fast at night along an unlit motorway. Cate wound down her window, undid the childlock from the outside and then tried to open the door. She had already unfastened her seat belt. Marina drove on.

We got back late at night and let ourselves in, very apprehensive about what we might find. To our surprise, the house was not in a terrible mess and was in fact quite tidy, but there were also some ominous signs. Cate's teddy was sitting in front of the television and wearing one of Marina's bras. This was Big Ted, the magic bear we'd bought to protect her from all things nasty, but there'd been no one to protect him. Paul found his snooker cue in a corner of the room and immediately began to howl with rage when he saw that deep notches had been cut into it. It was in the morning that we worked out what had happened. There were dirty plates upstairs and used condoms in one of the bedrooms, but the house was basically tidy because all the bottles and cans had carefully been placed in a dustbin and because someone had swept up. When we found the hole in the Perspex roof over the back porch, it all made sense. Kieran had been taken away by the police and returned to his carers, but he had then come back to the house and, no longer having a key, had broken in. He'd cleaned the house, and had spent a couple of days alone here; there were the remains of meals for one in what had been his bedroom. The little money we had left in the house was gone, including the commemorative crowns we'd bought to keep for the children, and so was a lot of the wine that had been in the cellar. Two half bottles of spirits had vanished from the kitchen.

We got back on Saturday night. On Monday morning, Paul went to the bank. He wanted to buy a computer game, and knew that he had over a hundred pounds in his account. Unlike Kieran and Cate, Paul is good with money and always knows just how much he has in his account, but the bank told him he had only six pounds and he came home in floods of tears. I hurried down to the bank to find out what had happened. A quick check of the history of Paul's account showed that the money had been withdrawn from the ATM in two instalments of fifty pounds. Only one person could have done this. It would not have been difficult for Kieran to find Paul's bank card, but we still don't know how he knew the matching PIN. As we were able to prove that Paul had been out of the country when his account was cleaned out, the bank eventually reimbursed him.

We called the police to report the burglary. Two police officers came to the house but refused to take any action because there had been no forced entry and because a key had obviously been used. Although it seemed blindingly obvious to us that Kieran was responsible, they argued that there was no positive proof that he, as opposed to one of his mates, had been the first to enter the house. Nor was there any real proof that it had been Kieran – and Kieran alone – who had broken in through the back porch. There was no proof that Kieran had taken Paul's money because, unfortunately, there was no CCTV outside the bank. The police agreed that Kieran had been in breach of his supervision order by being here but said that that was a matter for the Youth Offending Team. They also agreed that he had breached his order in another sense: as he was on the sex offenders' register, they should have been notified of any absence from his designated place of residence. That too was a matter for the YOT.

The police did subsequently interview Paul about the theft of his money, but only because the bank's security procedures meant that they had to. Their reaction left us totally bewildered. Why wasn't this being taken much more seriously? What did this child have to do before it was acknowledged that he was a danger to both himself and others? Who was going to stop him careering out of all control? The answer to that one appeared to be 'no one'. Kieran was living with remand carers who never seemed to know where he was, and had been able to go missing for five days. He had then been able to disappear again. When he was first given a supervision order, a police officer had told Kieran that his picture was now on the computer carried in all patrol cars and that if he was ever seen near our house, he could immediately be identified and arrested. That was simply not true, and Kieran had realised that it was not true; he had worked out that he risked nothing more than an extension to a supervision order that he felt free to ignore anyway. After all these encounters with the police, he must have thought that he would have to do something really serious before he was finally arrested, and that he had a lot of room for manoeuvre. I began to realise why so many of the kids waiting outside the Youth Court looked so indifferent to what was going on: all they risked was another slap on the wrist.

We had reached the point of no return. We were hurt, angry and totally confused. Paul was bitterly upset about his cue, but it was the money that really hurt. For the first time, he began to hate the brother he loved so much: 'He took my money. He took my money.' He never wanted to see Kieran again, and said so very clearly. Even when the money was reimbursed, it still hurt. Cate did not say much, but the message conveyed by the bra draped around her teddy was full of veiled sexual menace. The fact that Kieran had gone through her underwear drawer made Marina feel sick. This time, we could not take any more. None of us wanted to see Kieran ever again, and we made it quite clear to him that he was no longer welcome in our home. Perhaps we did over-react, but we were reacting to the cumulative effects of multiple acts of aggression and provocation. This had been going on for a long time now; there was no indication that things would improve, and we were convinced that they could only get worse.

In our calmer moments, it did seem even to us that our reaction was extreme. We'd remained in contact with Kieran after the discovery of the abuse a year earlier, but now we were reacting as though damage to our property and theft were more serious than the abuse itself. I was furious about the disappearance of the wine, and angry with myself for being furious. After all, what did bottles of wine matter?

We had now been seeing Vanessa and Catherine for several months and could begin to understand things in a different way by talking them through in a sympathetic forum. We could see that, although Kieran's abuse of Cate could not be condoned and had to be treated as a criminal offence, it was pathologically moti-vated and, in that sense, beyond his conscious control. The break-in and the damage, which was largely symbolic, did not come into quite the same category. They felt like calculated and deliberate acts motivated by pure malice, and whilst there was a compulsive element in Kieran's return to the house, there was nothing impul-sive about it. Draping the bra on Big Ted had taken some thought and the notches on the snooker cue – which was, as Kieran well knew, a treasured possession – had not been cut in an idle moment. We felt that we had been targeted.

At this point, I for some reason had a session alone with Catherine, and I used it to try to explore why I was so upset about all this, and especially about the theft of a few bottles of wine, and to think about why I felt so ashamed about being upset. As with Kieran's theft of money, my anger and hurt had a lot to do with the betrayal of trust involved in the break-in, but I also realised why having wine in the cellar was important to me. For most of my life, including my adult life, this was something I had not been able to have, and I enjoyed having it. It was not so much the wine itself; it was the spoiling of the enjoyment that hurt so much. Very quietly, Catherine told me that she thought this was a perfectly understandable reaction. The relief was immense. I had been beginning to feel as though I had lost all sense of emotional direction and it helped so much to be told that my reactions were not as disproportionate as I had thought. The loss of the wine and my enjoyment of it were also obviously linked to something more devastating. Many people experience an attack on their home and property as an attack on them, and it is not uncommon for a burglary to be experienced as an assault, or even as rape. We felt we had had been assaulted by a son who had already sexually assaulted our daughter. Everything took us back to that.

It must have been at about this time that we had to get in touch with Juliet, the social worker who had been with us so long and who had actually been present at our adoption hearing. It was nothing more important than a query about whether the letter-box contact with Viv was going to go ahead. We thought it only fair to let Juliet know that Kieran was no longer with us and that the adoption had broken down irrevocably. We did not say why. Juliet wrote back to say that she was very sorry to hear the bad news, and added, 'It was probably always inevitable, given his early history.' Many adoptive parents are told the same thing. After years of difficulty, they are told that their best efforts had always been doomed to fail. And then they are left to live with the shame and the guilt.

Over the next eighteen months, we had little or no direct contact with Kieran because we did not want any. He was still living with the same foster-carers and they passed on news via our social worker Daniel, but it was never good and kept getting worse. Kieran was arrested on a couple of occasions for shoplifting and then for being drunk and disorderly. He began to miss more and more of his sessions with Bernard, was taken back to court and had his supervision order extended again and again. He was still refusing to accept any responsibility for what he had done. For a few weeks, he had to wear an electronic tag on his ankle and was placed under a curfew. He was picked up in a car that a friend had 'taken without owner's consent', which made him what the police call 'a TWOC-carry'.

We were frightened for Kieran now. Every time the local paper ran the headline 'Teenager killed in stolen car', we were almost too afraid to buy it but we always did so. The story was never about Kieran, but we were convinced that the next one would be. Kieran's truanting was now so bad that he was at school in name only. He was fifteen and had effectively dropped out of school. He was obviously going to obtain no qualifications and had few prospects. What little money he did earn from casual jobs went on take-aways and alcohol. He appeared to be drifting into a petty criminality that looked like a prelude to a much more serious crime. Other than that, unemployment seemed to be the only prospect. Kieran's failure to show up for YOT sessions and his general reluctance even to talk seriously to Daniel indicated that he was deliberately rejecting the little help that was on offer. To make matters worse, he was living on the edge of one of the bleaker inner city areas. This was not a good place for him to be, and it was potentially dangerous for a boy behaving as Kieran was behaving because there were a lot of drugs around and because there was a pervasive semi-criminal street culture. We could do nothing. We were watching as a car went out of control and headed for the inevitable crash.

We began to feel that we were living in a perverse wonderland. Kieran had been sentenced by a court for a serious offence and was under a supervision order. He was blatantly ignoring its terms, but no one could or would do anything about this. We were dealing with a social worker who happily let Kieran stay away from his remand placement for days at a time without informing the police. We had contacted the police, but they would take no action against Kieran, who was being allowed to get away with it. We felt persecuted and harassed, but we knew that any further punishment would probably not change Kieran's behaviour and might even trigger a downward spiral of offending, punishment, more defiant offending and more punishment that would end with him in jail. We also knew that we wanted him off our backs, that we wanted to be left in peace and that we could not live with this level of tension. We wanted someone to tell him 'Stop' before it was too late. No one said it. Kieran went on turning up on or near the street; so far as he was concerned, it was his patch and nothing would keep him away. We did not see why Cate should have to worry about meeting him unexpectedly, or why Paul should have to run home to tell us he had just seen Kieran again. We reduced our contact with Kieran to an absolute minimum and ignored him as best we could when he was in our area.

A new school was found for Kieran but, as we might have predicted, it was not a success. Immediately after the beginning of the autumn term, he began to truant again and was regularly excluded from school for days at a time. An attempt was made to get him into a pupil referral unit for at least a couple of days a week to receive more individual attention and some much-needed help with his numeracy and literacy skills, but it got nowhere. Before long, Kieran was attending school so sporadically that his final expulsion was no more than a formality. There was now almost no structure to his life at all. He was seen hanging around the gates of his old school, waiting for his mates to come out. Cate could easily have bumped into him on her way home. All this was appalling enough, but it got worse. Kieran was, it seemed, being allowed to stay overnight at the home of friends for periods of up to fifteen days without the police being notified. There was vague talk of Kieran being allowed to go on holiday with another family with a boy of his age and younger children. I do not know if anyone had thought to tell the parents just why Kieran was in care.

Kieran's second remand-care placement lasted for about a year. It did not end with a quarrel but in what would have been farce, had it not been so serious. Remand-care placements are, for all the obvious reasons, usually made on a single-sex basis. On this occasion, someone in Social Services decided to ignore the rules and placed an under-age girl in the same home as Kieran. She had a reputation for sexual promiscuity – a vulnerable young girl in the same house as a vulnerable young boy who had been placed on the sex offenders' register after pleading guilty to charges of indecent assault. Neither Kieran's remand carers nor his social worker had thought fit to raise any objections. The police did, and a senior officer made it clear to all that the situation was quite unacceptable. He insisted that Kieran had to be moved immediately and would hear no arguments: alternative accommodation would be found.

The decision to place the girl in the same house as Kieran had put two young people at risk. According to most of the professionals involved with him, Kieran still posed a potential threat to a girl like this; she had only to accuse him of assault for all hell to be let loose. Even after Kieran's removal, the incident appeared to cause no great concern to anyone: it had just been an unfortunate mistake. Perhaps that was the case, but the mistake was made at Kieran's expense. Kieran was sorry to leave his placement because he had become quite attached to his carers. Living in this area had made him much more streetwise, and he was, not without reason, quite proud of the fact. He'd also learned to have a healthy respect for the black and Asian boys he played football with on the street: 'Very fast and strong. Faster than me, and I'm fast.'

Kieran was moved for a third time and was placed with a black woman who lives some distance away from us in Murton, which can never quite decide if it is a suburb of the city or a small town in its own right. Cora and Kieran hit it off from the start, and he remained with her until he left the care system at the age of eighteen. He is still in touch with her. I've met her on only a few occasions, but she is well regarded by those professionals who have had dealings with her. I have heard her described as being ever so slightly eccentric, 'probably a bit crazy', and a specialist in impromptu parties. She was a good friend to Kieran and gave him a lot of freedom, but it was a conditional freedom. She gave him no key to the door and made it quite clear that, if he got back after she had gone to bed, that was it: if he had not arranged to spend the night at a friend's home, he was locked out. And he did spend a few nights shivering on the doorstep as he waited for the day to break.

Kieran was being left to run wild, and we were getting no help with Paul and Cate, even though they were becoming more difficult almost by the day. We felt that the entire system, from the police to Social Services and the Youth Offending Team, was failing us. Vanessa encouraged us to start shouting as loudly as we could, so we began by writing to our MP. We met him and he strongly advised us to demand a meeting with the Director of Social Services and assured us that, if the Director would not listen to us, she would have to listen to an MP who was also a powerful figure in the local government unions. We demanded a meeting and we got it almost immediately. We sat around a polished oak table in an office in a tall block with stunning views of the city, and we were served tea and biscuits. We were joined by senior social workers, and even by the Deputy Director, who looked to us like affability personified. Vanessa later remarked that we had enjoyed the rare privilege of seeing a notoriously difficult young man on a charm offensive. It was clearly stated to us that there would be no more talk of sending Kieran on holiday. By the end of the meeting, a number of things were on offer. It should be possible to get Cate into a group that worked with sexually abused children. We could refer ourselves, and the children, to a Family Resource Centre, which might be able to help. Individual support workers would be found for Paul and Cate, though it might take a long time.

It did take a long time. Always in short supply, individual support workers are not social workers but 'paid volunteers' who have all manner of jobs and attempt to help children in need in their spare time. They are carefully vetted and given some professional training, and are answerable to a senior social worker who acts as a team leader. In our case, the senior social worker was the somewhat enigmatic Kenneth, a middle-aged man with a very gentle manner who used a very camp sense of irony to keep the world at bay. On the only visit he made to our home, he picked up a thriller lying on the table, glanced through the lurid blurb and put the book down with a fastidious gesture: 'Wouldn't have it in the house, myself.' I took that to be his way of saying that he too had an extensive collection of lurid thrillers. He went on to tell us about support workers. He thought he could match Paul with someone in the fairly near future. Tony would take Paul out for a few hours every week. He would be someone for Paul to talk to, go to the cinema with, and to eat burgers with. Tony would have no therapeutic or social work role and we would have no means of contacting him. He would phone us but if we wanted to reach him, we would have to leave a message with Kenneth's office.

Arrangements like this are inconvenient, but they are designed to protect men and women who have put themselves in the potentially dangerous position of being vulnerable to allegations of abuse from damaged children, and to violence at the hands of angry parents. Everyone who works with these children and their parents is at risk, and people who act as individual support workers deal with situations that are far removed from the experience of most of us; Tony told me of boys who could silently devour three burgers in a matter of minutes because they never got enough to eat at home, and of going to pick up children from homes which had almost no furniture, no paper on the walls and no carpets on the floor.

Kenneth went on to explain that it would be a while before we met Tony, who was currently working with another boy, and that, for the moment, he was sorry but he could think of no suitable worker for Cate. There was, however, another possibility. There was Keep Safe. This was a group run by a psychiatric social work team for children who have been sexually abused. The group of three girls and three boys, all aged thirteen or fourteen, met weekly over a period of eight weeks. Ironically, the group met in the One-Stop Centre where Marina and I had signed the papers that committed Kieran to local authority care. I took Cate along and sat in the waiting room for a couple of hours a week. Keep Safe had a high ratio of workers to children: six children and three workers – two women and one man. 'Just one. He's there to show that there are some good ones,' Kath told me. She said it with a smile, but there are those in the social work profession who passionately believe that no men should be involved in this type of work because all men pose a potential threat to children.

Cate got on fine with the other children, and certainly never showed any reluctance to go to Keep Safe but she said almost nothing about what went on in the group. We have never had any problems with that. If she had wanted to talk about it, she would have done so and we would have listened. I never talked to her about my sessions with Jan, and Cate has the same right to privacy as me. The little I did learn about the group comes from what I gleaned from a few conversations with Kath, who told me that Cate listened carefully to the others but said very little. Kath also told me that all six children had been abused by male relatives, and that they were all surprised to learn that the same thing had happened to the others. Despite their own experience, they shared the widespread belief that abuse is perpetrated mainly by strangers. One of the girls had been abused for a period of years by her grandfather, but she still loved him deeply. He was her abuser and she hated him for that, but he was also the lovely grandfather who took her to the park and bought her gifts. She cried bitterly when he was taken away by the police and she went on crying when she could not see him because he was in prison.

The child's affection is one of the abuser's sources of power and control, and the other is usually the coercive use of threats ('I'll tell your mother' or 'I'll kill you') or the even more insidious 'No one will believe you'. All too often, the abuser is right about that. Abusers can also exploit a child's natural need and desire for affection and attention. The 'affection' shown by the abuser is perverse; that felt by the child is not necessarily so. In some cases, the abuser is the only person to display any affection for the child, and the child responds accordingly. I suspect that Kieran was once in that position, and that his abuser was the only one who took any real notice of him; it is possible for a child to receive so little attention that he or she would rather be fucked than be ignored. One thing we do know about what went on in Keep Safe is that the group spent a lot of time thinking about the power of the abuser. An 'abuser' figure – a rag doll – was propped up on a tower of bricks and then pelted with bean bags until the tower collapsed to demonstrate that the power of the abuser could be destroyed. Cate laughed out loud when she told us about that. The group's last session took the form of a party with cakes and lots of pop and those six children certainly had something to celebrate. It is now over four years since Marina first discovered that Cate was being abused; the eight weekly sessions offered by Keep Safe are the only professional help she has had.

We finally met Tony after weeks of waiting. In theory, we knew next to nothing about him, and were told only that he works as a fire-fighter. Paul in fact learned a lot about him, and immediately passed it on as an ability to keep secrets is not one of his strengths. Tony was in his late thirties, divorced, lived with his lawyer girlfriend, had no children, played a lot of sport and liked a glass of Southern Comfort. Every week he turned up and took Paul off in his car. They played pool and took Tony's dog – a very large Alsatian – for walks. They went to McDonald's and they went for long runs together. They went to the cinema. Tony was wonderful.

People like him usually work with children for relatively short periods but Paul saw Tony weekly for almost two years until it was decided at a meeting with Kenneth, Tony, Vanessa and myself that it was time to bring the arrangement to a gentle end. We expected this to be difficult but it proved to be surprisingly easy. When they next met, Paul was told by Tony that he was getting older now and did not really need his help any more, and that other and younger boys needed it more. Paul accepted this very gracefully, but he did get Tony to promise to come back and take him out for a drink on his eighteenth birthday. As they finally said goodbye, Paul thanked Tony in such formal terms that he thought we must have coached him. Tony was a good adult friend to Paul, and I do think he helped him grow up a bit. Tony always turned up on time, or phoned to let us know when his job made it impossible to come. Paul was always ready far in advance when he knew he was going out with Tony, and would wait for him outside in the street, even when it was cold and raining. Tony had endless patience with him and listened without complaining as he reeled off the miles of football statistics that drive me mad.

It was about a year after our initial meeting with Kenneth that we were at last introduced to Sandy. We never learned much about her, and know only that she is my age and works with children and young people in some capacity. She took Cate shopping and bowling, and they went to the cinema together. The arrangement did not work as well as it did with Tony, who was very neutral and non-judgemental with Paul, because Sandy took a much more interventionist view of her role. In her view, a trip to the cinema was a reward that had to be earned, and no school meant no cinema but only a walk or window-shopping. Vanessa was very sceptical about all this: 'She's trying to cure Cate. It won't work. In any case, it's not her job.' Sandy was indeed trying to act as a quasi-therapist, but she did not 'cure' Cate and was not supposed to be trying to. The other problem was that Sandy was not reliable. Some dates were cancelled at very short notice, and sometimes she just did not turn up, which left us having to deal with an angry and disappointed girl who would take out her frustration on us and her brother. Eventually, the relationship broke down. Without explanation, Sandy stopped coming and never rang.

The approach to Marina's birthday was typical. Birthdays are important to all of us and we make a big fuss over them. The children have always made a huge effort to buy us, and each other, what they see as the best possible presents and Kieran, in particular, has a real talent for choosing appropriate gifts. Cate was looking forward to Marina's birthday, and going with Sandy to choose a present for her mum was not a trivial matter to her. Two days before Marina's birthday, Sandy rang to say she would have to break their date because something had cropped up at the last moment. She promised to come the next afternoon, meaning the day before Marina's birthday. By late afternoon, she had neither turned up nor rung, so I offered to take Cate to the shops. She would not listen: 'I'm going with Sandy.' I explained that it was beginning to look as though Sandy was not coming and that the shops would be closing soon; Cate again insisted she was going to buy a present with Sandy and not with me. Sandy finally rang to say she could not make it after all. I was furious with her and I did think of making a formal complaint, but did not do so as I knew that, despite everything, Sandy meant a lot to Cate. I now had to deal with a Cate who was angry and disappointed because she knew that she would be unable to take her mother a proper present when she woke her with a cup of tea in the morning. We at last found a way around the problem by buying a cheap card and a bar of chocolate from the corner shop. Cate had wanted to make a big fuss of her mum, but the token gifts were enough to delight Marina.

There was also an underlying pattern to all this. Something was being repeated. When she was very young, Cate would, as Kieran had sometimes done before her, often succeed in frustrating her wish for something nice or something that would make her happy. Either Marina or I would agree to take her out to buy something she said she wanted. As we trailed around the shops, her demands suddenly changed: she now wanted something else, and it was either quite unreasonably expensive or just impractical.

An argument would begin: 'No, you can't have the giant soft toy that costs over a hundred pounds. You can have what we came out for. That's what you wanted.' 'Don't want it now.' This could go on for so long that we would end up buying nothing at all and would come home with a girl who was boiling with frustrated anger because she had effectively sabotaged her own pleasure. When she refused to go shopping with me 'because I'm going with Sandy', she was repeating that pattern and proving all over again that she did not deserve to be happy because she was bad. She also told me: 'You wouldn't be like that if I was Paul. You're only like that with me,' and then: 'You wouldn't treat me like that if I was your real biological daughter.'

Cate's difficulties at secondary school began when she entered Year Seven as an eleven-year-old and things are no easier now that she is in Year Ten and almost sixteen. The excitement of going to a new school, of studying new things and just growing up soon gave way to the frustration of not being able to cope with school's demands. Paul has always had difficulties too, and he missed a lot of school but his statement of special needs did mean that appropriate arrangements were, whenever possible, made for him. Because she had no statement, Cate does not even get that degree of help; everything has had to be negotiated and renegotiated, and it always feels as though we are improvising.

One of the side-effects of all their problems is that Cate and Paul identify with their school to only a limited extent. There are now out-of-hours clubs of all kinds. There are sports clubs and a computer club. They could become involved in drama or music projects. One mother with a boy at this school tells me that she never sees him before five-thirty because he is always involved with one club or another. Cate and Paul are always home just after three and won't join in any activities. In many respects, this is a good school, as its standards and results are steadily improving, and its staff are committed and enthusiastic. But it has not met the needs of our children.

Over the years, we've been involved in the endless discussions with school that began when Kieran was there and that will not end until Cate leaves. We've had most of these discussions three times: about Kieran, about Paul and then about Cate. Our relationship with the school and its staff has often been antagonistic: the teachers feel that we are awkward and uncooperative; we know that the school is failing our children. Homework has always been an issue. We have, for instance, had to convince a school that our children's circumstances, background and history all mean that they cannot do real homework. Kieran, Paul and Cate just do not have the sense of 'my future' that is essential to all but the most immediate projects. They not understand why they should do homework. Paul and Cate also have learning difficulties. We tried and tried. We had rows and arguments with the children over homework so often that we gave up on the issue. The pattern has always been the same. Kieran, Paul or Cate would begin the task with enthusiasm, but at the first hint of difficulty, panic would set in: 'I can't do this. It's too hard for me. I can't do it.' If Marina or I told, say, Paul to try – 'Just try' – his temper would begin to flare and the tears would begin to flow, as he began to prove to himself that it was 'too hard'. At this point, we should have given up, but for a long time we tried to insist and the result was that a minor homework problem turned into another row between an angry and frustrated parent and an equally angry and frustrated child. It has taken us a long time to learn that, whilst some arguments may be worth having, an argument over Cate's history homework is not one of them. And then we had the rows and the arguments with school. To argue that our children should not be asked to do homework goes against the entire ethos of the teaching profession, and teachers seem to find it almost impossible to accept it. It feels wrong to me and to Marina too – we grew up on very generous helpings of homework – but we've accepted it in the end. The SENCO (Special Educational Needs Coordinator) we deal with finally gave in, but she did so with very bad grace. Homework is, in some ways, the least of our problems; we feel proud of ourselves if we succeed in getting our children into school.

When Cate was in her second year at high school we agreed to go in for regular meetings to discuss her and Paul's progress. Normally, we met Mrs Jackson, who is the school's SENCO, one or other of the learning mentors and the educational welfare officer. Marina's work commitments meant that she could not always go, so I usually went alone and sometimes with Vanessa, who came along to lend moral support whenever she could. What happened at the meetings varied. Some were very relaxed, but one afternoon we were faced with a full delegation of form teacher, SENCO, educational welfare officer, deputy head of year and two learning mentors. By chance, we had turned out in force too: both Marina and I were there, and Vanessa had turned up too.

This was the most hostile meeting we ever had, and we were warned that if our children's attendance did not improve, we could face prosecution under the Education Act for failing to ensure that they attended school. We said that we welcomed the prospect of a day in court, and I added that our defence would be based upon the Mental Health Act, and that we would be glad to have the opportunity to say in public just how badly our children were being failed by a system that could not meet their needs. There was no more talk of prosecution. It was a threat and nothing more than that. It was, however, revealing. We have often felt that the school was taking a somewhat arrogant stance towards us. The people in that meeting had obviously decided in advance that they should threaten and bully us. We were not afraid of them. We had learned that the only way to get what we want is to shout and fight back when we have to or when we are threatened.

I made another appointment to talk to Mrs Jackson. The autumn term had not been under way for long, but Cate – now aged fourteen – had already missed a week's school and we were growing worried. The school had made no real effort to contact us. It was not a difficult or unpleasant meeting; it was just deeply disappointing. I felt that we were starting all over again. It was as though no one had ever heard of Cate's problems. I was told once again that no individual support was available for Cate because her needs were 'not bad enough', and that there was therefore no point in even trying to have her statemented. Even though the school had known about Cate's problems for years, no arrangements had been made for the coming term. Her new form teacher did not know she had difficulties; no plans had been made for her to work in small groups with the learning mentors, and it had been forgotten that she no longer did Spanish. It was as though the school had no memory of the girl who had been having such difficulties for so long, as though the beginning of the term were the first day of some bizarre creation when everything started anew.

Earlier that week, I had to take Cate to see the doctor. She would not go to school because she was ill. And she really was ill. She had a nasty cough, her ears ached and her glands were slightly swollen. Dr G examined Cate, found that she had a slight ear and throat infection, and prescribed a short course of antibiotics. As we left, I whispered to Dr G: 'She's very good at this.' Obviously well aware of what she was dealing with, she laughed. Cate's symptoms were very real and they did respond to the antibiotics. They always do, but they are not caused by any physical problem. Cate was neither simulating nor malingering that morning: she was ill. Some strange inner mechanism translates her psychological problems about school into somatic symptoms. It can make her suffer from viral illnesses, and tonsillitis is a regular occurrence. Her temperature can rise to such an extent that she has to go to bed with a paracetemol. Mild forms of psychosomatic illness are quite common, and lots of people suddenly can come down with colds before they have to face something stressful, such as a job interview, but I have never known anyone like Cate. We sometimes joke that she is so good at producing symptoms that she should study for the stage and I swear that I have actually caught her psychosomatic infections. School makes her ill in the most physical and literal of senses.

His sister is the real expert but Paul can develop psychosomatic symptoms too. He complained one evening that his foot hurt, and he was indeed limping quite badly. There was no injury to his foot, but the pain was genuine, and so was his fear of playing football the next day.

The educational welfare officer I fell over on the doorstep three years ago was the first of the four we have had dealings with. They obviously just do not last. Linda, who is the current incumbent, started out well and we all appeared to be getting along fine together. The system of rewards she introduced worked for a while: Cate was awarded points for every day she attended and a certificate for a full week, but her fear of going to school eventually overcame the allure of hand-written personal certificates.

The second of Linda's proposed solutions ended in total disaster. One of Cate's closest friends – they've known each other since nursery class – was in the same form and was also showing signs of school phobia. Linda had discovered that Holly had to pass the end of our street on her way to school and suggested that it might be easier if the two of them met there and went in together. We should have known better but we went along with the suggestion. Holly is a girl with a huge number of problems, and that is one of the reasons why Cate likes her so much; our disturbed children are spontaneously drawn to other children who are as disturbed as they are and, although Holly is in some respects pleasant enough, she is also almost completely dysfunctional, as is her mother, who refuses to take any job that is not within walking distance of their home. Some mornings, Cate left the house quite happily, expecting to meet her friend. The phone would ring as soon as she had walked out of the door: 'Holly won't leave the house.' One of us would have to run and tell Cate not to wait. There were mornings when Cate reappeared after having shivered on the street corner for twenty or thirty minutes because Holly had not turned up. On days like that, Cate just would not go to school. She was disappointed and had been let down again, and she was afraid that she would get into trouble for being late. Although we never said it in so many words, we had to admit that we wouldn't have gone to school either on mornings like that. Holly was not even fifteen when she dropped out of the school system altogether. Cate regularly comes home with gossip and rumours about her: 'She's smoking cigarettes and drinking. She's got a boyfriend and has sex with him all the time.' The rumours are perfectly plausible and sound like excerpts from an early chapter in a story that will soon end very badly.

We have tried to use the meetings at school to convince teachers that, even if they think they are dealing with basically well-behaved children with some minor problems and parents who worry too much, we are struggling to bring up very difficult kids. One meeting turned to a discussion of our home life. It was very difficult. Marina had found Cate perched on the window-sill of her bedroom and threatening to jump. Very wisely, Marina ignored the plea for attention and left Cate where she was. She spontaneously knew what any fire-fighter would have told her: trying to grab someone sitting on a ledge or sill is almost guaranteed to make them fall. As it happens, the danger was more apparent than real. Cate's room is on the first floor and, if even she had fallen, she would most likely just have skidded off the roof over the bay window and crashed into the hedge on the other side of the drive. When we recounted this incident, a learning mentor who had so far been very vocal gasped, looked away and said not a word for the rest of the meeting. We don't know what raw nerve we had touched, but we have heard almost nothing from our learning mentor since then.

When I said that if the school did take us to court, I would use the Mental Health Act as a defence I was joking, but it was a somewhat twisted joke. When we first met Vanessa, I found her comment about our 'three mad children' hurtful but I eventually had to agree that it was accurate. They do have mental health problems. They suffer from attachment disorder, and there is a checklist of symptoms. Children with attachment disorder can be superficially charming and indiscriminately affectionate with strangers; at the same time they are unable to give or receive genuine affection, even though they can also be very clinging and demanding. They find it difficult to relate cause to effect, and their eating patterns are often abnormal. They have difficulty in establishing and maintaining peer relationships, and have little or no control over their impulses. They can be destructive and self-destructive, and are often cruel to animals. They are pathological liars and avoid eye contact (except when lying). They have no conscience and little empathy, and they are preoccupied with fire, blood and gore. There is a very real danger that their anti-social behaviour will escalate into violence or total isolation from society. These children do poorly at school and do not fulfil their potential. Virtually all adopted children display some of these symptoms, and they are particularly common in 'older' adoptees.

A child who exhibits all these symptoms must be impossible to live with. Neither Kieran, Paul nor Cate has ever been cruel to an animal. We do not have problems with eating disorders. None of our children is unduly preoccupied with fire, blood and gore. Kieran did go through a phase when he was obsessed with the wrestling on TV, but he appears to have grown out of it and, alarming as they may have been, his games with matches never escalated into fire-setting. I am convinced that Cate's obsession with Buffy the Vampire-Slayer is no more indicative of an alarming preoccupation with gore than my own enjoyment of horror movies is symptomatic of a taste for necrophilia. But discounting cruelty to animals, an unhealthy interest in violence, fire-setting and eating disorders, our three children have, between them, the full set of symptoms of attachment disorder.

They do not, of course, all present the same symptoms. Cate rarely lies but at times she is so clinging that she suffocates us, especially Marina. Paul does have a lot of difficulty with peer relationships and has poor control over his impulses but is not indiscriminately affectionate with strangers. For a long time Kieran was, and someone he had met five minutes ago was his best friend – but within the hour, he would have a new best friend. Cate's tendency to rush up to old ladies she did not know and start talking to them was endearing, but the occasions when she went up to male strangers to ask them to hold her hand and help her cross the road were alarming. Luckily, she always managed to pick 'good' male strangers. For years, Kieran could look us in the eye and tell the most outrageous lies. Cause-and-effect thinking is beyond all of them, though Kieran's ability to reason is improving. When Paul found himself locked out, kicked in the front door and smashed the lock, he failed to realise that he would be unable to lock the door behind him once he was inside the house. In varying degrees, all three children can be superficially charming and mask their disordered behaviour. No one outside the family ever saw the Kieran who could fly into violent rages, let alone the Kieran who could abuse his sister. Cate once locked herself out and had the sense to go to our next-door neighbour, who looked after her for a couple of hours. Leslie described her as 'a charming girl'. Half an hour later, the charming girl was screaming obscene abuse at us.

Children are not born like this, though there are rather dubious claims that there is such a thing as a genetic predisposition to attachment disorder. The causes can be many, and may include maternal ambivalence towards pregnancy, traumatic prenatal experience, in utero exposure to drugs or alcohol, neglect, abuse or abandonment, separation from birth parents, divorce, multiple moves or placements, or institutionalisation. Virtually all the older children who are looking for a forever family have experienced one or more of these things. Some have experienced all of them. These are the things Kieran experienced during the first three years of his life. Paul and then Cate were born into circumstances that made it impossible to develop healthy attachments with their birth mother. Tragically, attachment disorder is easy to induce. Child psychiatrists and other specialists can describe the symptoms and trace the probable causes and have devised therapeutic strategies for coping with it, but they cannot make it go away.

Attachment-disordered children are uncomfortable to live with and do not respond to what most people would regard as normal parenting. For these children, the ideal parents would be a cross between psychiatric nurses and mothers and fathers. We have had to learn the basics of what the professionals call therapeutic parenting. We often feel that we are our children's managers rather than their parents and we rarely relax. Still hyper-vigilant, we always plan for the worst-case scenario and constantly ask ourselves: 'What will we do if she . . .?'. We feel that we are living with time-bombs and we wait for them to explode. Learning even the basics has been difficult, but we have been helped to learn from our past mistakes. We sensed at a very early stage that attempting to discipline or punish Kieran was not working, but we had no idea why it did not work and therefore assumed that we were failing as parents. We have had to learn to accept that our children are, and always have been, emotionally and mentally damaged. We have learned to accept that they will not do well at school, and it has been agonising. Kieran is not doing much better than anyone could have expected, and Paul and Cate will never go to university; Marina and I cannot have the same ambitions as our middle-class friends, who find it quite natural that their children have got into Oxford or Cambridge. We have learned to accept that Paul will probably always find it difficult to relate to his peers and that his social skills will never be brilliant. We have learned to accept that, whilst she is very affectionate towards us, Cate is also monstrously selfish and as demanding as any baby. I am still learning, or trying to learn, that getting into arguments with her is absolutely futile, but I still do and end up screaming at her in inarticulate rage. I am always ashamed of myself after the event, but that does not stop me from doing it again. We have had to accept that our children have very little sense of the future and therefore find it very hard to look ahead into what their lives might be or might bring them.

And then there are the things that we have not had to accept. Accepting Cate for who and what she is has not meant accepting that, when she says she is going out, our fourteen-year-old is off for a night of drunken sex with multiple partners. We had serious problems with Kieran but we have never had to accept the fact that he was sniffing glue. Accepting Paul for what he is has never meant accepting the fact that he is regularly brought home in a police car, or that we will again have to collect him from a police station in the middle of the night.

Cate spent much of yesterday afternoon writing a letter to us. Unfortunately, she wrote it in red crayon on orange paper, so it was not easy to decipher and she had to read it aloud to me. It was a variant on the 'story for a very special lady' that she had written for Marina. That story was about a ten-year-old girl who lost her mother and was sent to a boarding school. Eventually, she met the prince of her dreams, proposed to him and married him. The couple could not have children of their own and decided to adopt. They found the perfect child, but he had a brother and a sister and they had to adopt them too. Since then, they have all lived a perfect life. In the letter she now read to me Cate wrote that we were the best mum and dad in the world, and that she loved us very much because we had rescued her from foster care.

She showed the letter to Marina when she came in from work at about six. There were cuddles all round. As we sat down for our evening meal just over an hour later, Cate and Paul began their usual bickering. Paul quickly retreated and took his meal to his bedroom. By now I was so pissed off with the pair of them that I'd begun to flick through a magazine. Cate did not like that. She began to grumble that we were no more than a 'fake family' because we couldn't have mealtime conversations 'like normal families do'. Within the space of just over an hour, Marina and I had gone from being the best parents in the world, and even the heroine and hero who had rescued Cate, to being members of a fake family.

VIII

Eighteen months ago, Vanessa suggested that Paul might like to join a psychotherapy group for adopted adolescents run by Catherine and a colleague we had never met, as she thought that he was now old enough to benefit from meeting other young people in a position similar to his own. We discussed the proposal with Paul, who was enthusiastic about joining the group and he has been going once a week ever since.

We get some feedback about what happens in the group from Catherine and Vanessa but not a lot, and Paul rarely says much about it though he certainly enjoys going. Apparently he contributes well to the group discussions and has no hesitation about speaking his mind; his problem with literacy is no disadvantage here, and Paul makes good use of his highly developed oral skills. That he was for a long time the only boy in a group of six girls never bothered him, and I think he was in fact slightly put out when another boy began to attend. Catherine tells me that the girls tend to make a pet of Paul, who was and will be a good-looking boy, but who is at the moment a mass of spots rather than a sex god in the making. He obviously enjoys being a pet, and described in very moving terms the session in which he became very upset about something and which ended with all the girls sitting around him and stroking his hands to calm him. Many boys of Paul's age would find these girls intimidating, if not downright frightening, as they are wild, loud and very streetwise for their age. He does complain about a couple of them – 'Won't bloody shut up, that one' – but he clearly gets on with them too. He has been able to talk about his situation with people of his own age and, perhaps more important, he has been able to compare his situation with theirs and has learned that it is not uniquely bad. The group is quite self-contained. The children are very actively discouraged from contacting each other outside it, even by phone or text; this is neither a social gathering nor a youth club.

On three Wednesdays in the month, I put Paul in a taxi to go to his group, but on the fourth I get into it with him. I'm on my way to our parents' group. The group is made up of the parents of kids in Paul's group, and those of children who have been in it and then moved on. We had known for a while that the local branch of one of the major adoption agencies ran a support group for parents, but we had never really contemplated going along because it met in the evening, and on the other side of the city; getting there and back would have been difficult, and we would have needed a baby-sitter. It is true that we often find it hard to go out in the evenings just because we are so tired, but looking back, I now think that these were very lame excuses. The real explanation for my own reluctance to join any support group was a mixture of shame, fear and self-protection. There were a lot of things I was still frightened to talk about in the open because they made me feel ashamed – the abuse, my response to it, the violence that had been unleashed, my fears for the future – and I did not want 'being-an-adoptive-father-with-problems' to become the whole of my existence. When we did join the parents' support group, we realised that we had needed something like this for a long time. Why did we go this time? Because we needed to and because Paul was going to his group, because the parents' group was facilitated by Vanessa and Sandra, because we now had total faith in them and Catherine, because we believed that the three of them could probably move mountains if they wanted to, and because we'd have agreed to almost anything they suggested.

The size of the group varies from month to month. Some of the people who were already going when we joined have since left; others have attended once or twice and have never been seen again. Perhaps we frightened them off. At our last meeting there were eight of us plus Vanessa and Sandra: three couples, one father on his own and one mother on her own. Our first meeting provided a simple but wonderful revelation: we were not the only ones. This is what the girl who suddenly learns that she is not the only lesbian on the Isle of Wight must feel, or the boy who discovers that he is not the only gay teenager in Northumberland: there are more of us. We are not the only adoptive parents to be living with difficulties that have all but destroyed us. On the contrary, there are a lot of us, and we can help each other. We know almost nothing about each other – I don't even know what most people do for a living – and might not even like each other outside the group. Inside it, we know one another very well indeed. We know what we are talking about: we've all been there and, whilst we all face different problems and difficulties, there are common patterns running through our experiences. Some of these people are dealing with things that happen only in our nightmares. They are really happening to them. Four years ago, when we first met Vanessa and Catherine, we were dealing with something that happened only in the nightmares of the other parents. We were the ones who were standing on the edge of the pit. We are all at different stages in broadly similar stories.

The group is a clearing house for horror stories about adoption. Most, if not all, of us have come perilously close to seeing an adoption end in disaster; some of us have, like Marina and myself, actually seen that happen. The group is also a forum for the discussion and comparison of the properties of various antidepressants, and these are very informed discussions; between us, we have a great deal of expertise. We exchange coping strategies and sources of information and help. There have been a lot of tears but there has also been a lot of laughter. And a lot of the stories are funny. There is something intrinsically comic about the tale of the boy who has been picked up by the police so often that he is on first-name terms with every officer who patrols the city centre, but probably only when the tale is told in the right setting. We have seen people coming to a group meeting in a terrible state – angry, frustrated, tearful – but we have never seen them leave in that state. We have heard people say dreadful things about the children who reject their love, and then seen them hugging and kissing these children as they pick them up from their group session.

Yet even in this supportive environment, it was very hard to tell anyone why Kieran is not living at home and to say just what happened to our family. For a long time, we said nothing specific and merely mumbled that Kieran was no longer with us, without going into any detail. In some ways, this was unfair on the other people in the group, but no one is actually under an obligation to speak and I don't suppose for one moment that everyone is 'telling all'. Our inability to say anything specific had been making me feel uncomfortable for some time and I did eventually speak out at a meeting that Marina, as it happened, was unable to attend. A couple had just joined us for the first time and we were all introducing ourselves, so it seemed like a good opportunity, but I still had be prompted by Vanessa before I could say anything and the words did not come easily. The response was a series of gasps followed by silence and then someone quietly said: 'It's not your fault.' We spend a lot of time telling each other that.

I finally met Jonathan – the other boy in the adolescents' group – as he and Paul came out of their group session and as I came out of our parents' group with his mum. We had all heard a lot about Jonathan, who was giving his parents a terrible time: he disappeared for days on end, returned drunk, filthy and evil-smelling, and then vanished again to run around with a group of kids who were in constant trouble with the police and who were suspected of being involved in a series of nasty muggings. We had heard so much about the boy that I thought I knew him: he was a big lad with a strong physical presence, and would make a useful rugby flanker. He was tall for his age and looked much older and more mature than he was. The Jonathan I finally met for a few moments was tiny, and the only thing that was big about him was his voice. It is only in his parents' minds that he was a big strong lad. He took up so much space inside their heads that he had become enormous, but he was in fact just a teenager who is small for his age. I have exactly the same problem with Cate.

One of the things we have learned from our group discussions is that, incredible as it seems, it could all be a lot worse. Neither Paul nor Cate has ever shown any interest in drugs. It would surprise me if Kieran has not experimented with cannabis and possibly worse. I am convinced, though, that it has gone no further than that, and he has nothing but contempt for crack and heroin users, and I am sure he has come across a few. Our children are not running around like headless chickens and they are not self-destructive. We have not overcome all our family's problems but we have found answers to some of them, and we have learned to live with the ones we cannot solve.

It was Christmas morning and the turkey in the oven was beginning to smell very interesting but I was very conscious of the fact that, for the second year running, I was making Christmas lunch for a family of four and not five. I had just started the messy business of making croquette potatoes and my hands were covered in a sticky mixture of potato, beaten egg and breadcrumbs when the phone rang, so it was Marina who answered it. It was Kieran. He had promised to phone to wish us 'Happy Christmas' but we had learned to take his promises with a pinch of salt, so this was a pleasant surprise. His foster-carers had gone away for a week and he was staying with his mate, who lived within walking distance of us, but he was not doing much and he'd just wondered . . . Marina immediately told him to come over.

Half an hour later, Kieran was on the doorstep, looking very apprehensive and unsure of what reception he would get. We were apprehensive too, as we had had only sporadic contact with Kieran for the best part of eighteen months and were not at all sure about who we had invited over, but it was just a taller Kieran who walked through the door. It was not the most relaxed of days, as we were all on edge and still wary of each other. Paul seemed pleased to see Kieran and made no mention of his stolen money, but I don't recall any particular reaction from Cate. Marina was more pleased to see Kieran than I was because I was still not comfortable about having him around the house and was quite suspicious of what he might do. We enjoyed our lunch and settled down to watch the video of *Gladiator* that was one of our

Christmas gifts to ourselves, and it was much better than I expected it to be. Kieran watched only half of it with us, and then went off to see a friend on the street, saying that he was bored with the film and wanted some fresh air. He did play football on the street with a friend for a while, but then disappeared into someone's house without telling us where he was going. 'Off out, again,' I grumbled to Marina, adding that this inability or reluctance just to relax with what was supposed to be his family was typical of the boy, but I later contrived to make light of his disappearance by telling Kieran that the second half was so much like the first that he had not missed a great deal. The rest of the day was just a pleasant Christmas blur of food and drink, and dozing off in front of the television. Kieran left in mid-evening to walk back to his friend's place.

Three or four days later, we had to attend a review meeting to discuss Kieran's progress with Bernard. When Kieran walked into the One-Stop Centre we were horrified to see that there were cuts and bruises to his face. He explained that, after leaving us, he had been jumped as he walked past a local pub. He had done nothing to provoke his attackers, but they knocked him to the ground, gave him a good kicking and took everything he had on him, including the cheque we'd given him. Kieran did not seem to be particularly surprised and obviously viewed the incident as just one of those things, but we were really shocked. Seeing him in that state hurt us both, and the pain we felt was a sign that something had changed, or perhaps that nothing had changed. The injured boy with the cut and bruised face was our son Kieran and our instinctive reaction was to help him and care for him. He had come to us, and we had taken him in. And now we were seeing a son who had been hurt. Despite all that had happened to us, we realised that we still had a deep sense of being a family and that our sense of belonging together had not been destroyed. There was also a sharp pang of guilt; we'd never even thought of offering to drive him home that night.

Kieran was still being accommodated by Social Services, was still in his remand-care placement and was still on his supervision order. He had never really gone back to school, had effectively fallen through the net, and his only qualification was a single GCSE. But he was surviving and was beginning to settle down. He was now working at a printers, in an unskilled capacity; the hours were long and the working conditions sounded so poor that they bordered on the dangerous. Social Services were covering his living costs and paying him a small allowance, but Kieran wanted to live the same life as his contemporaries. Most of the wages paid to him on Friday were gone by Monday morning, spent in clubs and pubs. His turnover of casual girlfriends sounded to be rapid. We could not have said that we approved of the way he was living his life, but we had to admire his survival instincts and wonder at the fact that he was not locked away in a prison cell. Kieran was still living in the immediate present and still had little or no vision of a future. He did, on the other hand, tell us that he was now attending his Youth Offending sessions on a much more regular basis; significantly, he was also beginning to speak of Bernard and his fellow workers in much more positive terms. Something was starting to change.

That Christmas Day marked the start of a slow process of reconciliation that has taken over two and a half years. It has not allowed us to restore our family to what it once was because that family has gone and cannot be rebuilt, and we have had to build a different one. We began to see more and more of Kieran and he soon started to come to the house for Sunday lunch. At first, he would disappear 'off out' immediately after lunch and we again had the 'Where's he got to this time?' problem. Conversations were not easy and rarely got beyond the mundane. I could find very little to say to Kieran, still found it hard to listen to the endless talk about football, and still did not want to be alone with him for any length of time. I still felt that I had to avoid leaving money anywhere he could see it, and we certainly could not leave him alone with Cate. We were very unhappy about the wrestling games he still played when we sometimes allowed his friends into the house. We could not give him a key (not that he asked for one) and we were reluctant to allow him to stay overnight. I am not in fact sure that we had any legal right to allow him to stay, but we eventually gave up worrying about that. On a couple of occasions, we had late-night phone calls from a drunken Kieran who had somehow become separated from his mates while they were out clubbing. Marina got the car out and went to pick him up. He spent the night on our sofa, the only alternative being a chilly few hours shivering on his remand-carer Cora's doorstep.

In some ways, it was easier to meet away from home. We began to go ten-pin bowling together. Kieran was now very skilled at it, but it often felt as though he was not playing with us, as though he was interested only in demonstrating how good he was. When it was someone else's turn to bowl, Kieran would disappear for a cigarette or just wander away, and he showed little interest in teaching his sister or brother how to improve their game, even though Paul was still so uncoordinated that it looked as though he would forget to let the ball go and slide headlong down the lane into the pins. The bowling, occasional trips to the cinema together and the regular Sunday lunches became the bases for the new relationship we gradually cobbled together. I obviously was not privy to all that was said in their exchanges, but I do know that Marina's 'no-eye-contact' discussions in the car were more intimate, and in the long run more productive, than the hesitant conversations I had with him.

When he was between jobs and at a loss for anything to do, Kieran became our cleaner. He would turn up once a week and clean the house, and we paid him the going rate for the job. He'd always been keen on cleaning and had often despaired of the chaos in which we usually live. After he had been, the kitchen sparkled, the bathroom shone and even Paul's bedroom was tidy. There were also disadvantages to having Kieran as a cleaner. It was not easy to find anything afterwards. Things would turn up in the strangest places: the cups were mixed up with the wine glasses, all the herbs and spices were in the wrong cupboard, and the washing powder was in the back porch. Kieran clearly still believed that 'tidy' meant 'out of sight' rather than 'out of sight and in the right place'. When he was young, his bedroom always looked impeccably tidy, but if we opened a drawer we would find that his dirty underwear and socks had been stuffed in with the newly ironed shirts.

Marina and I had always known that Kieran's cleaning was an attempt to win approval, but it was also a form of 'nesting', a way of creating an environment that was under his control. We now came to see that his obsession with tidying everything away was a way of controlling us; he was organising the way the house looked, and trying, probably without realising it, to organise and control our lives. By now, we'd reached the point where we could smile at that.

In fury, Cate broke up the jigsaw she had been trying to do for so long and scattered the pieces all over the room. A couple of hours later, she came back into the room. With a very sad concentration she began to pick up the pieces and start the puzzle again. Then she gave up in tears: 'Can't do it. It's too hard. It's too hard for me.'

This is the perfect metaphor for what we spend so much of our time on. We are constantly trying to put together the jigsaw and it keeps getting broken up again. Sometimes we scarcely begin because we can see no pattern. Sometimes we do well and then something happens to stop us going on. We argue or quarrel, and we break up the puzzle. And we've always known that there are pieces missing. There were always pieces missing.

The fact that things have improved vastly over the last couple of years does not mean that we have an easy life by any means. Paul and Cate fight almost constantly, and have done for years. Mealtimes and bath times are the usual flashpoints, but fights can break out at almost any time. They often begin as a rough game in which they pat or tap each other like young kittens, and then one of them will grab the fork that was given to the other, or pour out the drinks on an unfair basis. They will fight over who has first use of the bathroom, even though we have two bathrooms. The verbal skirmishing begins with 'fat', 'freak' or 'gay' as trigger words and the language gets worse. The inevitable response to 'fucking knobhead' is 'fat cunt', and off they go. Food will be thrown, and salt or a drink will be poured on to a plate of food. A piece of cutlery might be thrown, or perhaps a plate or a bottle of ketchup. By now, they are usually running around the kitchen screaming at each other. In the past, Paul has picked up big knives and threatened Cate with them. She has hurled a heavy frying pan at his head, missing him by inches. Glasses have been thrown, and so have lumps of lard: there is still one lump sticking to the ceiling. It is true that Paul and Cate have never actually hurt each other badly and that the worst injuries to have been inflicted are slight scratches, the odd bruise or the red marks left by pinching, but that does nothing to diminish our fear, as it would be all too easy for an angry child who is wielding a knife to make a mistake.

The fighting went on for over two years. If we told them to go to their separate bedrooms, things could get much worse as they then fought to get at each other.

Cate's bedroom door was kicked in; we've patched it up now, but for over a year the only closure was a sheet draped over the doorframe. Paul's door has been smashed and pulled off its hinges, and similar fights half-destroyed our bathroom door when Paul and Cate kicked the panels in. We gave up trying to repair it long ago, and at the moment the door is still patched up with a piece of hardboard where there used to be solid pine panels. This is particularly heartbreaking because the old doors were original fittings and had been beautifully stripped and sanded by the previous owners.

In one fit of rage, Kieran smashed the original glass panel in the front door. Several balusters on the stairs have been kicked out and, as it isn't worth replacing them, they will remain like that for the foreseeable future. We had to remove and hide potential weapons such as the ceremonial sword I was given by an aunt and the heavy flat irons that were, so long ago, one of my mother's wedding presents. They used to stand on the mantelpiece in our sitting room, but could not be left there after Cate picked one up and went for Paul.

The children have also damaged their own possessions in these battles, and Cate once tried to throw her computer monitor at Paul's head and narrowly missed him. It was only a cheap second-hand thing we bought so that she could play games, but it will not be replaced now that it has been wrecked. Of course she cried when she saw what she had done but, only days later, she tried to hurl the television at him. When Cate is angry, it is impossible to reason with her. She still cannot understand that a girl who destroys her computer by trying to hurl it at her brother will be a girl who can no longer play her favourite games.

These children have fought in the car, on buses, on campsites, in car parks and on cross-Channel ferries. We stopped being embarrassed about it long ago, and if anyone wants to stare, they can stare. We're past caring. They can stare at what happens when Cate locks herself in the car to escape and when Paul then physically attacks it in frustration. They can stare when she does the same. The car is now badly dented where Cate, wearing her heavy boots, kicked it, and it is beginning to rust where the paint-work has been scraped and scratched.

Friends with birth children cluck with sympathy and try to sympathise by telling us how their children fight. I'm sure they fight; children do. But I don't know many birth parents who have had to call the police because they are afraid that one of their children will seriously injure the other. We've often had to do so, and we've always felt the same terrible, painful relief when the patrol car pulls up outside and two officers get out and come to our door. Although we found dealing with the police very frustrating when we were trying to cope with Kieran, they have always been very good on these occasions. Other adoptive parents speak of police officers who have given them the scornful look that means: 'Can't you even control your own kids? What kind of parents are you?' We have never had that response, but we've often heard a man or woman in blue say, 'It's OK. I've got kids too. I'll talk to them.'

The policemen and policewomen we have had dealings with have always been patient, courteous and reassuring, and have never given the impression that they thought we were wasting their time. Their usual tactic has been to talk to the children sep-arately, and to spell out that this level of violence is not acceptable and will not be tolerated. Paul and Cate have been told what will happen if they are taken to the station: they will be locked in empty cells where they will have to sleep on thin mattresses on concrete platforms; they will be left there alone and the food will be almost inedible. It has been made very clear to them that if either Marina or I are even touched in anger, they will be arrest-ed. The visits from the police have always had the desired effect. The children have always calmed down, and have usually remained cowed and subdued for days afterwards.

After one particularly bad night of violence from Paul, we actu-ally said that we wanted him to be taken in and held overnight. One of the officers agreed that he could, if we insisted, arrest Paul for breach of the peace, which is something of a catch-all charge to be used when no more specific offence has been committed, but then pointed out that it was almost midnight on a bank holiday and the cells would be full of drunks. He asked if we really wanted to put a fourteen-year-old boy in with them for the night? After a moment's thought, we had to agree that we did not, and in any case, Paul was completely calm by then.

I now have a better opinion of police officers than I have of most social workers, but we are well aware of the fact that we have some advantages when it comes to dealing with the police. We are a white professional couple and we live in a good area; take away those advantages, and everything might well be very different. I suspect that the police might respond very differently if they were called to a rundown house on a poor estate. I am also aware that we have never had to face the level of violence that some adoptive parents encounter. I have never been afraid to leave Marina alone in the house with any of our children because one of them might attack and injure her, but we have heard of a woman who was absolutely terrified of being left alone with her adopted teenage son because he had already assaulted her more than once. That forever family broke up in disastrously violent circumstances and the boy – now a young man – is currently in prison for unrelated offences. His father visits him, but his mother does not.

I have often reached the point of throwing meals I have prepared into the bin in anger and frustration. Marina has more than once reached the point of getting out the car and driving around in tears until she could regain some composure after another eruption of violence. We have learned to read the signs and can usually sense when the storm will break: it feels as though we are out on a pleasant walk, and that we have suddenly been engulfed in cold, damp mist or fog. Sensing that the storm will come and knowing what to do about it are, unfortunately, two very different things. We tried various strategies. We tried to ignore the fights and the obscenities, and we tried to mock Paul and Cate into silence. We screamed and shouted at them, and we made threats. And we have learned our lesson: we should never make threats we cannot or will not implement. Trying to make a joke of the violence, we adopted a theme from *The Simpsons* and described the fights as episodes from 'The Itchy and Scratchy Show', in which Bart's favourite cartoon characters do terrible things to one another. This time, the children did at least laugh at themselves for a while, but we were soon back to 'fucking knobhead' and 'fat cunt'.

The fights are in part an expression of sibling rivalry taken to extremes. In many ways Paul and Cate are very, very close. They love each other, and they hate each other (and themselves) because they love each other. They enjoy their fights: they come alive when they are fighting, and it gives them a sense of intimacy. I can understand that because I have felt the fearfully intense intimacy such conflict brings in the rows I've had with Kieran and Cate, and I know that the adrenaline rush is so powerful that it becomes almost addictive. For a long time, I could not just walk away from it and even now I still find it difficult to do so; at times, Paul finds it easier to walk away from a row with Cate than I do.

Whilst Paul and Cate have always squabbled, the real violence began when Kieran was taken into care. Their perception is that we got rid of Kieran because he was naughty and they hate us for it. They also hate each other because they blame themselves (and each other) for having him sent away. Our relationship with Kieran did come to involve a degree of violence. The first baluster was kicked out by Kieran, who had been told to sit on the naughty stair for some misdemeanour or other. During another tantrum, he overturned the table in Marina's study; it took some doing, as the table is six foot by three and made of solid pine. Paul and Cate watched and learned.

It is relatively rare for Paul to be violent outside our home, and to my knowledge Cate never has been. Paul has occasionally been involved in scuffles with other kids on the street and in the school playground. There is nothing unusual in that, and he has never actually hurt anyone; he also threatens that he is going to tear the head off so-and-so at school, but the violence is just verbal. He has come home saying that he has thrown desks at teachers he doesn't like, but when we raise this at school we are greeted with puzzlement: 'Paul? No, he's never done anything of the kind.'

At one point, it was suggested to us by a social worker that Paul and Cate might benefit from anger-management classes. Having reached the point where we would accept any kind of help from any quarter, we took up the offer. For a few weeks – none of these things lasts very long – they went off, each with a social worker of the appropriate gender. Most of the sessions were one-to-one, but there were a couple of joint sessions, and Cate and Paul behaved impeccably throughout; the social workers involved reported no hint of violence or aggression. It was, we were told yet again, just sibling rivalry and they would grow out of it. Tony and Sandy, who were the children's individual support workers, never witnessed even a hint of violence from Paul or Cate.

Everyone outside the family encounters polite, well-behaved children who are well-spoken and never cause anyone any trouble, but they are not the children we have to live with. The final insult was the suggestion that Marina and I might do well to attend some parenting classes. Parenting classes might have been of some use years ago when we first became a family but we had been managing an impossibly difficult situation for a long time, and useful hints about bringing up birth children were not likely to help now. Vanessa was trying her best to teach us to be therapeutic parents, and no anger-management class was going to do that. I joked to Marina that perhaps Paul and Cate should be made to attend some 'childrening' classes instead. Everyone in our parents' group has described the same experience. We have all been told that there is nothing wrong, or that we are just imagining things, and we have all been made to feel that, if anything is wrong, it must be our fault. We have all had the same sinking feeling: 'They don't believe us.'

Paul and Cate are violent at home because it is safe to be violent here. Paul knows perfectly well what would happen if he did throw a desk at his geography teacher or did pull someone's head off in the playground. He may well be ambivalent about school, but the last thing he wants is to be permanently excluded. And

242

although both he and Cate are always trying to find the limit beyond which we will send them away, they both sense that we are not going to do so. And so they can be safely violent at home. We understand that and our understanding should allow us to absorb and neutralise the violence, the anger and the fear, and we can do that to some extent. We can often absorb what is flung in our faces. We just cannot do it all the time, day in, day out, week in, week out.

One of Vanessa's more startling pieces of advice was that we should just walk away from the fights: 'Go to the pub.' We stared at her in disbelief, but we did as she suggested one evening and went to the pub, which is just at the end of the street. That we had never set foot in the place in all the years we'd been living here was a measure of just how isolated and asocial we had become; that we were so horrified at the price of a pint and a half of lager showed how long it had been since we last went out for a drink. We sat in the bar for half an hour or so, feeling very nervous about what we might find when we went home and conjuring up visions of injured children, blood on the walls, ambulances and another trip to the A&E department at the hospital. We got home to find two very subdued children quietly watching television together.

We have had to go the pub like this on a number of occasions. Sometimes they were still fighting when we came back and, if they were, we went back to the pub. We went back four times on one particularly bad night and ended up half-drunk. They calmed down eventually. They always do. And they always know that we will come back.

When we mentioned our trips to the pub in the course a meeting with Kenneth, who organised the kids' Independent Support Workers, he was, to Vanessa's great amusement, quite horrified. He had spent a lot of his career trying to get parents out of the pub, and here we were going there on the advice of a psychotherapist. Going to the pub is now officially known as 'the White Horse strategy', and it has failed on only one occasion. Marina was away from home and I was alone with Paul and Cate, whose quarrel began in the usual way, and then turned physical. I walked out and went to the White Horse, but I simply could not bring myself to walk through the door and order a drink, so I ended up sitting in the dark in the garden, weeping in the rain.

Cate ran into the house in floods of tears. Between deep sobs, she told us that Becky and Owen had been nasty to her. Owen had punched and pinched her arm and made it all red. And Becky would not let her out of her house, where all three of them had been playing. Her arm was very red and sore. We hugged her and held her and told her everything would be fine. She wouldn't be consoled. Normally, we try not to make too much fuss about incidents like this but this time Marina thought that we had to do something. She went to talk to Owen's mother to ask her to speak to him. This was not the first time something like this had happened. Minutes later, Owen's mum was on our doorstep, demanding to see Cate. She could see no red marks or bruising, and she used to be a nurse. It was all in Marina's mind. We let it go.

Paul did not want to let it go. He wanted to kill Owen, who is usually one of his best friends. He would kill anyone who hurt his sister. So he went off to do precisely that. In fact he ran straight into the arms of his independent support worker, Tony, who had come to take him out. There was no revenge killing that night, but a lot of obscene abuse was hurled in the street.

Paul had done something like this before, a very long time ago. Shortly after the children were placed with us, we took them to visit an animal rescue centre. This was probably not the best of ideas but we did succeed in getting home without acquiring a kitten or a puppy (or the black pot-bellied pig that I rather took a fancy to). As we were getting ready to leave, we were attacked by a very large and very angry goose. Neck stretched out, wings flapping, it hissed as it *made for Cate, who immediately burst into tears. Paul, who was not yet four, immediately flung himself between Cate and the goose, unbuttoned his coat and flapped it at the bird. The bewildered goose retreated. This is the boy who says he wants to tear his sister's head off. He does want to do that. And he would also die, even kill, for her.*

Paul's anger and frustration at having to live with Cate became so intense that he said again and again that he did not want to be in the same house as 'that fat bitch', and he finally told us that he was going to leave home and find a flat of his own to get away from her. When we pointed out that he was still at school and had no money, he said he would find a job and that he would soon be sixteen and social security would get him a flat in any case.

A lot of sixteen-year-olds seem to have this strange fantasy, and Kieran came out with it on several occasions. I suppose it's a way of warding off the fear that comes with the desire to be an independent adult: 'I want to be alone, but I want someone to look after me too.' The flat fantasy also has a lot to do with Paul's identification with Kieran. Marina had to go to a meeting at school about Paul, whose behaviour did, for once, seem to be getting seriously out of hand. One of the members of staff had misinterpreted Paul's threat to go and get a knife and come back to kill everyone, and had taken it quite literally. She did not know Paul well and it was therefore an easy mistake to make, as his threat displays can be very convincing. During this discussion, a teaching assistant remarked, with genuine pity, that she felt sorry for Paul because he had to travel so far to get to school: 'He has to go into the city centre, change buses and come all the way out here. It's a long way from Murton, and it's an awkward journey.' Marina just stared, and then the penny dropped: Paul had told the school that his mum had kicked him out of the house and that he was living by himself in a flat. Murton is where Kieran lives.

We were not finding it easy to live with two warring children and were almost tempted to go along with Paul's fantasy of a flat, unrealistic as it may have been. In our discussions with Vanessa, the expression 'respite care' has often come up. There is such a thing, but it is very difficult to find. In theory, it might be possible to get someone – but who? – to take one or both of the children for a weekend or a few days, or perhaps to move in while the two of us went away for a weekend. We have no close relatives who could take them. My sister and her husband have no children of their own, and no sense of what these two can be like at their worst. I'm convinced that, if they took Paul or Cate for a weekend, not everyone would survive the experience. Marina did once half-seriously ask her brother if he and his family would take them for a weekend, but he just turned very pale. Although we've talked a lot about professional respite care, we've never looked into it very seriously. I suspect we would feel enormous guilt if we let a strange couple take the children away from us for a weekend and I know that the children would jump to the conclusion that they were being sent away again. If respite carers stayed in our house while Marina and I went away for a couple of days, they would probably conclude that we'd gone for good.

None of these discussions solved Paul's problem. A lot of his argument was based upon fantasy, but his desire to get away from Cate was real enough, and she would probably have waved him goodbye with great enthusiasm. And then Vanessa told us that she'd heard that the local branch of a national children's charity was trying to get a board-and-lodging scheme off the ground; children who were on the point of leaving care or having problems at home, but who were too young to live independently and who were still in full-time education or training, would temporarily be placed with families that could provide board and lodging. This sounded promising, and it might well have been suitable for a boy in Paul's position. We talked about it with Vanessa, and then raised the issue at home with Paul, who responded with enthusiasm, though I'm not quite sure he understood just what was on offer: all he saw was the possibility of getting away from

Cate. Vanessa got us an application form, and we read through it with Paul and left it with him. He filled in his name, address and date of birth. For weeks, the form had pride of place on the table in his room, but he never completed it. This was just what we thought would happen: we'd called his bluff and he quietly backed down. We have heard nothing more about flats.

Paul will be seventeen in ten weeks. Until very recently, he has shown no real interest in girls. He has friends who are girls, but no girlfriends. Girlfriends have never even appeared on the horizon. We've never worried about this because Paul has been slow to develop in other areas too but has always got there in the end. And now, something does appear to have changed.

Friday was a teachers' training day and he had the day off. Quite out of the blue, he announced that he was going out to meet a girl from school. She lives in a small town about ten miles away and getting there meant taking the bus by himself. He worked out which bus he needed, made sure he had some money and his mobile phone, and set off alone. He had never been to this town and had only a vague idea of where to get off the bus. He was gone all afternoon and got home at about seven, just in time for supper. A couple of months, or even weeks, ago, this would have been unimaginable. He would have found it very difficult, if not impossibly frightening, to get into the city centre and back under his own steam. And all of a sudden, he could do this with no difficulty.

One of the side-effects of the level of violence we live with is that we are now almost totally isolated. For a very long time, Marina and I felt unable to go out together, and Marina had to go to the opera alone because I was so afraid of what might happen if I left Paul and Cate on their own in the house. But we eventually summoned the courage to ask a neighbour's daughter to baby-sit for us. The first time Jess sat for us, everything went fine and Cate and Paul caused her no trouble whatsoever. The second time, they felt much more relaxed because Jess was no longer quite the stranger she had been, and they therefore felt able to fight. Jess was a quiet girl with two younger sisters and she was genuinely afraid that she would be unable to stop Paul from seriously hurting Cate.

The behaviour of our children means that we have no social life. We rarely feel relaxed enough to go out in the evening and have turned down so many invitations that we no longer get them, and we feel that we cannot invite anyone home for a meal, still less for the weekend. We are ashamed of the state of the house and we do not want anyone to see the smashed doors and balusters. We cannot bear the idea of sitting down to an evening meal with friends and having it interrupted by a chorus of obscenities. We invited no one to the house for years. And yet, when two friends did come for the weekend, nothing happened. We took the risk because Andrew and Charlotte are amongst our oldest friends. We do not meet very often, but we've known each other for so long that it feels like for ever and, when we do meet, we just pick up where we left off last time. We've been through a lot together, carried each other home drunk and held each other's heads while we were being sick. We've stayed with them, and they've seen the children fight, though they've never seen them at their very worst. Paul and Cate were charm personified. They did not fight and nor did they swear at each other. There is no guarantee that a second weekend with the same friends here will be so tranquil.

Kieran is nineteen now. He lives in a little flat he shares with his girlfriend Nikki, who is a couple of years older than him. She seems very nice; I say 'seems' because she has said so little to us that it is hard to tell. Kieran keeps the flat absolutely spotless and is almost absurdly house-proud as he shows off his new lampshades and other bits and pieces when we visit. He plays five-a-side football regularly and goes for a drink with his mates afterwards; he dresses well and cares for his appearance. He has just completed the second year of an IT course at the local College of Technology and is collecting modules that will lead to an National Vocational Qualification; he did very well in his exams and university is beginning to look like a real possibility. On Sundays, Kieran comes for lunch and spends most of the day with us, playing pool with Paul or just 'chilling', as he puts it. He brings his washing – and often Nikki's – with him, and puts it through the machine himself. He's come a long way. He is now so relaxed that he no longer feels the compulsion to clean the house, so it's filthy again.

We do not really know what brought about the transformation in Kieran, who has grown up to be a young man any parent would be proud of. We've missed out on a lot of his recent life, but we know that his remand carers, and especially Cora, have helped him a lot, as have Bernard and the other Youth Offending Team workers. As he approached eighteen, social workers from a 'leaving care' team helped him to find and move into the flat. Marina and I agreed to act as financial guarantors, but he has never failed to pay the rent or to meet any of his other commitments. The boy who used to steal money compulsively is now a young man who complains because his credit rating is much lower than he thinks it should be. But no one could have done anything to help Kieran if he had not wanted to change. He had to want to change his life; he had to want to write the letter to Cate in which he apologised for what he did to her over the long period of abuse, and before he could even think of writing it he had to say, to himself and others: 'I did that.' No one could make him think that or write that, and I do not think that anyone even suggested to him that he should do so. And neither Marina nor I made Cate write the note in which she accepted his apology, forgave him and told him he was the best brother in the world. I do not really think that Marina and I can take much credit for a transformation that has been almost miraculous. I do like to think that it is at least in part because we did give him a stable – if difficult – family life for as long as we did that he could transform himself, albeit with a great deal of professional help.

I spent Sunday afternoon building a futon with Kieran. I have enormous problems with flat-pack furniture. I look at the assembly diagram, panic and have no idea of what to do. It's almost like a bizarre form of dyslexia. Kieran takes one look at the diagram and knows precisely what to do. Sometimes, he can actually do without the diagram. When he was eleven and starting high school, we bought him a flat-pack desk. Without even looking at the instructions, he put it together without any difficulty.

I've come to rely on him for things like this. Trying to build the futon with Marina would have been disastrous. We do not work well together. We're about as good as Laurel and Hardy and always end up screaming at each other. Kieran and I can work together. It took a while to put the thing together and there were so many screws involved that we both ended up with blisters on the palms of our hands, but working at it together felt good. And now there will be a proper bed for him if he wants to stay overnight.

Last summer, Paul was quite adamant that he did not want to go on holiday with us, or rather that he did not want to go on holiday with 'that fat bitch Cate'. We quickly sensed that there was no point in arguing with him; he wouldn't go, and that was all there was to it. After what seemed like endless and rather directionless discussions, Marina and I decided that we had to take the risk. We badly needed at least a short break after what felt like a long, hard year, and there was, after all, a possible solution to hand: Kieran could move in with Paul while we went away. Paul thought this was a wonderful idea. Kieran was happy with the suggestion, and quite delighted when we agreed that his girlfriend could come to stay too. They promised that they would look after the house and the four cats and insisted that they would be fine on their own.

Very nervous and apprehensive, we went off with Cate for a week's holiday in County Kerry, where we'd found a cottage to rent at the last moment. We had some rows and a lot of grumbling from Cate, but we enjoyed ourselves in very undramatic ways by going on boat trips to see the seals at close quarters, and getting very wet in the warm soft rain as we walked along the beach. Cate was very annoyed that she was not allowed to drink Guinness in the pubs, but grinned with delight when we let her have a quiet sip when no one was looking. On the way back to Dublin to catch the Liverpool ferry, we broke the journey and stayed overnight in a bed-and-breakfast. Cate had a room of her own, and spent all night alone in it, tucked up in a double bed that was so large that she almost disappeared into the pillows. That was a first.

We phoned home every day, never quite knowing what to expect and haunted by grim visions of the debris of teenage parties and of all the damage that might have been done. An hour from home, we used the mobile to say we were on our way. As we nervously rang the doorbell, we could smell cooking; Kieran was making a meal for us and had already opened a bottle of wine. The three of them had cleaned the house from top to bottom. Paul had been treated to what Kieran called a funky haircut and new jeans; both made a great improvement to his appearance. The three of them had been to a party given by Kieran's former carer Cora and come home by taxi at three in the morning. They had spent all the money we had left them in record time. The cats were well, though they had missed a few meals when everyone forgot to feed them.

That week was important. Paul and Kieran clearly had a wonderful time together. Kieran was able to enjoy being the big brother in the family, whilst Paul could happily luxuriate in the role of younger brother. They've been able to build on this. They now go to football matches together and go off to play pool and snooker. It's good for both of them; it is also good for Marina and me. This year, Paul is going to stay with Kieran and Nikki while we go away on holiday with Cate, and we are going for a fortnight.

So where are we now, fourteen years since Marina and I decided in bed one night that we could do anything? It would be nice to say that we are all living happily ever after, and there are days when we are, but there also days when that is far from being the case. We continue to live in an emotional war zone, even though it is true that the outbreaks of peace now last longer than they once did. Cate and Paul still fight, but they now do so less frequently and the violence usually remains at a verbal level. We still live with children who were badly damaged when they were very young and who are still hurt, and we continue to live in a very fragile situation. We live with many fears. I am not convinced that Cate and Paul will ever be able to live truly independent lives. Vanessa tries to assure me that they will find their niche, and I just pray she's right. They are both still very naive and therefore very vulnerable, but Vanessa is no doubt right to point out that Paul's ability to handle money is a very good sign. I don't know how they will cope with the strains of the sexual relationships they will soon be involved in. At the moment, Kieran is flying, but I suspect that it would not take much to send him off the rails again, and I dread to think what will happen if he and Nikki break up as they probably will in the long term, if only because they are so very young.

The story is not over yet and we still have a long way to go. We have been through experiences that have almost destroyed us. We have lived through the disaster that ended our adoption of Kieran, and Marina and I came perilously close to breaking up more than once. To be more accurate and honest, I have come perilously close to leaving my wife and family more than once, and I have told my children to their faces that I could not going on living with them any longer. I have hit our children and we have had to live with their violence too. We have lived twice with the effects of sexual abuse: we have lived with a boy who was abused, and who went on to abuse his half-sister. Marina and I have screamed obscenities at each other and at our children, who have screamed them back. We have all cried ourselves to sleep. I have never believed that pain makes any one stronger, and I now know that it does not: it hurts, and that is all it does.

These have been long, difficult years and they have been years of frustration. For long periods of time, we have felt that we had been completely abandoned and there have been moments when we've felt we were caught up in some sadistic experiment: 'Let's see what happens when the adoption of three children begins to go wrong. And then let's see what happens when we tell the parents that they were always going to fail, and that we knew it.' There have been the cold, bleak times when we stared into a void that had no name and faced the fear we could barely voice: we are going to lose our forever family. We have feared that we were going to lose everything, and that there would be no 'us'. There have been moments when I thought I was going to break down and go mad, and perhaps I did for a while. There have been days when I have hated our children, times when I have hit them, and times when I have loved them without liking them one little bit. We've been to some bad places. We've had to contemplate things we thought we'd never see, and I wish we hadn't seen them. We have a knowledge we do not want, and it will not go away. We have needed a lot of help and we will go on needing it. Without Vanessa and Catherine, it would have become impossible and we could not have survived as a family. Without Jan, I would have been overwhelmed by the depression. We have not done it on our own. We have soaked up resources, financial, human and emotional. This family has cost society a lot.

I do not know what is going to happen to us. There are still days when it all feels hopeless because everything is just so bloody hard and when I again think I should leave – because I can't stand it any longer, because I can't improve things or because I think my presence is just making everything worse. On better days, everything seems possible.

I am optimistic about Kieran's future. He's done well and we're proud of him simply because he is now leading the life of a normal young man of his age. I worry about Paul and Cate.

Paul is making progress and received a 'most improved student' award from school this year. It was the first award he has ever received; when he read the letter telling him about it, he danced around the kitchen. His vision of the future, however, is still quite unrealistic. Ask him what he wants to do, and he will say 'something to do with sport'. He loves football, is very knowledgeable about it and talks about it endlessly, but the boy who wants to have a career in sport has never even tried to join a team, and will not wear boots when he plays football ('they hurt my feet'). Paul is also the boy who can be so tenderly patient with a girl who has to live in a wheelchair and who tries so hard to help her. The boy who once found it so hard to go to school now has an attendance rate of 100 per cent.

Cate is even further removed from the real world. For a long time I thought she really had given up on school, and that school had quite lost interest in her; she was rising late and spending whole days watching television, and one of the reasons why she was so ready to pick fights with Paul was that she was simply bored. For reasons that none of us can understand, she suddenly decided to go back to school, and has been attending regularly for weeks now, but she is out of her depth with the work and is beginning to drown again. It will not be long, I fear, before she refuses to leave the house once more, but I may be wrong. She goes on being as demanding as a tiny baby. Cate is also the girl who displays such affection to us that it almost hurts and who worries so much that I will not look after myself properly when I'm away from home.

I do not know what lies ahead. Looking back, I do not really know how we got here or how we survived. I do not know how we coped, but I know that Marina and I have been through so much together that nothing can divide us. All I know is that there are five of us and that it is going to stay that way. We are a forever family.

Notes

Unless otherwise stated, all statistics cited are taken from government sources (especially www.dfes.gov.uk/adoption) and materials published by British Agencies for Adoption and Fostering or made available on its website (www.baaf.org.uk). BAAF's *Surveying Adoption* (2000) provides a comprehensive account of the adoption of children from local authority care in 1998–99. Other useful sites include www/adoptionuk.com and www/ postadoptioncentre.org.uk.

page 9 For the present legal framework for adoption, see Fergus Smith and Roy Stewart, with Deborah Cullen, *Adoption Now: Current Law Including Regulations, Guidance and Standards* (London: BAAF, 2003).

-9 For a moving account of the adoption of babies in this period, see David Howe, Phillida Sawbridge and Diana Hinings, *Half a Million Women: Mothers Who Lose Their Children by Adoption* (Harmondsworth: Penguin, 1992). At the time of writing, a 'Tenth Anniversary Reprint' was available from the Post-Adoption Centre, 5 Torriano Mews, Torriano Avenue, London NW5 2RZ.

11 Statistics on Ritalin: *Observer*, 17 August 2003.

33 'National Adoption Standards': see *Adoption Now*.

50 On hyper-vigilance and the other effects of living with traumatised children, see Megan Hirst, *Loving and Living with Traumatised Children: Reflections by Adoptive Parents* (London: BAAF, 2005). 'Megan Hirst' is the collective pseudonym adopted by a group of adoptive parents.

57 On disruption, see John Fitzgerald, *Understanding Disruption* (London: BAAF, 1990, second edition); Sheila Smith, *Learning from Disruption: Making Better Placements* (London: BAAF, 1994).

104 The classic formulations on attachment and attachment disorder
are to be found in the work of John Bowlby, especially the three
volumes of his *Attachment and Loss: Attachment* (London:
Hogarth Press, 1969); *Separation: Anxiety and Anger* (London:
Hogarth Press, 1973); and *Loss: Sadness and Depression* (1980).
Shorter accounts will be found in his *A Secure Base: Clinical
Applications of Attachment Theory* (London: Routledge, 1998).
For a very good introduction, see Jeremy Holmes, *John Bowlby and
Attachment Theory* (London: Routledge, 1993). A wonderfully
insightful account of parenting attachment-disordered children is
provided by Kate Cairns in her *Attachment, Trauma and Resilience:
Therapeutic Caring for Children* (London: BAAF, 2002). Sue
Gerhardt's *Why Love Matters: How Affection Shapes a Baby's
Brain* (Hove: Brunner-Routledge, 2004) successfully integrates
attachment theory with more recent neurological theory, demonstrating that early emotional experiences have effects on the development of the brain.

167 Statistics on antidepressants: *The Times*, 20 October 2003.

175 According to the British psychoanalyst and therapist D. W.
Winnicott, 'holding' is a vital aspect of the function of what he calls
the 'good-enough' mother who provides her child with a safe environment. Faulty holding results in extreme distress, a sense of going
to pieces or falling for ever, and the belief that external reality cannot be a source of reassurance. See, for instance, the essays collected in Winnicott's *The Family and Individual Development*
(London: Tavistock, 1965). On Winnicott, see Madeleine Davis and
David Wallbridge, *Boundary and Space: An Introduction to the
Work of D. W. Winnicott* (Harmondsworth: Penguin, 1983).